PRISON AND THOUGHT

PRISON AND THOUGHT

TESTIMONIES OF A CUBAN POLITICAL PRISONER

Pedro Santos Gallardo

ALEXANDRIA LIBRARY
PUBLISHING HOUSE
MIAMI

@ Pedro Santos Gallardo, 2018

ISBN: 978-1546897149

Library of Congress Control Number: 2017943703

Alexandria Library Publishing House
www.alexlib.com
info@alexlib.com
305-469-6796

CONTENTS

CONTENTS	5
AUTHOR'S NOTE	7
PROLOGUE	9
INTRODUCTION	11
THE FAITH	13
THE TRUTH	49
BAY OF PIGS	54
THE BRIGADIST	57
THE HATE IN ACTION	60
THE OCTOBER CRISIS	65
THE DISEASES	69
THE MURDERERS	72
A WORLD OF TERROR	77
THE SLAVERY	82
THE PLAN OF FORCED LABOR	85
THE POWER OF GOD	94
THE NAKEDNESS	101
THE MOTHERS	118
THE HONESTY	120
THE INVINCIBLE	128
MAN OF HONOR	137
THE REASON	157
THE GLADIATORS	169
THE INFAMY	183
THE DUTY	194
THE PROGRESSIVE PLAN	200
THE CONCERN	209
THE TRAGEDY	212
THE HUMILITY	215
THE HISTORY	218
THE CUBAN GENOCIDE	222

AUTHOR'S NOTE

Don't want to be vain or appear as a hero to the write my odyssey in the jails and prisons of Castro Communism, and for this reason, I wish with complete transparency to express my Prison and Thought: 1. Assuming the condition of humble spokesman those like me, suffered the horror of prison, and whose voices were severed by hatred and revenge: 2. Animated by a desire to fulfill my consciousness as a political prisoner in rebelliousness. These conditions forced me to tell the world, convincingly, the truth the Cuban gulag and the crimes committed there in me and the tens of thousands of my colleagues, during the period of deprivation of liberty, in various prisons scattered throughout the country, which were not differing one from others in terms of the cruelty with the political prisoners.

As already have started to consider, my readers, the idea that life in the jails and prisons are worse than the convicts to hell described by Dante in his anthological work in the Divine Comedy, the jails and prisons are a monstrosity in Cuba communist. Are hell and literary nonfiction, where the abuse of the government was cruel, the repression, the oppression, experiments physical and psychological and, of course because they virtually did not exist in the inducements. That is part from the psychological torture? No, the compassion not existed with the political prisoners.

An example of the above, experiments with the Presidio Politico and the naked that were banished to the notorious prison of Puerto Boniato, in Santiago de Cuba, Oriente Province. In that dark enclosure we were confined in sealed cells and horrifying-

doors and windows with metal plates —without electricity, ventilation, or enough water for our basic needs. In those filthy cells physically, totally unarmed, but heavily armed by faith in God, we faced isolation the hermetic, the retrograde obscurantism, individual and collective's beatings, the genocide dietary experiments, biological, lack of medical care, Without medicine. Also we beat to death by Starvation or own bullets of our enemies, because those who died will live forever in the history of Cuba and the consciousness of the all people that love the fatherland.

Now the reader will as, how many real situations we overcome and survive death in absentia to entire ordeal in political prisoner? I say with full conviction that the profession of religious faith is the answer to our strength and our victory. Indeed, we are irrefutable proof of this assertion.

For example, I am a believer in God, with faith and hope. I began to struggle against the communist regime, atheist and shameful. I experienced a sense of security and confidence. I was more involved committed to the fight. My arrest and in solitary confinements in the dungeons of State Security, the violent interrogations, day, night and early morning, threats of death by firing squad, the trial proceeding without warranty of any kind, caused a strong impact on my consciousness. It was a call that caught my attention on objective existence of "something" that kept my feet on the earth and put prudence in my lips.

After trial, I was plunged into the dark uncertainly of a sentence that was left unfinished, pending the issuance of a decision subject to the whims of my executioners. Again I left the presence of the "something" said, Peter you have wielded the sword of divine justice. Your cause will triumph, because it is the cause of God! At that exact moment was that my parents understood what I defined as firmness of conviction. And I became strong in adversity, faith and hope ran through my veins, and myself absolutely to the belief of the righteousness of God, and my soul became rock and bastion of my strength and maturity, against my enemies. But my big win was had became in militant faithful God's justice. I believe that the same must have occurred too many of my colleagues, of whom I differ on rock and impregnable of the bastion resistance.

PROLOGUE

I could not reproduce textually, because the letter, because the letter written in green ink would become me a free man. The letter remained in the archives of the political police. But I mentioned to Pedro Santos Gallardo in that letter. And I know because it was one of the moments of truth! That set off my path to personal freedom in a totalitarian regimen.

Well, if I remember in December 1979, one of those mild winter days Cuban. His niece Cristina Gonzalez goes to visit her uncle, the mother of my daughter Aliadna Cartaya, I had heard about him, always quietly, because we were both recent graduates of journalism. We had found work in official media.

Then once seemed impossible for us to meet with Pedro, but in 1978 the unexpected happened. The dialogue came, community trips and the pardons. Cristina that day of December asked me if I wanted to meet her uncle. She goes to visit him that afternoon at the Hotel Plaza, across from Central Park. I said yes and I went to see him with her.

The lobby was crowded and poorly illumination, but it was easy to find him, because she had told me that Pedro Santos Gallardo was in a wheelchair, the result of many hungers strikes during, his long ordeal of 17 years in prison.

I said it was for me a moment of truth, because everything had been destroyed in half hour all the propaganda that had been absorbed to across throughout my life about terrorists and CIA agents that assassinated innocent children for money. I found in front of me, a man, humble, wise, forgiving, and had accepted to stay anchored to a wheelchair rather than give up their dignity, without hate, their ideals and his motherland.

I got there after my last moment of truth, acts of repudiation that followed the events of the Embassy of Peru. I informed in a letter written in green ink, the fascism in my homeland.

If many prisoners of conscience of my generation could survive on the prison, their privations and his men, it was because of the tradition that started Pedro Santos Gallardo. When nobody listened, they had faith in the righteousness of their struggle and resisted a life without to see relatives and without communicate with them, like beasts, in dark cells, with no lighter than that which comes from heaven and emanating from the stars that illuminates and kill.

God bless these pages and Pedro Santos Gallardo.

Rolando Cartaya
Journalist former Cuban political prisoner
January 2012.

INTRODUCTION

I want to be as explicit and simple explanation of my testimony to my readers to have an appropriate information so that everyone do their own analysis and come to their own conclusions about the historical truth of what was the life of political prisoners in Cuba enslaved by communism. It is supposed I decided to write my Prison and Thought, full of that spirit, that all know and understand the reality of the adverse and difficult conditions in which I had to live during my long years in jails and prisons, where I went sent by try to free my people and my country, both subjected to the most brutal oppression of the communist system.

The tyranny of a despotic regime atheist, and wicked only creates misery, starvation, torture, murder, terrorism, ideological slavery and segregation, as a form of racism consisting regarding ideological and illegal torture of the human condition, of us noncommunist therefore lacked the most basic rights, such as the simple right to be born free. This granted, with the truth, being understood that concept of ideological discrimination and reactionary, is easy to assume that the dungeons and prisons in the communist regimen have the sole purpose of destroying us physically and psychological the human beings, to make us to languish slowly and kill us from starvation, without medicine care, without medicine and without the resources needed to survive in this world of cruelty applied sternly to the Political prisoners.

More or less the chronology of this barbaric prison, where had thousands of political prisoners officially in the prison of the Isle of Pines. There began the communist system implemented the prison system, which some variants in all prisons in the country, as part of the Russification of Cuba, a process to which I was opposed to the Revolution when installed in power.

There, in the Isle of Pines, the men were subject to the cruelty of forced labor on farms or concentration camps of that scattered throughout the country, farms or camps concentration that imposed by the government communist in sealed cells of punishment and impossibility of seeing the family for many years. Farms and concentration camps where the men died assassinated. By all hatred and terror created by the wild communists. But faith, hope and belief in God strengthened our hearts from the terror, shame, alienation and death.

But our ordeal was very difficult, but the men were full of peace in that ignominy of an uncertain fate, where thousands of political prisoners we were in conditions totally aggravated by prolonged hunger strikes we held with the patriotism of those who love the motherland giving their life for her, the men hunger strikes who, in my case, were made with an awareness of interpretation of spiritual fasting, abstinence during which I gave to religious contemplation and meditation.

The fight was predictable. The dead were always in our group. Our skin lacerated by blows of the bayonets, our body was the one who received the beatings, we were the objects of repression, oppression and punishment, far from giving in, we became against the oppressors stronger. But, they were felt powerless before us.

Our martyrs have spilled their blood on the Isle of Pines. In the circulars, stone quarries and forced labor camps. In each province of Cuba jails and prisons, farms and fields concentration with respective areas of forced labor of these enclosures. This experience was collected in my Prison and Thought. This is my testimony of my real life. I have waited more than five decades with faith, hope and belief in God, to make them known.

I understand that the stories are sad and my Prison and Thought is based on everything I have gone through long years of captivity, in that shadowy world where a man dies without asking for clemency.

THE FAITH

For Human Being the faith is essential in life and not only leads to knowledge, decisions and actions of growth, but also binds to hope, optimism and confidence. Confidence is our belief in have faith in something and the confidence this way is absolutely basic to human life.

My faith in God made me a free man. Let no one doubt. Because God is gave me strength to overcome the horror that was living. I would say that sometimes God chooses his sons to withstand human evil. The victims are chosen as test and more strengthened in spirit and noblest feelings than ever. God is the reason, when I go to sleep, feel a special peace in my soul because he is at my side at all times. Helping me spiritually to my soul assimilate the suffering caused for the pain that exists in humanity.

I reiterate. The faith and hope I learned were crucial in the years that I have lived especially at critical moments in captivity, where there was no pity or respect for men of ideals who love the motherland. How without my faith in God could endured so much suffering? The heart felt so much pain in difficult times with the shame and slavery by a cruel system that is not in keeping with human beings.

This concept of inheritance became part of my mental structure, which was built by my family for the cause of Independence of Cuba as colony of Spain, logical reason of the behavior of rebellion I assumed from the revolution communist who seized power, thus the fate of Cuba would inevitably, annexation to the Union of Soviet Socialist Republic. Not a Republic of State, but as a colony. So I responded to the empire of my blood and of my consciousness.

I "Pedro S. Gallardo" was born on August 1, 1936 in Ciego de Avila, Cuba. My Parents Fabio Gallardo and Pura Rosa Batista come from a family of veterans of the War of Independence of 1895. That war, militarily, was led by Maximo Gomez with Antonio Maceo, which in turn was also chief military of the War of Independence. The Big War of Ten Years (1868-1878), which failed, with signing the Pact of the Zanjon, Maceo was forcing before the signing of the Covenant. Then, these heroes had to go into exile, where Gomez and Maceo prepare invasions unsuccessfully. They tried to organize but fail the desired purpose. Until commanded by our Apostle Jose Marti organizes the insurrection and rebellion in Cuba with invasions from abroad.

Under the command of those heroic veterans, the Army fought heroically in the battlefields, open to Cuba's Independence with the Grito of Baire, on February 24, 1895, with the cry, and the load to the Machete. In the Ten Years War that Gomez taught to the Liberation Army. Antonio Maceo had been one of its most outstanding Generals, now, almost 17 years later, returns to the scene of the war. Gomez and Maceo heads of the cavalry did Mambi Army that shiver the Spanish Army. And never knew how to counter to the Mambi Army to the Machete charges that he caused many casualties. This time, between the new students of Gomez and Maceo is found Tomas Batista, Josefa Gallardo, Mariana Gallardo and Leonila Gallardo. Gomez and Maceo had taught the art of war and the cry of the Machete.

This war began in the Eastern Province with the launch the Grito of Baire on February 24, 1895, concluded by the military intervention of the United Stated, which became involved after the decree of February 15, 1898. These is a mysterious explosion of the Battleship Marine, anchored off the city of Havana, where he had arrived at the request of the American Consul, Fitzhugh Lee, fearing for the safety of the U.S citizens in Cuba, threatened by a rare anti-American profile that looting in the complex manifestations of protests, riots and looting because of the laws publication-too late-, issued by Spain, granting autonomy in Cuba.

Spanish mobs of radical consist, first, of irreconcilable elements with any concession to the colonized Cuba and on the other hand, components of the Volunteer Corps — a paramilitary group that gun in hand, and by the Spanish Army, fighting to the death against the Cuban Independence insurgents. Also expressed, but civilly, on one hand, Cubans compromised with the withdrawal of Spain and the absolute Independence of Cuba and, Spanish proponents of autonomy.

Of the 354 crew members of the ship of war, 266 were killed in the incident. On April 11 the U.S. President William McKinley, who since coming to the White House came pressuring to Spain to negotiate a solution with Cambyses the Independence, authority asks Congress to take action in the Cuban conflict. The Congress response was immediate, and 19 of that month proceed to the approval of a Joint Resolution, proclaiming... The Island of Cuba are and of right ought to be free and Independent it was the duty of the United States require that the Spanish government to unilaterally renounce its authority and government in Cuba must withdraw of its land and naval forces from the island; that for this purpose the President of the United States was authorized to use the army and navy of the nation and the United States denied any intension sovereignty over the island, and affirmed their determination to leave the government of it to the people Cuban. On 20 McKinley signed the resolution and an ultimatum to the Spanish government, with 21 broke the relations between the two countries, the 25 the Congress declares the state of war and the 27 is ordered to proceed to block with Navy Cuban shores.

McKinley directs the U.S. Army Chief, General Nelson Miles, who communicated in America with Don Tomas Estrada Palma — abroad Delegate of Cuba in Arms— and within the island with the General Maximo Gomez Baez and Major General Calixto Garcia Iñiguez. By dark, but well premeditated reasons, was ignored which should be the central figure of that process interventionist Major General Bartolome Maso Marquez President of the Government of Cuba in Arms, elected in full Managua. Absurdly, General Nelson Miles could not contact Maximo Gomez-Army Chief General Liberator —and if the most difficult to find of the two, with Calixto Garcia the President and the Chief of Army insurgent of Cuba, were excluded from the Plan.

The General Miles, with Lieutenant Adrew S. Rowan, sent a dispatch to the Cuban Calixto Garcia informing decisions made by the United States and requesting their support and collaboration with the American forces — this office is known in the history of Cuba as a message to Garcia.

Achieved contacts, made the ties and under the protection of the troops of Calixto Garcia, on the coast between Cuba and Guantanamo, Santiago. Ground units were coming commanded by General William R. Shafter and marines were led by William T. Tompson. From the landing, all military operations that took place in the Theatre of War, culminating in the defeat of the Spanish forces, had the decisive participation of plans General Garcia in the preparation of plans and execution of the attacks themselves, on the other hand, the modern American Navy in a naval battle that lasted about an hour and a half to put out of action the old Spanish Army against the port of Santiago of Cuba giving the coup of grace to the colonial rule of Spain in Cuba.

Now all that battlefield covering Santiago of Cub and surroundings not only did the defeated of Spain thanks to the Cuban veterans led by Calixto Garcia in Cuba, but it must also be recognized the operations by reinforcement to the besieged Spanish in Santiago. Spain was defeated, leaving Cuba as interventional under the jurisdiction of the United States of America. During of four years cemented appropriated conditions of pre-institutionalization of the Republic who left established the first democratic Republic and Representative of Cuba, the historic May 20, 1902.

War veterans of the 68 and 95 — and within the latter, I mention my family, Tomas Batista, Josefa Gallardo, Mariana Gallardo and Leonila Gallardo, men and women who had devoted their lives to the side of General Maximo Gomez, fought in the fields of battles, practically wearing with rags, barefoot, poorly fed, but imbued with patriotism, with many deprivations or sacrifice, when they reach the freedom of the Cuban nation. Now were in the streets, with pride of their struggle and joy and happiness to see how the people cheered the victory of the War of Independence.

That was the biggest show of the gratitude offered in Havana to the Patriot General Maximo Gomez and his veterans. Although, they were crying for those that died fighting on the battlefields without seeing the victory of their efforts and bravery. However, soon to General Calixto Garcia made a management requesting to President of the United States aid for the Liberators that had not clothes, nor food, whose donation was notified by General Maximo Gomez, who with the most good faith accepted the gift of Three million dollars. Maximo Gomez reported the donation to the Assembly of the Cerro, which was used with attack to Maximo Gomez. Maximo Gomez reported the donation to the Assembly of the Cerro, which was used with arrack to Maximo Gomez. Maximo Gomez renounced all his posts.

That situation forced the General Maximo Gomez to reject the donation Calixto Garcia had asked the President of the United States. The General Gomez said to the retired: "Here I post all my charges, I am a foreigner. If someday I need to go back to Cuba again I will return serve it". That was how he was dismissed from the Assembly of the Cerro. Maximo Gomez, General in Chief of the Liberation Army. The negative reaction to the unjust measure was immediate and massive. Thousands of Cubans cheered to Maximo Gomez and condemned the decision of the Assembly of the Cerro.

For this reason Maximo Gomez, Tomas Batista, Josefa Gallardo, Marian Gallardo and Leonila Gallardo and most of the veterans were retired the ranks of the Liberation Army. Furthermore, the town was in constant protest, marching against that dismissed. Simultaneously, the press and civil society joined the protest. Given the unanimity of popular repudiation, the Assembly of the Cerro was forced to dissolve. The reason of that Assembly was that Washington determined the conditions and arrangements as Cubans participate in the structure created by government intervention.

Clarified that the Assembly was inadmissible against Gomez, was unfair, ingratitude, immorality, myopia, and lack of patriotism, when Gomez had —and there are and will— We have to keep eternal gratitude to Maximo Gomez. The Republic of Cuba and Cubans are eternally forced with our Liberator.

Another impact was that of our parents and other family members of veterans of the War of Independence 1895, was that they defended to Maximo Gomez for his honesty with the Republic of Cuba. When Gomez's offer he rejected to be candidate to First President of Cuba. Maximo Gomez said, should be a Cuban and not a foreigner, and therefore, I recommended to General Tomas Estrada Palma.

He was occupying the office of the Cuban Revolutionary Party Delegate abroad since the death in combat of the Apostle Jose Marti. There was another presidential aspirant, General Bartolome Maso, President of the Republic of Cuba in Arms to the end of the Independence War because, knew better that anyone the needs of Cuban.

But as the General Maximo Gomez recommended to Tomas Estrada Palma, General Maso and his supporters had criticized severely to Maximo Gomez by the process of the elections. Bartolome Maso withdraws from the election. He abstained from participation in the elections, calling into question the fairness of the process and he withdraws not to suffer the shame of defeat at the polls. My parent explained that Bartolome Maso was immaculate and appropriate as President of the Republic of Cuba. But at the end of the war, his candidacy for President of the Republic of Cuba was not supported by Maximo Gomez.

According to my parents explained to me, that he preferred that Maximo Gomez will not endorse to Don Tomas Estrada Palma. But Maximo Gomez gave his supported at Don Tomas Estrada Palma. Thus was it promoted the candidacy of Estrada Palma in an act of patriotism for Maximo Gomez, Marti by right full natural and legal, would be elect First President of Cuba. So, Maximo Gomez understood that should be done and so he did.

His honesty and his pure incorruptible sense of justice, which had characterized by the war, Maximo Gomez kept them in peace unharmed, despite all the ingratitude, as that patent holder of the cute child of Washington. Tomas Estrada Palma was not elect by Washington support, but from Maximo Gomez, who was to be the First President of Cuba as a Republic, until one day they both attended a reception. The Liberator was so enthusiastically acclaimed and applauded by the public, that the salutation to the

President was obscured. The reaction of evil successor of Marti was the envy. And envy is the expression of meanness in the souls. Don Tomas Estrada Palma did not return to leave with Maximo Gomez, nor socialize with him, or appear in public with General Maximo Gomez.

Once demobilized veterans return to civilian life, and thus return to their abandoned homes and lands. And they were to work to rebuild their properties. They knew that in addition to participating in the national reconstruction were building a Democratic Republic and Cuba as Representative, surrendering to work with the same vehemence that fought for the freedom of the fatherland.

So the years passed and in 1920 Fabio Gallardo and Pura Batista, my parents started a family with 8 children: Miguel, Rafaela, Ramona, Emelina, Eduardo, Pedro, Santo and Cornelio. Family knew to bread, maintain and direct with the principles of love and civility patriotic acquired both in the jungle redemptive, as in the run of the Republic of Cuba.

The family was immune to the virus of the political passions; our parent said that the political began to sicken his mind of the Republic since its birth, not being further back. The example cited as General Maximo Gomez was his central figure, as well as other similar examples cited of what they were witnesses, were constant reminders our parents made us to ensure that the lessons forget. With such teachers, our approach could not be other —while fulfilling our duties as citizens— never participate in any that would undermine or denigrates the good name of Cuban or any right blocked to the democratic and constitutional order in Cuba. For these and other reasons and principles, our family has stayed out of charges political and uniforms military, and their children did the same.

My family had to work from dawn until the afternoons to carry the food for their children they had at least slice of bread and a glass of sugar water to not go lie down without eating, exactly. The family had nothing but was a family very harmonious and very united through thick and thin, as it should be, as we have always been and as we wanted it to be the Cuban family, for the good of all.

The decades of the 1920, 1930 and 1940 were very difficult years for the family, whose economic resources not were enough. Occasionally we were going to see our grandparents and to eat with them that day, or if we were not going to the homes of my aunts, also veterans of the War of Independence of 1895, to lunch with our aunts. They had not very much in their houses, but the few they had. They had lovingly shared it with us. They were times of hardship that I keep in the memory forever. But in 1940 there was a painfully day and taxed in my soul with the same intensity as if it had been by the application of a Kalimba, the hot iron those cattle is marked. Here is the story: My dear mother, Pura Batista, went to the winery (grocery stores) and asked the cellar man and owner of the establishment, if he could to sell on credit 5 pounds of corn meal, the cost was one penny. Nene - nicknamed him. This guy and subject, without considerations, with the cruel replies to my dear mother who could not sell the flour and that he had already eaten and the people too.

My mother come home and hugged my two youngest brothers. We went to the bed without to have eaten. My mother never forgot that embarrassment caused by the cynical words that heartless man had said.

I am six years old and had never quarreled with anyone nor knew the feeling of anger. However, in that terrible moment, I felt possessed of tremendous anger and wanted to be big in size to punish the cellar man who caused so much pain and tears of my mother. I confess that this dramatic event had castrated my childish illusions. Stop being a child, and though I was a young. I started thinking about adult and I resolved to work, to study and do not go to the bed with the stomach empty, and never to see my mother mourn for such a reason. The purpose became for me a kind of leitmotiv.

I started working when I was back from school. I went with my father, I did not care that I was very young. The important was to bring something, if only slightly, as well as did my older brothers, also boys still. Life is very difficult when you are living in poverty and the misery. The worker and the peasant are exploited by settlers, ranchers, businessmen, the corrupt Government and essentially by the communist.

Unfortunately, this problem still has not changed much in these early years of this country. Humanity continues to live in poverty by the uncontrollable ambitions of the interests. The workers, the farmer does not get paid a fair wage, by the work that make. Families who work the land live in dismal conditions. All of this due the corruption of our governments, and of course, is terribly worse in communist countries. They steal all the treasure of the nation to enslave its people, as happened in Spain. During the leftist socialist government communist of the Republic II (April 14, 1931 - April 1, 1939) then ruled by a leftist-socialist alliance communist-anarchist who was defeated by General Francisco Franco Bahamonte, and the fact degenerated into a bloody civil war (July 17, 1936 – April 1, 1939 that is internationalized.

It involves military intelligence soldiers and the Soviet Union, who was already in Spain before the uprising, and which shared a subtle process of Russification of the country and murder of opponents. This presence are added tens of thousands of members of the International Brigades, created for the purpose by Soviet Union in October 1936, composed mostly of Communists of various nationalities and military, there were thousands of other foreigners who presented without Brigades. Then they call the socialists, leftists, communist and anarchists.

Many of these were in Spain before the military pronouncements. The rebels were supported by the royalists, rightists of the country and abroad with the help of Nazi Germany of Adolf Hitler and Benito Mussolini's fascist Italy. These two countries were provided and transport, warplanes, artillery, machine guns, rifles, ammunition and logistics. Italy also sent a combat unit.

At five months into the conflict, it is discovered that the rumors were indeed that Spain was being sacked by the Socialist-Communist Government, and the fact became apparent when on 28 September of that year, four patent freighters of Russia Mediterranean in the of Cartagena in the region of Marcia is carrying 510 tones of gold, 72.6 percent of the gold reserves stored in the vaults of the Bank of Spain. This laid bare the intentions of the Russians. For Spanish communist found it easier to loot the public treasure that to rob every house in the country. They hoped that if is lost the war, they and have to leave to the abroad, with gold in Russia. They had any problem or convenient.

Meanwhile Joseph Stalin, the Soviet tyrant and dictator of the international communism, had decided to steal to Spain gold as cooperation not agreed by the military and was sent, initially in secret, Spain received combat aircraft and transport, artillery antiaircraft, taxis, tanks, armored cars, tanks assaults, trucks, jeeps, motorcycles, guns, rifles, pistols, ammunition, drugs, advisors and technicians.

But these were not the only wealth that socialists and communists stole. Spain was not only shipment. During the Civil War, and principally on the eve of his final vandalism with dependent groups, did not fail to steal the wealth to the people and the Spanish State, looting homes, jewelry, churches, convents, monasteries, museums, art galleries, gold, jewels, objects, paintings, relics, shipped through the same port, but with different destination and secure.

Mexico was the most favored of these destinations, given the multifaceted, support open to the socialist Spain. The President, General Lazaro Cardenas gave to Spain men, arms, money, political and diplomatic support. Furthermore, Lazaro Cardenas had offered him political asylum to government and their socialist-communist partisans and defeated. They make shipments originated toward Aztec land. When the military rebellion triumphed, the Socialist-Communist government flees to Mexico and there established a Government of the Republic of Spain in the abroad.

So, the years passed and Fulgencio Batista in 1952, with the support of the Armed Forces, had overthrown the constitutional government of Carlos Prio Socarras, Fulgencio Batista was unable to measure the consequences of reactionary the elements communists that wanted to overthrow by armed struggle the unconditional government that had taken power.

On July 26, 1953, a group of Communists attacked the barrack and the hospital Moncada. They murdered in the Barrack in Santiago of Cuba, with knife and guns fire to the militaries that were in their sick beds. The communists had committed the most heinous crimes in the history of Cuba. In addition, opposition groups clustered in secret cells with the full support of the House of Representatives to the rebels in prison. It took 21 months and the guerrillas of the Communist Party who attached the headquarters Moncada are released by the benches of the House of Representative, whose president was Rafael Lincoln Diaz Balart that was opposed to the law passed by a majority of the Legislative to his release to the rebels who had attacked the Moncada Barracks.

However, Rafael Lincoln Diaz Balart signed the Act of Pardon the Communists who had committed dozens of crimes against humanity. They were released. Of course, Fidel Castro the motherfucker was his brother in law and had to release him with all who attacked the Moncada Barracks. The protest is not valid because he signed the law that the legislators gave him and he not used his Veto, as Chairman of the House Representatives. However, the Senate, the Executive and the Judiciary signed the law of pardon. That's the truth that not said.

Years later I began studies at the Academy of the Dr. Kindelan and Dr. Morales in The Havana, Cuba. I study three years at that institution. Years later the Kindelan and the Morales my teachers. They gave me a letter of recommendation to the Committee at the Business School for the fall course where I was to continue my studies. Without loss of time I go to school and the secretary told me, the tests begin in two weeks. Time passed quickly, but I had not said anything to my sister Ramona Gallardo of my studies at the School of Commerce, because I did not know if could pass the exams. Then I would have to return to the Academy with teachers Kindelan and Morales.

In two weeks we turned up 45 students in the Business School, all younger than I, they came from Catholic Schools, Private Schools and Public Schools. Minutes after teachers entered the classroom. They gave us a sheet accounting. The teachers explained what we had to do and how we had to fill the boxes for the columns of Income and Expense. They told us we breathe deeply for one minute. A minute later they gave us accounting exams, mathematics, history, geography, civics and politics, in the classroom all was very an impressive the silence. Two hours after we deliver the exams and we returned to our homes.

A week later we return to School to see if we had passed the examinations. Upon arrival we saw the forms on the walls and each one checks his name. Many of them were happy, while others were very sad. Only we had approved 21 of the 45 students. In the School of Commerce, we gave to the students that had disapproved encouragement them to come back the next semester and to study everything can for the upcoming exams.

My friend Concepcion was crying and I embrace and dry the tears and told her that I would help the next semester to pass the exam. She gave me a kiss and returned home very sad, because she had disapproved the examinations in business school. She returned four months later and successfully approved exams. She was happy and was my best friend at school.

I came back to my sister's house; I said I went to begin studies at the School of Commerce. However, she ignored me, thinking I was joking. I told her, I go to the store to buy the Uniform. She did not believe me, but when I returned from the store with the uniform she told me, you are a genius. Because you have done studies in record time and gave me a kiss and a hug.

The next day I went to see my teachers Kindelan and Morales to tell them that I had passed the examinations. When I arrived, I found to the professor Kindelan in his office. I greeted him and I said, Professor, I passed the exams. I thanked him for all he had helped me in the years in his Academy. He was very happy to see that I had passed the exams in just three years of study. The teacher called to Morales. The Dr. Morales gave me a hug that I could have broken a rib. So were these two sages of the science and arts of teaching.

Another important fact was that since 1952, the University Student Federation (FEU) was a terrorist organization and we knew that the communists were infiltrated at the University Student Federation. These men had a history of involvement in gangsterism and were under communist influence.

What I can say is the when Fidel Castro landed in Cuba and when was in the Sierra Maestra of the Republic of Cuba in December 1956. From that moment there is not stability in Cuba and the situation of the country was affected by the attack on the Presidential Palace on March 13, 1957. Attack directed by

Jose Antonio Echeverria Vianchi where he died at University of Havana and the rest conducted that action trying to overthrow the President unconstitutional of the Republic of Cuba. So, the time passed and terrorist guerrillas invaded the island of Cuba.

In 1958 the communists in the Sierra Maestra were organized with the full support of the capitalists, businessmen, intellectuals, professionals, representatives of the camera of the Legislative and Executive that they had joined with some of the administration officials in 1958. The government made the elections peacefully and Andres Rivero Aguero was elected the candidate of the administration in power. Dr. Marquez Sterling, Free Party candidate, ranked second and the Authentic Party candidate, Dr. Ramon Grau San Martin in the third place.

As we know, Dr. Andres Rivero Aguero won the victory in the Eastern Province and the Villas, where almost the people no vote, because people failed to vote. Dr. Marquez Sterling won in Camaguey, Matanzas, Havana and Pinar del Rio. According to Dr. Marquez Sterling had lost the elections by fraud at the polls. You may have been so, because he won in four provinces and essentially in Havana and Camaguey having a population around one million inhabitants in each one.

The situation was extremely difficult for the candidates who had dabbled in politics and essentially for the Republic of Cuba, because the corruption grew in the rank of the governors that and were bought with thousands of dollars for that the guerrillas will pass through the provinces of Cuba with the columns of men were under arms in exchange of the silence. So the Governors do not allow to the Army of the Republic of Cuba will take action against the guerrillas and their commanders. Who left to operate freely throughout the territory of the Republic of Cuba? However, the people did not care about the events in the country, with hundreds of guerrillas that were invading the territory, due to the irresponsibility of some soldiers, priests and the ruling administration in 1958. In reality, the Governors were a scoundrel and miserable.

All this was due to the Judiciary, House of Representatives, but the Senate was not impartial. The results were catastrophic for the Cuban nation with the coming to power of the guerrillas who were aided to invade Cuba with arms of the United States, Colombia, Costa Rica, Mexico, Venezuela and other nations when they were in the mountains of Santiago de Cuba, Camaguey, Santa Clara, Matanzas and Pinar del Rio, the guerrillas were invading the territory national of the Republic of Cuba.

Months later the Government of Cuba preferred to relinquish on January 1, 1959. The government gave the power at the communist's guerrillas. They were throughout in the territory of the Republic of Cuba without opposition from the military to avoid bloodshed. The President unconstitutional Fulgencio Batista flees with his wife, Dr. Andres Rivero Aguero, who had won the elections in 1958, but this man was a coward with other members had been taken exile in the Dominican Republic. Two other planes came to the United States with the sons of Fulgencio Batista and some close associates of the government.

The remaining militaries eaters of Alfalfa remained in Cuba as the General Cantillo, who was appointed Chief of Staff of the Army by the Army General Francisco Tabernilla Dolz. As well, Colonel Barquin, who was in charge of the armed forces and in command of Camp Columbia at the time arrived the guerrilla army led by Camilo Cienfuegos, arrived at city of Havana? Colonel Barquin opened the gates of the Camp Columbia at the time that the guerrilla army led by Camilo Cienfuegos at the city of Havana? The Colonel Barquin opened the gates of the Camp of Columbia welcomed the army of Camilo Cienfuegos. The Colonel Barquin was a motherfucker with the General Eugenio Cantillo. At the end of Havana "Che" Guevara and his troop's terrorists had taken command of the fortress of The Cabaña.

The transfer of power of the Republic of Cuba led the country to into chaos, with thousands of murders in the firing squads. Since then ran rivers of blood with the coming to power of the communist Castro regime, the internationalist criminal that stole all the wealth of the Republic of Cuba. That's how the guerrillas came to power, committing all kinds of crimes and have continued to do so since 1959. The wretches that delivered power are dead. All of them are living with Satan in the hell.

The coward's dogs communists of the regime dictatorial of Fidel Castro. The guerrillas triumphed and took office on

January 1, 1959. Everything was a mess in the Cuban nation with the overthrow of the government that was in power. Thus passed the days of January, when Emelio Fraga of the secret cells of the Communist Party was arrest me, because I did not agree with Marxist-Leninist ideals when the guerrillas were in the Sierra Maestra, Oriente Province. I know that Emelio Fraga and Juan Fernandez, owner of the company where I worked belonged to the Popular Socialist Party (PSP) for several years.

Fraga was not agreeing with me. But, if he was agreeing with the guerrillas who were in the country. I was disagreed with violence, assassinations and bombs that exploded in Havana. Terrorism had no mercy on the citizens of the country. That brought grave consequences when communist guerrillas triumphed. Fraga with degrees of sergeant was to arrest me. But I was not at work that day, January 2, 1959, because my sister Ramona Gallardo called me by phone to I go her home until the country is normalize.

Thus the months passed and I continued with my work, not well paid when Emelio Fraga came with military uniform and grades of sergeant and said me, "You know that if you are working that day when I came to arrest you. You would not pass moments happy in the jail. I said to him: We have not had any problems that I know. He continued No, but not you like to speak of the guerrillas in the Sierra Maestra." I replied, that is true, and now you are in power neither I like. Emelio Fraga looked at me and said: We the socialists we will make a modern nation where we will have everything. I listened to his lecture and I say to him, this is not for me and we know me seven years ago. Yes or not. He said, yes.

Fraga answered me saying, "We go to have everything. And to this today that I am writing this book, in my country there is a total destruction throughout in the nation. The population lives in poor conditions, because the only thing the communists built is the slavery, the misery, the hunger, the destruction, assassinate in the firing squads, the torture, the isolation, the terrorism, jails and prisons. Fraga might not have imagined this terror, poor man without brain.

I would not like to be one of the thousands of innocent's victims, if I am arrested by the Sergeant Fraga in 1959, when

Ernesto Guevara de la Serna "Che", massacring hundreds of prisoners in the prison of The Cabaña in the firing squads. The communists have shed much blood of innocent victims throughout the Cuban Nation.

The entire country became a hell with the massive detentions in Cuba. All of the detention had been caused by the communists who had taken power through violent struggle. Since that time the Cuban people fell under the terror of slavery, misery, torture murders, executions and imprisonment. So the years passed and the island of Cuba became a prison with more than 300 prisons at the country, from East to West.

The island of Ciba had become a holocaust of tremendous proportions, by assassinations of innocent men and the hatred that had the communists against the Cuban people. That was the blindness of evil that sees everything in black and white. So, we had to live in those years of terror that have continued for over 50 years.

The executions continued in the firing squads of the colonial fortress of The Cabaña, where Ernesto Guevara, "Che", was massacring hundreds of innocent's men without having committed any crime and did so only by hatred and revenge. That's what makes men miserable. And when they fall in mud, they cannot get out. They are only cowards using the evil to continue doing the crime. They never find honesty, shame, decency, honor, faith, and hope in their hearts because they feel hatred and resentment. Because they have never saw the light with the precious pearl necklaces and the dark nights illuminated that nature gives us all humans.

The Island of Cuba has fallen in a Chaos, for the murders committed; as the Che Guevara and Fidel Castro in the fortress of The Cabaña. These men are communists and internationalist criminals. The pleasure was to kill to implant terror in the Cuban population by hatred and revenge? The executions were daily throughout the country under the command of Fidel Castro, terrorist and criminal; That is the true who want to hide all over the world since the Communists took power in the Republic of Cuba in 1959. Since that time the Cuban people have had to live more than half a century of slave only with hope and faith in

God. A people generous and good, who have never forgotten their ancestors and tear for freedom of the Fatherland, these murderers will be incinerated one day in the fire if the hell.

The people have had to suffer the most difficult moments of history since the discovery of the Americas by the instability in the nation since the overthrow of Cuban President Gerardo Machado. From that moment there is not stability in Cuba by the political ambitions in Cuba from the colony of Spain until 2013. For this reason I am reflecting on the horror that I have had to live by the political instability of the Marxist-Leninist government and military deciles and scoundrel with the rabble and the cruelty of the assassin system of Fidel Castro, Raul Castro and Ramiro Valdes.

Cuba never had political stability for more than 12 years in the history of the Nation. However, Cuba was the paradise in the Caribbean and always at the head of the nations of the Americas with the exception of the industrialized nations, the Republic of Cuba with 6,3 million inhabitants in 1959. The growing economic, today could be on top of the other nations `of the Americas, Thus, the political prisoners that we were in the jails and prisons, we had to listen to the download of the military rifles killing the heroes of the Fatherland.

In addition, those have not experienced the horror and crime of the communist's systems of mass executions for more than half a century. Knowing as are the miserable-fascists-Marxist-Leninist-Communist in reality. The truth is that Fidel Castro, Raul Castro, Ramiro Valdes and the militaries are murderers, scoundrel miserable offender internationalists.

Cuba has made many spectacular advances in many fields: the destruction of the economy, agriculture, communication and transportation, narcotic traffic of cocaine and marijuana, poverty, famine, slavery, ostracism, imprisonment, repression, terrorism, massacres in firing squads, murders in Forced Labor, the assassination in jails and prisons, the huger strikes, the physical and psychological torture. These are the achievements that earned the most offensive communist system of the universe for more than half a century of crimes against humanity and with Cuban people, generous and good.

The Platt Amendment, annex tax Cuban of the Constitution of 1901 at the request of U.S Senator Orville H. Platt cede to the United States of America (USA) the control of Cuba foreign policy and the right to military intervention in the island. However, the big mistake of Cuban politicians was to repeal it in 1934, left unprotected the island of Cuba. Of course, the men who ruled in that time did not think about the future of the Cuban nation. This Amendments could be reformed by other amendments and laws, rather than repeal it in entirely the Amendment and to protect the security of the island of Cuba. Years later lost everything by the inability of the Representatives, Senators, the Executive and the Judiciary Power.

Since that time the Communist Party found within the government of Fulgencio Batista and Zaldivar, Ramon Grau San Martin and Carlos Prio Socarras. The communist began to create the conditions to destabilize the Cuban nation. So, it was like year later the Senate, the House of Representatives, the Executive and the Judiciary gave him the power to the communists to massacre thousands of men in the firing squads with their brutal methods to assassinate too many innocent men. That was how we had to live with the world's cruelest system when took power. Therefore we cannot forgive mistakes and betrayals of men full of ambition and responsible of the greatest genocide in the history of the Republic of Ciba.

But the saddest thing of all was that the administration of Fulgencio Batista gave to power to the communist's guerrillas with only 1,839 guerrillas. Addition, we can add that for more than 54 years, the communist government of Fidel Castro has murdered over 100,000 Cubans. However, free and democratic governments of the world covered the eyes, ears and mouth to the reality of the Cuban people. So with that sadness, Pedro Santos Gallardo and all Cubans have had to live with hope, the faith, the illusion, the joy, the optimism, the belief in God and the freedom of the Fatherland.

We all know that faith is the response of man in mind and will to God's power. When we have faith and hope are as a dream, when we in peace? I believe that faith and hope come after exploring as we are and what are the deeper interventions in our live.

That is how we see the world with hope and faith that one day will be change for futures generations can live like a big family in the universe created by God. So, we live in peace and love without suffering the horrors of the war and the mothers happy with their loved ones. That is the love that we all want. However, we are experiencing difficult times and we not realize that our life on earth is a few hours and we spend a third working, other third sleeping and the other third watching the sky, taking care of the family and entertainment. So, we spent a lifetime full of hope and faith without definition, only with the illusion, the hope and the faith in God, because, practically we are not living the beauty of the nature with the cold night and the wonderful days.

All reminds me of my grandfather Tomas Batista, who fought heroically alongside Maximo Gomez and Antonio Maceo. Tomas was very strict, but very noble with the family and friends. Tomas never flaunted of his battles against Spanish Army. He spoke of his friends who had fallen in the battlefields and never said a word against their enemies. Tomas told me, they were brave, but the strongest could overcome the other. Tomas said, my classmates were unforgettable martyrs. They fought bravely in every battle, but fate had reserved them the eternal rest, at the end of the War of Independence. They were extraordinary men and on the battlefield were always up front with heroism and bravery. They demonstrated their patriotism in all the bloody battles against the Spanish Army.

If we think in politics, we see the diversity of political and militaries men, who mostly have destroyed the Republic of Cuba. For example, the presidents, Tomas Estrada Palma, Jose Miguel Gomez, Mario Aurelio Garcia Menocal, Alfredo Zayas Alfonso, Gerardo Machado and Morales, Fulgencio Batista and Zaldivar, Ramon Grau San Martin and Carlos Prio Socarras were men thinking dark with the country. Men frustrated without much love for the country by and ended only with ambition of the power.

When the Communists took the power in Cuba the jails and prisons where full of political prisoners. We had to live in overcrowded prisons with thousands of soiled bedding and bugs. We could not sleep in the beds full of insects we could not eradicate because we had not insecticide. The cruelty was unbounded in those difficult times for prisoners in all prisons of Cuba.

In 1959 and 1960 thousands of men and women left the country. A stampede as pack animals, so great that almost changed the color of the sea in a dark yellow. By their bad deeds and ambitions had destroyed to the Cuban nation.

Thus began the stampede by air and sea, for not having enough courage to defend his country when was in danger. No, not I am saying lie. It was a nation with more than 60,000 men in the power. That is, they gave power; they were demoralized men in the Army, Police and Marine. That is, they were without forces to struggle in the Sierra Maestra against the communists.

The leader of the guerrilla belonged to the Communist Party with other members: Fidel Castro PC, Raul Castro PC, Camilo Cienfuegos of the PSP, Ernesto Guevara "el Che" PC, Huber Matos Benitez PSP, Ramiro Valdes of PSP, Sergio del Valle PSP, Aidee Santa Maria Cuadrado PSP, Juan Almeida Bosque PSP, Aldo Santa Maria PSP, Raul Roa PSP, Blas Roca PSP, Carlos Rafael Rodriguez PSP, Lazaro Peña PSP, Joaquin Ordoqui PSP, Antonio Nuñez Jimenez PSP, Jose Pardo LLada PC, Osmani Cienfuegos PSP, Manuel Piñeiro "Red beard" PSP, Jose Abrabte PSP, Eloy Guitierrez Menoyo Spanish PSP, Anibal Escalante PSP, Isidoro Malmierca PSP, Juan Marinello PSP, Universo Sanchez PSP, Fulgencio Batista PSP, David Salvador PSP, Jesus Menendez PSP, Ydalmiro Retano PSP, and Julio Antonio Mella PSP.

This is a partial list of some of the top leaders of the Communist Party who were before the guerrilla uprisings throughout the country. However, there are many who argue that revolution was not a Communist. I do know who said that lie. But they knew the true. When in 1940 he had changed the name the Communist Party (PC) by the Popular Socialist Party (PSP). Not, not new that this was done to disguise the Communist Party.

The settlers, farmers, entrepreneurs, capitalists and professionals, intellectuals had given his unconditional support for the Communists. However, years later have fled from the clutches of those who had supported to destroy the country in the political, economic social.

After analyzing the mental problems that have consolidated these men and fundamentally predominant pathological problems and developed where there is no mercy, no trace of compassion with the perversion and systematically aggressive manifestation without ideological identity with neurotic traits connected to mental suffering mixed with unbridled brutality of barbarism and savagery of cruelty to become executioner of his own people with the transformation of subjective gratification absolute of the sadism of evil and hatred against humanity.

To Fidel Castro does not like the sages, hates the old man and admires the docile and the members of the Central Committee, the commanders, the colonels and generals. And no one can contradict his words or give an opinion and everyone has to be submissive and obedient. They will not oppose his words and everything he says, like all submissive and miserable. That is evidenced by officials working abroad as international espionage spies, and essentially in democratic countries like the United States and European countries.

Castro expressed his hatred of the U.S. government and against the Cuban people to justify the genocide committed and supported by Raul Castro, Che Guevara, Ramiro Valdes and the whole communist elite is in the power. The peasants massacred by oppose to the system communist. It is unforgivable that wants to subdue a people, because they are in disagree with such a brutal regime, whose commanders are the executioners of the Cuban people. That's the really of these evil men that carry in their hatred and revenge soul. As human vultures.

The men docile and with trembling lips: as Ariel Alarcon Ramirez, Rafael del Pino, Marzo Fernandez, Delfin Fernandez, Ramiro Valdes Jr. Francisco Aruca, Edmundo Garcia, Andres Gomez, Max Lesnick, Lorenzo Gonzalo, Ydalmiro Retano, Roberto Solis, Jose Quevedo Perez, Carlos Calvo and many more that we do not know if they are double agents of Cuba and the United States. But if we are convinced that Ramiro Valdes Jr. Edmundo Garcia and Ydalmiro Retano Jr. they are sons of the three terrorists, cowards, communist and murderers who have slaughtered thousands of men in the firing squad tragically, innocent heroes who died for only defend democracy, freedom and the homeland. Protagonists of the cruelest epic story of a brave people gave their best warriors when they were just beginning to enjoy their lives. The Youth loves a better world. Meanwhile, others are indifferent in the world, because are only spectators. Nevertheless, many men were massacred in the firing squad by Ydalmiro Retano, Garcia Frias and Ramiro Valdes. Three internationalist murderers killed thousands of brave men and especially innocents.

In the Communist dictatorship, the man is slave by birth, subjected to all kinds of control and abuse under the oppressor regime which develops, grow and die slaves, with all the restrictions applied by the system communist and scoundrels. Nor has the right to education, private work, to medical care, hospitalization, food resources, private property, capital, clothes and shoes. That is, not entitled to anything, because only receive what gives the government. The government has the control of the intentionally population. If you buy or sell something, you go to the jail between 10 by 12 years, without parole, by being a slave of communist rule.

Over times we can see Fidel Castro a few years before of his death that he moves with slow dull steps and with body bent like a camel, unconscious on the earth and the fainting in the pulpit before the crowd and breaking his knee and arm. He was the laughingstock of the humanity with his the speeches obsolete with mind lost in space and time, with unfinished words could not remember what he was saying, with the creaking teeth and the saliva going out from the mouth, with rough hands, eyes wise, with black outs and senile dementia, believing that it could dominate everything without knowing that his madness would lead him to hell to purge all the evil he has done for uncontrollable hatred that is eating his soul slowly, full of deceases and suffering, because it is a man and diabolical villain.

Also, his hate and uncontrollable nervousness, pulling the hairs of the beards, the full head dye, with the gray hair covered with Clairol visible in the few hairs remaining on his head, the talc used to cover wrinkles and freckles reflecting a gaunt face where the death lurks. Suffers incurable diseases like Joseph Stalin, Adolf Hitler and Yasser Arafat by the wrong he has done in his bitter life hatred and mass murder by violence to a humble working people and uncontrollable ambitions.

What is going to bring in his death with the contempt of his own people he has killed, in his life decrepit of suffering and as punishment for their wickedness? This is how this miserable murderer terrorist and thief die; and when beech gone to the grave, the earth shall tremble of horror with the monster full of diseases.

Fidel Castro was the laughingstock of the rulers of Mexico, essentially with President Fox that said in his face that did not want him at the Summit of the Presidents in Mexico. The President Fox said. Do would like one lamb to eat that he had prepared for you and Castro went because there he was not welcome in Mexico. Castro had to leave Mexico reeling. That is, they threw him as a dog murderer and miserable with the communist plebs that accompanied him.

In this universe, people are subjected to the barbarism of slavery with such brutality that characterized the criminal to torture of a humble people with the savagery against innocent men and women to terrorize by violence to people defenseless as punishment for disagreeing with the executioners. The people have undergone the ordeal of the communists. Nevertheless, they can fight in against the assassin, the massacres, the malnutrition, the disease, the lack of adequate food and medicine. For that reason Government has committed the genocide against populations across the country because they not struggle.

That is how this mob of the century XX and XXI committed the darker genocide in the Cuban nation to seize power and bring ostracism absolute millions of human beings. The Cuban Genocide was the total isolations human beings. The Cuban Genocide was the total isolation of families, the murders, destruction of the country and holocaust that have overcome wars in our Western Hemisphere to assassinate the heroes of the Fatherland.

Extermination committed by the Marxist-Leninist guerrillas-communists. Thousands of brothers and parents were massacred.

Men killed to implement terror. Fidel Castro has the absolute liabilities with the complicity of the military for having murdered in the firing squads to many thousands of men heroics. The labor forced camps on the Isle of Pines and the Isla of Cuba were fields of men massacred.

Fidel Castro and his elite criminals have murdered children in High Sea. That was bringing the Communist Party had brought to the Cuban people led by Blas Roca Calderio, Carlos Rafael Rodriguez, Lazaro Peña, Joaquin Ordoqui, Jesus Menendez, Anibal Escalante and Raul Roa. They were the ones who brought violence, assassination and isolation of the Cuban people.

The delivery was completed with the full support of government officials who were in power in 1959. Professionals, capitalists, and socialists all handed over power to the Marxists-Leninists who filled thousands of Cuban families of mourning throughout the country. Yes, they were responsible massacres that have been committed in the Cuban nation, and then flee desperately for the mistake they committed against their own race and fill in mourning thousands of Cuban Mothers.

Cowardice was so great that they gave the businesses, house; all types of object by leave the country trembling with fear and terror. That's what these sages did who has mostly died in exile and others have committed suicides.

The rest are in the last days of their life living with pain by to have destroyed the country and will disappear gradually without seeing the holocaust committed by the communist criminals. That is what they have received all wise scholars who helped to destroy the Republic of Cuba and enslave its own people.

Many of them walk through the streets of the world's nations powerless as Rafael Del Pino, Huber Matos Benitez, Fidel Castro Ruz, Raul Castro Ruz, Ramiro Valdez Menendez, Ernesto Guevara de la Serna "el Che" and Ariel Alarcon Ramirez "Benigno the terrorist". Seven coward's murderers that look at the sky and looking for a place to live eternal life in this world of peace where they go all the disappeared and never will return to the earth, because Satan have them in hell.

There you can see all the evil against a humble and generous people that not be deserving to have been slave with the forces arms. The people live in confinement, in misery, the huger, the homelessness, the torture and no resources to feed their children, the terrible poverty is experienced by the Cuban people. The pain the Cubans that are suffering the bitterness of the murders of their loved ones who gave their lives so that the people would not suffer slavery that has suffered for more than half a century with the most barbaric dictatorship that exists on earth. The terrorism was created by all these criminals who destroyed the growing technological, economic and social development of the Cuban people where evil without precedent in the history of the Republic of Cuba.

I was punished brutally in my long years in prison for political reasons. I had to sleep on the floor for 14 months and I had to heat the floor with my body, because the cell had no canvas bed for sleeping. That does not exist in the punishment cells, dungeons without water for bathing. The water not existed for every month we were in them. With what cruelty, I had to live for the whole period of the punishment.

The floor of the dungeons wet sand-like where the body never dry and slowly deteriorates. You will sick without surrender of your ideology by which you fought. So, our life has been. All have had to live with the brutality of the communists for many years and see how their fellows starved in the cells of punishment. That was the method used by the communist regime's henchmen. The punishment is more severe and without piety. That is the cruelty that uses the communist system and terrorist.

Dungeons floors wet sand-like, so that your body never dry, I slowly deteriorate, no that you get sick and surrender of ideology for which you fought. So life has been all we have had to live with the brutality of the communists for many years, and see how your fellow starved. That was the method used by the communist regime's henchmen so that the punishment was more severe. That is the cruelty that uses the communist system.

When you have to live in punishment cells, dungeon, hunger strikes, denial of food ordered by Fidel Castro, the galleys infested with insects, without medicine or medical care, isolated without seeing the family during 9, 12 and 14 years. That brutal punishment was applied and applied with sternly when we were cut off from the outside world. This savagery is used in all the jails and prison of Cuba.

The pain and suffering I went through in my long years without seeing the family, only because he disagreed with the barbaric methods of the communist system. But we are living away from reality, thinking that foreign governments will help us to free ourselves from slavery and monstrosity. The communists impose by force, mass murder. The Marxist tyranny of Fidel Castro, wretched and coward with the bloodshed of the Cuban people, the crime, the slavery, the impunity, the poverty, the torture, the revenge, the hatred, the injustice, the malice, the shamelessness, the indignity, the huger, the murder and the terrorism. The Communists have had some success to the terror and the devastation across the country. That is what built the communist in Cuba.

I understand that Cuba will not have a space for criminals Marxists-Leninists who swarm around the world. Every crime has its price and very high.

Inevitably that happen a day the return in mass to the homeland, that took many men to the battlefields across the Republic of Cuba to release it from the fascist mobs. Heroes who were stripped of their earths and duties as the country required its best sons to defend the fatherland against the regime atheist and without awareness.

Will definitely for those who have survived the long years of waiting and are not instruments of international terrorism, let alone those who have massacred their own people. Those who have been stained by the blood of thousands of heroes, has no return until the last day to close their eyes.

We will come back the sacrificed his life and his youth, and the men of good will can live in the country. The country will not be for all, only for those who have not defiled with bloodshed of his best sons that are waiting by their relatives and friends in their graves, with a bouquet of flowers.

The Fatherland expects; as the mother to her son that went and spent many years, and the mother could not sleep at night endless, waiting to see the beloved son of her heart. And when she sees him to arrive tired, the mother with open arms hugs him and kisses him again and again like a baby, with the affection and love of the mother that never forgot from him.

The son tells his beloved mother, mother forgive me for all the pain that I have caused in these long years of absence. The mother takes him in her arms and says lovingly. Do not you realize that when you leave of the home, even if you live in a palace in silk beds you go to miss your house?

No matter if you have to sleep on a barbecue where the rain makes that the sleep be deep and when wake you feel happy with the breeze the calm and the dew and the sun caressing your face. The son hugging the mother and she will not reproach word of the son beloved. Because it is part of her live. The country is waiting by you to give you the welcome by the time you have been away from it. The man must be true to their ideals in order to fulfill the dream of seeing a world more united and without injustice.

The fatherland is and always will be the same, although they try to subdue. She will prevail from hate, the deviant men, the injustice, of the monstrosity of the man that thinks he can devour everything and does not realize that he is going to be devoured by nature, No, you cannot distort the truth of the genocide committed against the Cuban people. The pain and suffering of the Cuban people have been and will be memorable by generations to come. The hatred, malice and revenge are unparalleled in the history of the Cuban nation. They committed many crimes and not have had piety the suffering of the Cuban people.

The happiness of the return represents the memory of the human beings, which has never been forgotten through the years of torture and murders caused by the tyranny communist and so much pain in their lives.

We can see the night, the day, the moon, the stars; the sun, the water, the earth and the beauty of the sky that reflects the rainbow of nature, the cloud and thunderheads irrigate the land with rain and coolness, to give life to all that exists on earth and in the sea. Earthly paradise created by God, whose Holy spirit is like the air we breathe and can no see. However, that gives us life, because without oxygen there would be no life on earth.

What sadness is live with so much selfishness in the world full of incurable diseases? Ah, but the man does not want to understand that we come into this world full of mystery to spend a few short days between suffering and pain until our departure is definitely of this worldly world.

The minority is like Pontius Pilate, Barrabas, Cain and Satan, Cain and Satan, causing much pain, so many crimes and infamy for their ambitions uncontrollable cruelty.

There are many men who use blackmail, cowardice, malice, revenge, and crime because they are cruel and scoundrels, crime is his profession and torture is their happiness because they are cowards and do not look good man's greatness. They do not want to acknowledge that they have come into this world for a few days.

The ordeal not over and continue to die at sea slaughtered by Marxists-Leninists to men, women, elderly and children that cannot reach the land of liberty because were massacred in the sea in their rustic rafts. That is the truth what is happening in Cuba for more than half a century.

About this I can add that the Cuban administration in 1958, by the lack of political vision of Fulgencio Batista with the General Francisco Tabernilla Dolz and the elected President Rivero Aguero had delivered the power to the communists. But, Rivero Aguero was a coward, had not the courage to take power and to rush out the country with panic that had and die of grief and suffering for not having the gallantry to defend the homeland. For that was that the communist killed thousands of innocents in the firing squads, led by Fidel Castro the terrorist and his gangster brother Raul Castro, better known as the "Duck".

The dictators and thieves like Fidel Castro, Raul Castro, Pol Pot, Benito Mussolini, Yasser Arafat, Saddam Husaym, Adolf Hitler, Joseph Stalin, Ho Chi Ming, Rafael Trujillo, Francisco Franco, Mao Set Tung, Muammar al Gaddafi, Augusto Pinochet, Marcos Perez Jimenez, Pol Pot, Idi Amin Dada, Slobadan Milosevic, Saddam Husaym, Hali Mohammad Suharto, Kim Jong Il, Omar Hasan Admad al-Bashir, Osama bin Laden, Hugo Chavez Frias, Emperor Herohito had dragged the masses as robotics machinery; as if were hypnotized without knowing in the world that were living. And when they wake of hypnotism is like to live in the world that does not know, as if time had stopped for them in his youth. They had lived the horror and helped massacre by his blindness.

View as the women, the men, the elderly, youth and children killed by the militaries coast guard. Only they wanted freedom and found the death in the sea.

The border guard with water hose had sunk the Remorcador March 13, on July13, 1994, where hundreds of people traveled of which more than 40 were killed, including several children. The Boat Cojimar was sunk into the Ocean. The Brothers to the Rescue had been pulverized by the Mig 29. All of them are found in the seabed where they rest eternally. However, these bastards think they will escape justice. But come to comply with the laws of God.

Thousands of martyrs are in the places that neither relatives know where they are because the communist government has not told where their loved ones. That's the scariest cruelty there are in these criminal's systems. The heroes gave their lives fighting for the freedom of the Fatherland. The communists are cowards unprecedented in the history of Cuba. Fidel Castro with his communism has committed all the atrocities unimaginable with the human beings. Castro, with his communism has committed many atrocities with heroic men.

All this is because the Communists are infamous, slanderers, terrorists, opportunists, corrupt, mafia, criminals, thieves, liars, murderers, scoundrels, firebrand, cowards, gangsters, atheists, and drug dealers.

Everyone think is going forget what was wrong. See and not intervene in the events is like living without hope without faith and without honor.

We must face the truth of the facts to say we have done what I corresponded. God knows that this is the law and applied always to all the levels. We must have honor, principle and respect with who do not struggle. For that reason, everybody can be free and happy, but never to be spectator, because that is not good for the human beings.

Fidel Castro is the monster and thief of the century XX and XXI. He has destroyed the Republic of Cuba from East to West in more than half a century of dictatorship communist, the most beautiful country in the world. It was total devastation throughout the Republic of Cuba as if as earthquake had happened, with his absolute power where no one is entitled to anything. But if claiming, he will kill him as he has done throughout his life gangster. But almost all the communists have died in the century XX and XXI. And the few that remain are in the last years of their lives. All of them filled of failures and defeats in all parts of the world. That's what they have achieved these brainless evils.

In a population of 11, 5 million of habitants and only 20 percent is next to the dictatorship. Because they have crimes, have tortured and beaten to their own people. These men are so vile, miserable, cowards and full of mud, the enslaved people and the largest holocaust in the history of the Republic of Cuba.

They murdered thousands of men, women, children and elderly because they wanted to be free and live in a better life. These criminals hate life of the human beings because they wanted to see them in the misery without future the innocent children who were massacred at Sea.

Thank God we give because most of them have died and those who remain are like Fidel Castro is drooling and shuffling no strength to stand, when they go to sleep asking God a few more days of life, and also to all saints more day of life. They are afraid of the hell, where Satan is waiting them.

The Dinosaur in his old age, full of illnesses will die defeated by not have obtained any achievements in his life of terrorist and criminal. Fidel Castro has been so criminal as Joseph Stalin, Benito Mussolini, Pol Pot, Adolf Hitler, Yasser Arafat, Saddam Husayn and Mao Set Tung. The comparisons with all of these criminals not exist. Fidel Castro has committed genocide very heartbreaking in the history of Cuba. Massacring tens thousands of men innocent victims and oppress the Cuban people, the torture, the slavery, the misery, the imprisonment, the murders and devastation of the Cuban nation. Those are the achievements of this miserable, motherfucker and coward.

Fidel Castro and his communist system and the army have subdued the Cuban people in poverty for more than 54 years. Without food, without medicine and with a salary that cannot meet their basic needs, let alone buy their foods. No, they cannot buy because the items are to be purchased with the ration book of barely is not enough for two weeks. And to top in with water and salt regulated. So, they have to live only with the few foods that they receive. Who can have everything, are the commanders, colonels and generals that buy freely in the market.

But, this criminal named Fidel Castro takes away food and medicine of the Cuban people to be sending to other countries to develop terrorism, murder and subversion throughout the world.

Besides, I am saying that when Fidel Castro, Raul Castro "The goose" and Ramiro Valdes "the alcoholic and assassin". They disappear from the face of the earth, the terror will finish. These scoundrels have developed all kind of terrorism from that they took the power in 1959. The Cuban people have lived more than half century of torture, misery, hunger, slavery, the imprisonments and suffering.

In 1920 the communists were a little group disorganized. The Socialist Popular Party (PSP), was named, Popular Communist Party (PCP) when it was founded in 1925. However, they were struggling in organizing workers. The Confederation of Workers of Cuba (CTC) in 1939.

In those years began the tragedy of the Cuban people. Years passed and Fulgencio Batista legalized the Communist Party. In 1943 Cuba and the Soviet Union established diplomatic relations. Blas Roca was a member of the Communist Party since 1934. He was elected as Party General Secretary Communist since 1940-1952, who served in the House of Representatives. The other was Carlos Rafael Rodriguez, a leader of the Communist Party. Lawyer and Economist, who became a prominent politician, He was an opponent against the administration of Gerardo Machado, along with the group of Communist of the gay life. Carlos Rafael was Mayor in Cienfuegos in 1931. He joined the Socialist Party and was elected to the Central Committee in 1943 and 1944. He served as a lawyer in the Court of Havana. He was Minister without Portfolio and member of the National Committee during the postwar years in the government of Fulgencio Batista. This man always stood by Fidel Castro as lead counsel in the affairs of the Communist Party until his dead and with the beards of goat that always he used.

The communists are not human beings, they are just criminal's terrorists, murderers, corrupt, thieves and do not deserve the forgiveness for Satan. Those who have died embrace Marxist-Leninist doctrine full of hatred and revenge for being cowards and with much resentment.

Essentially, Fidel Castro "the thief" is always surrounded of criminals to kill and destroy everything in their path with irresponsible terrorism. They have a docile and subservient behavior very weak. They still roam by worldwide looking for a place to rest, Fidel Castro with his anger in his soul of vulture without the support of the masses of peasants and workers. Everyone knows that neither worker nor peasants backed him when he was in the Sierra Maestra hiding in the cave of the mountain where communist guerrillas were operating.

The farmer refused to cooperate with the communist Castro and all those weak men of the Popular Socialist Party (PSP) with his irrepressible resentment. Evicted of the land from the Escambray to the peninsula of Pinar del Rio, place they could not enter nor leave, where had lived for centuries.

That was Castro's revenge because farmers did not cooperate nor bowed to the cowardice of the guerrillas, who did not promise anything to favor the workers peasants. There resentment began and essentially the communist Fidel Castro. Who never can get that the farmers cooperate with its communist doctrine? For Castro is essential and never is satisfied because he sees everything in black and white.

To all these crimes was joined by a group of soldiers with Captain Jose Quevedo Perez who meekly led the combat against the guerrillas who were in the mountains of the Sierra Maestra. This man of immoral conduct surrendered with his soldiers docile to the ranks of the Communists. That is cowardice of these men without honor. They surrendered to the ranks of the Communists without analyze the consequences and your irresponsibility against the Cuban people, who did not understand the politic and its development. Men despicable were carrying their own friends to death in firing squad. Many martyrs shed their blood the sake of freedom. Heroes unforgettable that raise their arms in their graves to do justice for all the miserable bastards that destroyed the land where they birthed.

Men cowards negate who have committed the massacres made by more than 50 years. These men still have the shamelessness to come and live in a democratic country after they are skeletons that are on the verge of death and to have committed the genocide darkest in the history of the Cuban people. So are all these scoundrels who have no shame or decency because they are dark men.

All we know that it these men have fought for the social injustice and never for social justice for the people. This is due to a depraved mind and corrupt life of the communists which support all evil that exists in earth. Men miserable have assassinated to a noble and generous people who are not capable of defend the society of all the cruelty of those who destroy everything in their path. This kind of damn curse had created a danger in the people because they are living in slavery. The Cuban people not have anything and only receive the misery that gave these miserable. Castro is a son of bitch and assassin. That is the truth.

The pain and suffering of people dying of hunger, the misery, the poverty and slavery and walks the streets powerless and unable to get something to survive to the horrible famine. This is the most heartbreaking crime that humans have lived in the history of mankind.

Men are without shame in their souls. Their eyes shine with the blood spilled, the hatred, the falsehood, the mercantilism, the blindness, the pain to a humble people. So was like they destroyed the Republic of Cuba these criminals' internationalists.

The terror and barbarism as much committed by youth 18 and 20 years who belonged to compulsory military service and the armed forces. The youths shed much blood of brave men without any justification by committing crimes against humanity of men heroic, brave but essentially honest, generous and heroes, brave but essentially honest, generous and heroic.

Many martyrs shed their blood the sake of freedom. Heroes unforgettable that they lift the arms from their graves to do justice for all the miserable bastards that destroyed the land of their ancestors.

Those who have not experienced the horror of genocide Cuban do not know what freedom and democracy. All these criminals will die with his eyes open as fish on market by all the crimes they committed and commit. These murderers have committed all kind of crimes against the Cuban people, the savagery, the cruelty and the massacres.

These generations of 1920, 1930 and 1940 will disappear all communists. The Cuban nation with social and economy ideas will grow in the XXI century. The young people will build a nation free of all suffering, the horror, the genocide, the famine, the slavery, the torture, the murder and will carry in their hearts all the pain and suffering of his ancestors who lived through the disaster of the Cuban nation that was decimated by Marxists-Leninists. Because the youth they were not agree with Communist dictatorship that converted the country into rubble and debris.

This new generation of the century XXI, they can develop the technology, the economy and social progress for the new generations to come. The nation will grow without hate, without revenge, without slavery and suffering of all Cubans, where can build a better world to live for centuries.

Man had been unfeeling. He just thought and watches others with indifference. The man is cruel and believes that is invincible and that he can control everything. And other mistakes of the men.

The envious man does not respect to the others, speak ill of the neighbor lives and does not look his spots. He is a reckless and often uses violence to get what he wants. Violence that leads to death or to the suffering if left alive.

The man is very smart to be selfish, violent, cruel, rebel, dirty, miserable, coward, liar, criminal, corrupt, gangster, thief, abuser, irresponsible, mean, scoundrel, without honor. Without decency, without ideals, traitor and few more things we could say about the man and the lepers essentially communists.

The leaders of the Cuban communist system have no brain to think and all say the same thing that your boss. They are all murderers and none can contradict the communist dictator Fidel Castro as known as the thief and assassin. They are cowards, docile, criminals, atheist and scoundrels.

I see the poison in the blood inoculated with these thugs and communist's geese. They will not be able to erase from his mind what he was taught and that no man could contradict their leader and weaknesses homosexuals to be obedient their leader with the weaknesses homosexuals to the obedient, docile and subservient as Ramiro Valdes in his of motherfucker life and drunk.

These types of men are controlled by the Ministry of the Armed Forces and their control is absolute and no one can give a personal opinion to express their anger within the ranks of the Communist Party. Of course, they have a defeatist mentality, men humiliated, powerless and without mental capacity.

The life of these men is the extortion, the corruption and evil, since they got the first barking, when bitches mothers gave birth to them for crime, destruction, slavery, poverty and terrorism around the world. Unjustified actions for all that have suffered the torture of an evil regime, bloodthirsty bastards. Men who carry on his face the blood of the heroes of the motherland. These terrorists hate because are coward with the children aged of 9, 10, 11, 12, 13, 14 and 15 years old, because they did not accept the communist government. No, you cannot deny the reality and let alone the truth that hurts in the soul.

All I am telling you is what has happened since communism took power in 1959 with only 1,839 guerrillas that almost all were intellectuals and professionals who came down from the Sierra Maestra where Fidel Castro was hiding in the mountains of Cuba, to covert the island of Cuba in a dumpster full of debris. These are the achievements of these wild and wicked monsters. Who can deny that the jail and bivouac full of children and young people were wildly beaten by mobs military on cold nights to the one or two in the morning.

These who have lived all this cruelty in jails and prisons we cannot forget the thugs who committed these horrible crimes to innocent children. It was extremely difficult to emerge unscathed from the mob of soldiers who quench their hatred against defenseless men and boy. Beatings were every day, revenge of those despicable military. The epic that with honor and decorum political prisoners in default we can say that these wretches are butcher's terror of the worst kind that may exist in the universe.

The mass destruction caused by these criminals, only for hatred and revenge, they did every day crueler and coward, starting with the executioner Ramiro Valdes, murderer, alcoholic, assassin, terrorist, thief, coward, miserable communist had assassinated thousands of people in 1959, 1960, 1961, 1962, 1963 this bastard and scoundrel.

The political prisoners have experienced the cruelest process of the history of the Republic of Cuba. The heroic political prisoners were abandoned in the most critical moments of their lives. We all know that crime creates to execute by the hatred that feels the communist. That is what they carry in their souls these criminals. All of them are cruel against the Cuban people. We see the men with the mental problem, emotional and sentimental. All of them have to massacre the people of Cuba that was blameless. Men with beards and long hair have made the massacred thousands of men, women, elderly and children in the history of Cuba.

THE TRUTH

The Truth of a child that sees to a different world whose thinking was beyond of my imagination. He called me because he wanted to talk to me in the mid-1960. Cornelio Gallardo said with his brief words full of wisdom all that was happening in the country. My brother Cornelio expressed wisely the situation of the country and we had to have very careful with what was happening. He said in his conversation, the sky every day is darker and does not look anything good for the nation.

Pedro: The sky is always the same. Nevertheless, the human beings have many ambitions, because we do not understand the reality of the life. Nevertheless, we destroyed everything because we not think in the future.

Cornelio: He with his genius and wisdom natural he replied. "You know better nobody that the Cuban nation is on a very narrow road and very difficult to transit and in nothing good is going to end, because they are doing things against God".

Pedro: All I see with many stains and we will become a filthy homeless for everything that is happening right now.

Cornelio: You are talking like a wise, and I like talking with you so that you are smart and do not forget me in any time because I will always be by your side. Although there are many obstacles on the road, all win.

Pedro: However, the fruit is not ripe to reap the harvest, because the trees have not grown.

Cornelio: He actually laughed and said, "The harvest will be not for now, you and I, we know. The trees shall grow and many will die, because they lacked the sap, rain and roots will dry and the tree will fall.

Pedro: I understood what he was saying with his wisdom of his words and I kept thinking about knowledge and wisdom without knowing I was going to respond.

Cornelio: He looked at me and said: "We are living like a desert and the rain does not appear, because never in history hah had this immorality, the abuse of the society, all social and moral principles."

Pedro: I listened to his words with the wisdom as an angel who shed their light on the earth and left me thinking in those crucial moments of his short life as could see a different world, with sadness in his eyes, so was happening in our country. He analyzed every detail from their short years of the life and how could see in his imagination what would happen in our fatherland when generations will pass. And everything would in the past, like a dream, when you wake up that not remember nothing, just the memory of the dream.

Cornelio: with his genius and wisdom toll me, "You know, I would go to do, but for now I cannot. Nevertheless, I will be very close to you, and we will have to wait for a new dawn as a child at birth and mother hugs him and he is happy. So, it will be when this is over. Though, the snow will cover our scalps through the years. Besides, you will have to go through hard times and no one will arrive to you because I will be with you. You do not know the path that you go to cover. But you arrive on time. Nevertheless, the nature has in store a special place for your old age. The new trees wait you arrive. They see you very tired and many will admire you as an unknown hero for everything you did for them and will follow you steps as an example of love for the Fatherland.

He kept talking and said: "Look how strong I am," and shook my hand and squeezed as if to say goodbye. "And remember that every work that begins must end it." That's what my brother said with his words and prophecies in the years of the childhood, with the vision to see what I had to pass before to arrive to the end of the road. Said one month before his eternal rest

Pedro: He sees a different world with his mentality when started the suffering and pain of Cuban mothers crying for their children who had left, never to return, because had been assassinated in the firing squads. Cornelio had expressed many truths in every words and every thought to see what would happen for generations. That was the understanding. He did not speak rudely of the men that fill the earth of debris, the death of Fidel Castro with the diseases and suffering, where Satan waits for him in the caldera of hell by his ambitions outside the law of God. So Cornelio Gallardo was and never forgets this ordeal.

But the most important thing is that often live illusions and we are not aware of reality. He said, I want to tell you something that go to live for future generations, when you finish all this tragedy, will come three elderly, after half century, very tired, but with a lot of history. They will govern for a short time. Cuban people's worship and in its few years of life create a new nation flourishing. That is what goes to happen. We are experiencing the mass destruction. I want to tell you that never miss the faith or the hope. Because you will live a better world and the stars will dance as precious pearl necklaces at night, and the days will be bright with cumulus of clouds that irrigate earth with its rain, and flowers beautify the landscape and everyone will be happy.

Pedro: We must all prepare ourselves intellectually to make our lives less sacrifices because we expected an uncertain world and that is what we must avoid.

Cornelio: "Intelligence is natural in the people and develops his knowledge at the universities where intellectuals through the studies can express your ideas and knowledge. This does not mean that people who have not attended at the Universities cannot do the same. Whether cannot read or write has as much talent as the who has made a career of Law, Medicine, Economics, Education, Journalism, Engineering, Sciences, History and many more that exist and the human beings can to develop their knowledge. But the most important thing is to have God in your heart and the tree to grow and will give flower and fruit and never missing. The man's greatness is his generosity and not in those with an empty soul because they have never harvested nothing."

Pedro: I was surprised as child express in detail what I had never imagined. He told me many truths in his childhood that one has to think because there is always something better in the life.

Cornelio: "The human being is able to experience many emotions, hate, failure, frustration, revenge, love, gratitude, sadness and pain. But the love is the greatest feeling because it covers the entire world. And remember that when you love is closer to God, who is the Supreme Being in all. Is eternal, omnipotent, knows everything, all things owe their existence to him, their presence is everywhere, if we are further we encounter with God. Nevertheless, the biggest thing in the man is the soul, and the biggest thing in the soul is God."

Love is a feeling of the spirit that has to be expressed. Expresses love and giving of himself. If there is love always gives you something to be loved. God not only has, but has given. God gave us hope, faith, love, joy, family, night, day, wisdom and dream for us to rest."

"God gives us life, and gives us that air we breathe, the land we support, the light, day, wisdom, and dream for us to rest. God gives us life and gives us oxygen we breathe, the land we support, the light us illuminate, the heat and cold. But God gave us his son Jesus Christ, who is the greatest gift we can have. Christ is worth more than all the treasures that may exist in this world, poor and rich, ignorant and the learned, weak and powerful, sinner and saint, children, men and women, The earth will receive to all individually or collective and each will be classifies accord to the law of God. Cornelio said many truths with his natural intelligence of human being and as a genius who comes to earth with the wisdom to know what is happening around us. I want to say something, "I know you are not going to like my words. But you will understand when you finish the Cuban people genocide that you go to live. And remember that when you return home you will not find what you left."

Those were the last words of Cornelio Gallardo when he went to rest eternally. I was very impressed with all points of view and knowledge beyond what I could imagine. Cornelio told me many interesting things that I have not forgotten like my brain is a tape recorder so that I never forgot what he had said in his childhood in the most difficult moments of his short life.

I think life teaches us wonderful things to humans. So many years passed until one day I started to think of all that I had passed in my life and I remembered what my brother Cornelio had told me in 1960. However, I had never thought those words unpredictable. But the most interesting of all is that he has not been wrong in what he said ago more than half a century, an unforgettable reality in all my life.

BAY OF PIGS

The Collapse of Playa Giron and the surrender of Brigade 2506 created a lot of confusion in the country, where the underground Organizations November 30 Movement (M-30-11), People Revolutionary Movement (MRP), Revolutionary Recovery Movement (MRR), Cuban Democratic Movement (MDC), Insurrectional Revolutionary Movement (MIR), and dozens of organizations were abandoned because their leaders had been arrested and others had left to the exile.

While all this was going on April 18, 1961 with the failure and the surrender of Brigade 2506 in Playa Giron, political prisoners of the Isle of Pines prison struggling to free itself from the dozens of tons of dynamite installed in the four tunnels of the circular. That work was extremely difficult and crucial to the political prisoners to achieve the facilities where they were the tens of tons of explosives to disconnect wires electronics connected to the dynamite.

No, it was not easy to build tunnels in the solid walls of concrete and granite floods to reach the 220-volt electrical cables. A mistake with the detonators connected to tons of dynamite would produce an explosion of catastrophic magnitudes and would disappear from the face of the earth more than 5,000 political prisoners. We were living on a powder keg for over a year waiting for the dead slowly but surely.

The catastrophe of the facilities of the Isle of Pines prison was imminent and had to act quickly on the job to disconnect electric cables. It was cruel and monstrous with savagery of the terrorist regime to massacre the population of Cuban Political Prisoners.

The political prisoners with courage and heroism, opens tunnels to reach the facilities where the detonators were. Without to sleep, after so many hours of work, and without testing night and day, the political prisoners had been able to reach the facility and had disconnected the electronic cables of the detonators. Heroically brave men who rushed to save the Presidio Politico of the monstrosity and to eliminate all political prisoners of the Isle of Pines.

The political prisoners had succeeded in his mission. In the most difficult times risked their lives to save the prisoners of the Isle of Pines prison. That was a time of reflection, joy and peace, where a group of men can arrive and to deactivate tens of tons of dynamite. That was almost a mission impossible, not to have the resources necessary to drill the solid concrete walls. That was brave and heroics feat, rushing to save the Presidio Politico Cuban, with more than 5,000 inmates in its facilities.

All was joy when so huge number of tons of dynamite was deactivated. Now we had to wait between walls in of Isle of Pines prison. Only God could stop the genocide that Castro had planned to remove the Presidio Politico Cuban if the Brigade of Bay of Pigs triumphed.

The days passed quickly, and we did not know if the Communists were going to bomb the facilities of the Isle of Pines. Only we had to wait the outcome of the Bay of Pigs Invasion, and members Brigade 2506.

The 2506 Brigade had surrendered unconditionally in Playa Giron in less than 72 hours by a lack of logistical support and without ammunition, water and food. The U.S. administration had left them alone on April 17, 1961. The Brigade 2506 surrendered for the superiority in weapons and dozens of men in the battlefield. They fought heroically against the communist system. But, they were alone and defeated.

68 Brigade were killed in combat and another 19 were killed, nine in the Sea and 10 in the Truck of death. The rest, up to 101, were shot in the firing squads in the prison of The Cabaña, and others died of starvation in the jails and prisons without medical assistance.

The hope had disappeared with the surrender of Brigade 2506 in the Bay of Pigs Invasion, the timing of the overthrow of communism and all its criminals' terrorists, Marxist-Leninists was lost.

A week after the communist government decided to withdraw all the tons of dynamite from the four circulars the Isle of Pines. The thief Castro comes with his terrorism murder, the massacres of tens of thousands of men in the firing squads, imprisonment, drug trafficking and the guerrilla in Central America, South America and Caribbean.

Who were the young boys who threw to death without being certain of success? Only in exchange for a long shot that existed at that time, because Castro's communist government knew would Brigade 2506 Bay of Pigs would land and were waiting in the coast of Playa Giron.

Those who have committed the infamy of not communicating to the Brigade of Bay of Pigs Invasion the disembarking will not have peace on earth. The abortive disembarking had been rejected by Pentagon and signed by President John F. Kennedy. They were men with hope in victory that for them was almost certain. But the leaders of the Brigade 2506 ignored him the speech of President John F. Kennedy five days before the Bay of Pigs landing.

Where were Jose Miro Cardona, Rafael Lincoln Diaz Balart, Jose Antonio de Varona and Carlos Prios Socarras, when the young were dying of Brigade 2506? There are many questions and few answer and tell not the truth. They rest in peace and anybody will know the Truth hidden of the Bay of Pigs Invasion, because, they are living the eternal life.

THE BRIGADIST

The Bay of Pigs all it did was to consolidate the communist system, enslaving the Cuban people and submit to the barbarity of the famine. But around this dilemma are interesting and wonderful things. For example, a few days after that the Brigade 2506 was had been surrendered. A man arrived (Brigadist) named Rolando, I do not Know if that was his name or not.

What I can say is the he was 25 or 30 years old. The Brigadist told me that he needs to see his girlfriend who lived in the Vedado La Havana. I told him, I have no problems with that. When you want could go see his bride. Choose the day.

Three days later we went to see his beloved girlfriend that she did not know he had been in the Invasion of Playa Giron. The Brigadist, the driver of the black race and I arrived at the house of the bride. I get off the Truck where we were going the three. I headed home to his girlfriend.

When I get to the home, the sister of the bride of the Brigadist was with her boyfriend, a lieutenant of the Army. I asked her if her sister was in the house. Yes, she said, she was in the dining room with her dad. Without saying a word, I went where they were and told the father and daughter that wanted to talk with them.

They went with me to the street and there, I told them that Rolando was waiting. She opened her eyes and told me. He was in the United States. I replied that he was waiting them. We walked until we got where he expected.

She was overjoyed when she saw him and talked a few minutes on the street. They agreed to be in the Film 23 and Zapata. The Brigadist, the driver and I left for the Cinema where we had to wait for bride and father will arrive several minutes later. As was my habit I stayed street waiting the bride and father of the Brigadist, because we have to take precaution of someone were looking at the three in the truck. We had to avoid any problem So that the driver and Brigadist can leave quickly the place where they were awaiting the arrival of bride and father.

A few minute after they arrived. She had changed her dress and came very elegant to the Cinema, But I for precaution. I stayed a block from Brigadist and driver.

Minutes after the father and daughter joined me and we all gathered in the Cinema. We entered the Cinema and they spent an hour together until the movie ended. Maybe, they were talking about their future marriage in the United States.

When we entered, I was surprised because were putting the movie of Bay of Pigs and when the movie ended we all go out and Roland explained that the Invasion of Bay of Pigs or playa Giron had been a failure. But he had escaped of the hell without any type of experience in the place boggy where the men were dying in the battlefields without aerial support. His partners were dying because they had no air cover and were slaughtering the enemy in the battlefield.

She was very happy and his father as well, and between kisses and hugs goodbye, perhaps for the purpose of getting married in exile when she will arrive for the United States. She was happy to see her love, like a child when see the father comes and he kiss him when takes many hours outside without seeing him. That was one of the most wonderful experiences of my life to see this woman so full of joy knowing that had man of her life near her.

The day that Rolando went for the embassy, he does not know that I had gone very early to the home of a friend who had come from the Escambray to seek some medical supplies and some ammunitions he needed. I just could not tell the Brigadist of Bay of Pigs that a friend had come from the Escambray. I could not say anything for the failure of the Brigade 2506. I had to remain in silent with him, where he was hiding.

So, spent hidden the last day and when I came back it was gone, had sought asylum in the embassy. Rolando not knew in what place he could find me. That is the greatness of the men who fight and are virtually anonymous to other that are not within of that small that a detail. You can go you to jail for many years, as it happened to me, or perhaps, lose the life with Fidel Castro and Ernesto Guevara "Che" in the firing squads.

When you are young you risk all hazards and the life is different thing when you already have a mature age. We are more conservatives.

I admire the young because they are determined, and when they are in combat are brave and not afraid of the enemy's bullet in the battle.

I do not know if this man lives or has died in combat in other countries, as they have been thousands of Cubans who have integrated the U.S. Army Forces, and only we spoke of a dozen of them. The rest are anonymous men such as me. I cannot see reports in the media of radio, television and print media. I tried in silence and work to the enemy when working in silence and work is efficient, when you feel done to comply with the duty imposed on us by the homeland and to pursue it in the most difficult times, remembering that the Homeland is only a as is the mother.

Actually I have never seen in the U.S. Rolando, nor have I wondered why the FBI does not give information but you are a reporter, or a government official. Perhaps you have the information. I guess the Brigadist Rolando the Bay of Pigs Invasion is alive.

There are thousands of anonymous men and women, that npbody know about them. I am sure they want to their country and their hearts are always watching and observing others who betrayed the motherland. They never had been joined the ranks of the enemies and traitors for executed many thousands of martyrs in the firing squads.

See a world filled with sadness and pain when the stars and beauty of light of the sky reflects the nostalgia of the night with the necklaces of precious pearls and when the morning comes and the light of the sun caress the face of the heroic men. They were able to defend Fatherland proudly. But Che Guevara and Fidel Castro took their lives without giving them a chance to see the light of day.

THE HATE IN ACTION

On January 1962, after that all the prisoners of the Bay of Pigs Invasion were in the circulars of Isle of Pines prison. The terror began before the start of the Summit of Punta Del Este, on February 24, 1962. The circulars of the Isle of Pines were crowded with thousands of pounds of Trinitrotoluene (TNT) in the tunnels of the four circulars. However, the situation worsened when the military started drilling holes in the walls of the circulars for several months to install the cables, with 32 tons of TNT round four of the circulars of the prison.

The military had drilled the walls to place the entire monstrosity of TNT, when the meeting began in Punta Del Este. The tunnels were filled with tons of TNT. So immense that had not the remotest possibility to save the life of that monstrosity of tons of TNT. All would miss in Nueva Gerona. Nueva Gerona would be totally devastated with this impact of the explosion of 32 tons of TNT.

The political prisoners risked their lives with that huge mountain of tons of TNT and detonators in the tunnels of the prison of the Isle of Pines. The technicians were imposed mission of die or to save the prison population with more than 5,000 political prisoners in its facilities.

No, it was not easy to build tunnels in solid concrete walls to reach electronics cables. An error in to the disconnect detonators would be an explosion of catastrophic explosion magnitudes. The prison of the Isle of Pines would disappear from the face of the earth with more than 5,000 political prisoners.

The work was exhausting to make the tunnels, and holes in walls and floors granite. The Isle of Pines prison to disconnect the cables connected to electronic detonators and the mountain of Trinitrotoluene TNT with many tons in each circular. The work was extremely hard, and we had to live in a powder keg of large proportions of several tons of TNT.

The catastrophe of the Isle of Pines facilities was imminent and we had to act fast to clear monstrosity and savagery of the terrorist regime that wanted to massacre the population of Cuban Political Prisoners with tens tons of dynamites.

Inmates political with bravery and heroism pierced the walls of the tunnels to get to the facilities and the tens of tons of TNT that were in the tunnels of the four circulars to disconnect the power cables to the detonators. Men with Heroics had saved the Presidio Politico of the monstrosity that the communist government had created to eliminate all political prisoners of the Isle of Pines.

Trinitrotoluene (TNT) (Notation JEPAG) is an aromatic hydrocarbon pale yellow, crystalline, melting at 81° C. Is a chemical compound of several explosive mixtures, for example, Amatol is obtained by mixing ammonium nitrate. Is prepared by the nitration of Toluene ($C_6H_2CH_2$), has chemical formula $C_6H_2(NO_2)_3CH_3$.

Is its refined form, Trinitrotoluene is quite stable and, unlike Nitroglycerin, is relatively insensitive to friction, shock or agitation. Explodes when an object of 2 kg of dough falls on it from 35 cm height (ie. 2 kg at a speed of 2.62 m/s, or force of 19.6 Newktons, with an energy of 6.86 Joules), the temperature of explosion, when anhydride is 470° C. This means that the toy must use a detonator.

Does not reach with metals or absorbs water, so it is very stable for storage for long periods of time, unlike of the dynamite.

German chemist Joseph W. Wilbrand TNT first manufactured in 1863. It was used as a yellow dye. Is potential as an explosive was not apparent until after many years, especially for being more difficult compared with other detonation explosives and less powerful than other alternatives.

The political prisoners succeeded in their mission. In the most difficult times risked their lives to save the political prisoners of penitentiary of Isle of Pines. A group of men managed what was almost a mission impossible by not having the resources necessary to pierce of solid concrete walls under the stairs, to perform such a heroic and courageous that, rushing in to die to save the Presidio Politico Cubano with more than 32 tons of Trinitrotoluene TNT in all circulars with more than 5,000 political prisoners in its facilities.

The city of Nueva Gerona would disappear with all its inhabitants with such an immense load of TNT placed in the circulars buildings of the Isle of Pines prison. The consequences of the explosion would be devastating population the Isle of Pines for many years due to contamination. The population could die of cancer through the years by the monstrosity and cruelty. Fidel Castro has been worse that Satan and the international communism.

No, that was never spoken in the nations in the world, because really not were interested in the life of the Cuban people and much less with the men who had risked their lives defending democracy and international interests of all nations.

Among its advantages, however, was the ease of liquefied securely using steam or hot water could be introduced in liquid form inside the pods of artillery shells. It is also very stable, in 1910 was removed from British Explosives Act 1975, losing the consideration of explosive manufacturing and storage effect.

The German Army adopted it for its artillery in 1902. The armor-piercing projectiles exploded after penetrating inside the main British warships filled with Lilita tended to explode when hitting the shields wasted of his energy on the outside of the ship. The British began to use it as a substitute for Lidita in 1907.

Due to the high demand for explosives in World War II TNT often mixed with 40-80 percent of Ammonium Nitrate, producing an explosive was called Amatol. Although practically was as strong as TNT and much cheaper, the Amatol had the slight disadvantage of being hygroscopic (has an affinity for absorbing water). Variation Minol lowland, consisting Amatol with about

20 percent of Aluminum powder, was used by the British in the mines and depth charges.

Although TNT blocks are available in various sizes (250, 500, 1000 gr.) is most commonly found in a number of other components. Some examples of explosive containing TNT are Amatol, Baratol, Composition B, Actol, Pentolite, Tompex, Trinotal and Dinotal.

B. Amatol, experts in explosives, Isle of Pines would be a ghost town because its population would be decimated in the face of the earth for many years and with a high percentage of pollution that would make inhabitable the Isle of Pines for generations. The chemist, scientist the German explosives expert Joseph Lee "Chinese" hired by the government of Fulgencio Batista before he came the guerrilla of Castro government, said he could not do anything because everything would disappear in seconds by the huge amount of Trinitrotoluene TNT that had been installed in the tunnels of the circulars of the Isle of Pines. That everything would be like a desert by the monstrosity of all the tons of TNT in the tunnels of the Circulars.

All this was what you wanted to use to eliminate Political Prisoners in Isle of Pines in February 1962, when governments met on February 24, 1962, in Punta Del Este. They were supporting the subversion of all the countries that were against of the government of the United States. And essentially the government of Cuba and by the international Marxist-Leninist and had been supported by Fidel Castro the assassin and terrorist and his brother "The Duck)."

If TNT had been activated Nueva Gerona and the population of the Isle of Pines prison and the other cities of the territory of the Isle, through the years the effect of the pollution the Isle of Pines would be an uninhabitable place for years if the attack was would have occurred against the political prisoners in 1062, with more than 32 tons of TNT, when the terrorist government of Fidel Castro was in Punta of Este.

We would be still suffering the consequences of the Holocaust of the population of Isle of Pines. The population of the Isle of Pines would live with cancer for many years, where thousands of heroes gave their lives for the fatherland. That was what happened in the Isle of Pines in 1962, thousands of pounds of TNT during a year. Yes, with that monstrosity in the twentieth. That is the truth of our life in jails and prisons.

THE OCTOBER CRISIS

The crisis began on October 14, 1962 with flights of U-2 plane over Western Cuba. The reconnaissance mission by Major Richard Heyser, was the first strategic air command mission after the authority on flights was transferred from the Air Force of the CIA. The photos taken by the mission provided the first evidence of MRBM in Cuba.

The reading fast team in the interpretation of the National Center Agency Photographs (ANPIC) in Washington analyzed photos taken by U-2 mission of Richard Heyser. Later one of the teams showed pictures of major component of the Soviet MRBM in a field of San Cristobal, Pinar del Rio also identified another shipment with 24 SAM-2 type rockets. Another photograph from the San Julian showed an IL-28 light bomber dismantled. However, the explanation why no McGeorge Bundy informed President Kennedy of missiles in Cuba was because he had spent the night out dated and did not give the information to the other day in the morning of October 16, 1962. Men like these endanger the lives of millions of human beings.

On October 16, 1962 McGeorge Bundy informed the President Kennedy that he had strong evidence, obtained by the photographs, that Cuba had Soviet MRBM. John McCloy, a Republican lawyer who acted as a private consultant to President Kennedy, recommended that the President take strong actions to remove the missiles, by the gravity of an air strike and Invasion.

Actually, talking a lot, but the situation of the missile crisis of October 1962 is getting worse by the indecision of the Pentagon's Strategic Command. That always happens in this Department when you have to make immediate decisions that left as if the problem was not urgent.

The Congress and House of Representatives and the United Nations were trembling jaws and teeth crunched not let them think what they were doing at the time of the October crisis.

The days passed and all of run of a place to another without knowing how they would solve the problem of the missiles and the crisis between Cuba, the Soviet Union and the United States.

Photos taken by the mission of the U-2 piloted by Richard Heyser showed the major component of Soviet MRBM fields of San Cristobal, Pinar del Rio.

Afternoon flight are sorted and six reconnaissance U-2, so made during the day. The situation with the Cubans became more difficult. The only option left was a single air raid on bases surgical missiles, a series of attacks for a comprehensive invasion and blockade of Cuba.

The day went by and the missile crisis in Cuba stretched no solution to the problem created by Castro and his elite commanders unconditional without brains who thought only in international terrorism.

The B-52 nuclear bombers were about to take off with passive attacks to destroy all military and civilian airport. All aircraft were armed with nuclear weapons, the gravity of the missile crisis in Cuba. It seemed that there was no solution to conflicts created by the communist government of Cuba.

Negotiations with both the Governor Soviet and U.S. were enforced, without having to negotiate with Cuba's communist government. That made the thief Castro hatred of the United States that has not left him sleep at night because he did not have between the United Sates and the Soviet Union. So you have to die this terrorist thief and drug dealer.

The decision taken by the United Sates was applying a naval quarantine on Cuba effectively. Suddenly the news came on November 12, 1962. The Premier Nikita Khrushchev had confirmed the extraction of the missiles from Cuba.

Yes, all offensive weapons were withdrawn from Cuba and outside the Western Hemisphere. Hopes that Cuba was free of communism had vanished and political prisoners Isle of Pines had been completely abandoned by the decision of foreign governments in final to convert the Island of Cuba in a focus subversive guerrillas in the Western Hemisphere and unprotected for political prisoners who fought for freedom and democracy to the Cuban people were not subjected to slavery, misery, poverty, hunger, physical prisoners were totally stranded with tens of thousands across the country of the Republic of Cuba.

The Soviet Union had taken the lead in defense of Cuba. However, the administration of the United States, accommodating to the Soviet, they accept everything proposed by the Soviet minister. Both administrations, they agreed to resolve the problem created by the Cuban administration.

The timing of the overthrow of the dictatorship of Cuba was lost with the negotiations between the United States and the Soviet Union. The leaders of the United Sates and the Soviet Union were without Castro, who in the middle of the negotiations of the two most powerful world powers.

The October 1962 crisis put the world on the brink of World War III. The United States, the Soviet Union and European countries for a country that meant a lot of to Western democracy and much to the Soviet Union caused by blackmail communist dictator of the Republic of Cuba. Also, knowing how act the Soviet Union and the United States, which have always been an inseparable marriage, everything looked like it would be a divorce between them. But like any marriage, after launching many indirect reached reconciliation and settle their differences on the bed, when it seemed that the world tells on them. They agreed to a settlement and that no more talk between the two lovers who love each other forever.

Thus, Marriage is inseparable from the United States and the Soviet Union, we always help each other in times difficult and inconveniences the fixed to monitor arms until death do you part.

But the most interesting part is that if the Soviet Union attacks a country by force, or does the United States, comes the kicking and even seems to be definitely fight. However, love is stranger than force. Days later made an invitation and sit at a sumptuous banquet with silverware and glasses of champagne, and nothing has happened here, always the losers are the people who have to lie to shoulder the entire burden of what they left inseparable lovers.

The consolidation of Marxism-Leninism by the defeat of Playa Giron and neglect of those who ought to overthrow the communist government was the result of total dedication to such a brutal system of Soviet-American negotiation.

The delivery of the Island of Cuba to Communism was one of the most devastating blows in the history of the Republic of Cuba, which did not respect the right of Cubans by government around the world.

The pain goes to the Cuban people, who had not harmed any government of Western Hemisphere. Yes, have been cruel to the Republic of Cuba and the most generous people in the world. Only God can forgive you for everything you have done a noble people suffer, but brave like no other in the world.

The Cuban People will not forget how it was left to his own devices by weak and complacent with communism and corruption all universal. Thus, the Cuban people will have to live in bondage fiercest Marxist-Leninist of Western Hemisphere by the irresponsibility of governments envious. But Cuba will be free very soon and many will have to mourn.

THE DISEASES

In the Isle of Pines and in every prison in the country was a great famine in 1963. I was not the only patient, in the Isle of Pines. Pinar del Rio, The Havana, Matanzas, Santa Clara, Camaguey and Santiago de Cuba political prisoners were sick and dehydrated. Food and medicine where absent on a scale I had never seen before in my life.

We had not developed immunity against amoebas and bacteria from drinking contaminated water. The bathrooms were infested with bacteria from the outbreaks by not have the necessary hygiene by the absence of detergents to remove infectious foci that existed in the bathrooms.

The most common diseases were the inflammation, related to the lack of protein in our diets, and possibly by high salt proportion at the dinner, instead to be thin like normal person. The political prisoners were usually swell in the legs and other body part. And we feel sorry for what we have.

The proportion of infectious diseases was amazing. Skin injury are common, essentially fungus. We were always exposed to moisture our skin and had not chance to dry. There were cases of Pneumonia and Tuberculosis.

Almost all political prisoners had diarrhea commons and many had dysentery, caused by improperly cooked food and water contaminated when our defenses were down.

The government gave not us any antibiotics or medicine treatments for dysentery. That was the cruelty that the Ministry of Health used headed by the thief, murder and terrorist Fidel Castro with that gang of criminals of the Armed Forces and the

Ministry of Interior led by Ramiro Valdes, Sergio Del Valle, Jose Abrantes and Raul Castro.

I was ashamed of my dysentery, is an ugly and humiliating disease. I thought that was going to die and that it was over for me.

Something feels when one is on a hunger strike for several days and begins to think of the roast, vegetables, fruits, salads, milk, breads, cheese, sweets and when the hunger strike is over. We begin to live another reality, of the fantasy of dream on an empty stomach and on the verge of death during six hunger strikes after to be 7, 9, 11, 20, 35 and 46 days in each hunger strike in a state of dehydration.

These have been the most official moments I have had in my life. They are unforgettable and God only half the strength to overcome all evil that most cruel system of Planet Earth. The legs will tremble because muscles have no strength to support the weight of your body after losing 40, 50, 60 and 70 pounds so violently in a few days.

So the years passed and the majority of the political prisoners in rebelliousness had saved the lives of the most horrible ordeals in jails and prisons with the massacres of thousands of political prisoners in the firing squads. The Forced Labor Plan Camilo Cienfuegos, hunger strikes, isolation, nudity and murders in the punishment cells without medical assistance, in filthy, completely dark, and full of microbes, unhygienic, dilated pupils in the darkness of the sealed cells with metal plates.

When, we went out the light was like if you prick with pins the eyes due from years we are living in dark cells of punishment, with the brutality and savagery of the criminal and savage mental weaknesses communists and terrorists.

The monstrosity of the executioners Marxist-Leninist was so fierce that the political prisoners in rebelliousness were living Naked in the filthy cells, as in the primitive slavery, where the slave chained dies wildly of starvation and cold. So, we had to live without being able to cover our body with a towel or shirt for the cold and humidity or die of hypothermia because of the savagery used by Interior Ministry.

That barbarism we have lived all political prisoners in rebelliousness because of communist, terrorist and murderers who submit the most impoverished people into poverty. Poverty and hunger have been more heartbreaking crimes committed by officials of the communist system in Cuba and Fidel Castro mainly, the criminal and thief internationalist with the plague of scoundrels and murderers Cubans., the nation has become a dumping ground of rubble.

Unfortunately, I had to live all the events, or nearly all, in the jails and prisons of Cuba. I, as political prisoner was in rebelliousness, food shortages, illness and lack of medications in the punishment cells. All the political prisoners were cut off from their families for more than 9 and 12 years in cells completely dark without artificial light without light of the Heaven with doors and windows of iron by many years. We had to live the political prisoners.

Diseases of heart diseases, hyperthermia, hypertension, stomach infections, fungal infections, tuberculosis, pneumonia, eye diseases, paralysis, ulcer diseases and many more very serious sicknesses by the lack of food and medicine. I have had to live with all that in my long years in jails and prisons in Cuba.

Faith and hope by which man lives today and oppression of thought that we all feel, is conditioned by the experience of man by his own balance, instinct, thought and emotion. However, my faith and hope in God was more powerful than all the tortures that they applied my enemies for so many years, perhaps, to die of starvation, cold, without enough alimentation and without medicine. That is the reality of my life. I have lived and suffered the evil of men cruel and cowardly, because, they are devils worse than Satan.

THE MURDERERS

The monstrosity of the murder of the Cuban people is unprecedented in the history of Cuba from the Spanish colonialists, slavery that massacred the three tribes that lived peacefully to along and width of the Republic of Cuba. The Guanahatabeyes, Siboneyes and Tainos lived in the earth more beautiful of the world, when were assassinated by the Spain colonialists. However, after 467 years arrived to power the communists, the criminals, the terrorists, the assassins of the Planet Earth. They became in coward's delinquents and ran rivers of blood in the Republic of Cuba. Angry men committed the most horrible holocaust of a people humble and generous by not accept a terrorist regime. Thousands of men and women were killed in the firing squads for opposing the communist system. The country was destroyed from East to West. The man from birth until his death is a slave. Here are the most barbaric murderers of the world.

Acebo Cortiñas, Miguel
Acevedo González, Enrique
Acevedo González, Rogelio
Alarcón de Quesada, Ricardo
Aldana Escalante, Carlos
Alegret Fernández, Vecino
Alespurúa Rodríguez., Juan C.
Alfonso Borges, Rolando
Almaguer Vidal, Orlando
Almeida Bosques, Juan

Álvarez Blanco, Julián
Álvarez Cambras, Rodrigo
Álvarez de la Nuez, Luis E.
Álvarez Gil, Abelardo
Álvaro Crespo, Vicente
Anastasio Ávila, Mario
Andollo Valdés, Leonardo
Andollo Valdés, Ramón
Araze Hernández, Filiberto
Aspolea Ruíg, Jorge Luis

Azoy Quintana, Gilda Glenda
Balaguer Cabrera, José R.
Batista Santana, Sixto
Bermúdez Castillo, Jesús
Betancourt, Abelino S.
Bonachea Valdés, José
Borroto Nordelo, Carlos
Bouza González, Heriberto
Bravo Martell, Orestes
Cabello Morales, Mario
Cabrisas Ruíz, Ricardo
Camacho Aguilera, Julio
Campa Huergo, Concepción
Cardozo Pereira, Hortensia
Carneado, José F.
Carrera Montes, Amparo Zaida
Carreras Rodríguez, Lino
Carreras Rolas, Enrique
Carriere Hernández, Sergio
Carrizo Estévez, Juan D.
Casas Regueiro, Senén
Casas Reguero, Julio
Casillas Palenzuela, Ernesto
Castaños Lage, Raúl
Castilla Más, Belarmino
Castillo Cuesta., Bárbara
Castro Ruz, Fidel
Castro Ruz, Raúl
Cienfuegos Gorriarán, Camilo
Cienfuegos Gorriarán, Osmany
Cintra Frías, Leopoldo
Cobos Conte, Miriam Isabel
Colás Sánchez, Silvino
Colomé Ibarra, Abelardo
Collazo Malos, Enrique
Confino Asian, Juan
Cortina García, Josefita L.
Crombet, Jaime

Cubelas Secades, Rolando
Cuervos Ibáñez, Eugenio
Cuevas Ramos, Jorge
Curbelo Morales, Raúl
Chávez, Pedro M.
Chomón Mediavilla, Faure
de la Guardia, Antonio
de la Guardia, Patricio
de la Rosa Hilario, Jorge L.
del Pino, Rafael
del Toro, Ulises Rosales
del Valle Jiménez, Sergio
Delgado Pérez, Manuel E.
Díaz Barrunco, Carlos
Díaz Bermudez, Miguel Mario
Díaz Cabrera, Debys I.
Díaz Denís, Vladimir
Díaz González, Manuel
Díaz Suárez, Adolfo A.
Díaz, Roberto T.
Diego Bello, Caridad del R.
Domenech Benítez, Joel
Domínguez González, Gilberto
Dotres Martínez, Carlos Pablo
Drecke Cruz, Víctor E.
Elías Iglesias, Arabel
Encono Valle, Lucio
Enoz Barceleta, Fernando R.
Escalante, Aníbal
Escalona Reguera, Juan
Espín Guilloys, Vilma
Espinosa Martín, Ramón
Estrada Nelson, Rafaela
Febles Rodríguez, Juan P.
Fernández Álvarez, José R.
Fernández Báez, Oscar
Fernández Font, Marcelo
Fernández Godín, Carlos

Fernández Mell, Oscar
Fernández Rodríguez., Herminia
Fernández Sánchez, Julio A.
Fernández Suárez, René
Fernando Silvio, Fladio T.
Ferre Gómez, Yolanda
Ferrer Martínez, Haroldo
Franks Pardo, Humberto
Frómeta Ponz, Idalme E.
Gálvez Tauples, Luis O.
Gallaego Busch, María D.
García Álvarez, María A.
García Arango, Felipe
García Carballo, Rubén S.
García de la Cruz, Teófilo
García Díaz, Roberto F.
García Fernández, Rigoberto
García Ferrer, Francisco
García Frías, Guillermo
García Laseran, Jacinto
García León, Rodrigo
García Martínez, Calixto
García Vera, Yadira
Gómez Gutiérrez, Luis Ignacio
González Albear, Víctor M.
González Farral, Emilio
González Pérez, Irán
González Pérez, Tania A.
González Vega, Rodolfo
González.López, Francisco
Grobart, Fabio
Guerra Bernejo, Raúl
Guerra González, Orestes
Guerra Hidalgo, Secundino
Guevara Valdés, Alfredo
Guín, Ramón
Gutiérrez Calzado, Carlos
Gutiérrez Cepero, Carmen

Gutiérrez Menoyo, Eloy
Gutiérrez Torres, Juan
Hallara Santana, Sixto
Haranda Calumble, Félix
Hart Dávalos, Armando
Hernández Fiffe, Ramón
Hernández García, Nelce
Hernández Gutiérrez, Ada Caridad
Hernández Pérez, Digna R.
Hernández Rodríguez, Ernio
Hernández Rodríguez, Melba
Herrera Navarro, Juan
Hidalgo Basulto, Alcibíades
Hondel González, Alfredo
Ido Morgodo, Arquímedes
Iglesias Leyva, José
Iser Mojena, Omar H.
Jiménez Lage, Reineiro
Jollamonte Vidal, Manuel
Jordan Morales, Alfredo
Junco del Pino, Juan M.
Kindelán Bles, Rolando
Lage Dávila, Agustín
Lage Dávila, Carlos
Lazo Hernández, Esteban
Leal Spangler, Eusebio
Legró Sauquet, José
Lemus Rivera, Victoriano
León Aguiar, Roberto
Leyva García, José A.
Lezcano Pérez, Jorge
Linares Culvo, Francisco
López Cuba, Néstor
López García, María E.
López Hermández, Julián
López Miera, Álvaro
López Olivera, Claudio
López Rodríguez, Wilfredo R.

Lugo Fonte, Orlando
Lussón Batlle, Antonio E.
Luzardo García, Manuel
Llanusa Gobel, José
Machado Peñalver, Francisco
Machado Ventura, José R.
Machado, Darío J.
Machín Fernández, Sonia
Malmierca Peoli, Isidoro
Malrmierca Peoli, Isidoro
Marín Pérez, Miguel
Marinello Vidaurreta, Juan
Marrero Camacho, José
Martín Muñoz, Juan C.
Martínez Corona, Conrado
Martínez Puente, Rubén
Martínez Vázquez, María C.
Martínez, María C.
Matar Franye, José
Matos Benítez, Huber
Mejías Jomarrón, Mario
Méndez Cominche, Joaquín
Mendoza, Jorge E.
Menéndez Castellanos, Manuel
Menéndez Pérez, Iris
Menéndez Puente, Rubén
Menéndez Tomassevich, Raúl
Michel Vargas, Raúl
Migra Álvarez, Eugenio L.
Milián Pino, José J.
Millán Castro, Armando
Mir Marrero, Carlos
Miret Prieto, Pedro
Miyar Barrueco, José M.
Molinelo Hernández, Isabel
Montané Oropesa, Jesús
Montseny Villa, Demetrio
Moracen Limonta, Rafael

Morales Cartaya, Alfredo
Morgas, William
Muruarte, Teresita M.
Naranjo Morales, José A.
Núñez Jiménez, Antonio
Ochoa Sánchez, Arnaldo T.
Oliva Pérez, Mario
Oliver López, Sonia
Olivera Moya, Filiberto
Palmero Hernández, Cándido
Pardo Guerra, Ramón
Pardo Lazo, Anicia
Patiño Alfonso, Osvaldo
Pausa Bello, Evelio
Pedraza Rodríguez, Lina O.
Peña González, Lázaro
Peña Osorio, Tomás G.
Pérez Betancourt, Pedro
Pérez Hernández, Faustino
Pérez Herrero, Antonio
Pérez Rodríguez, Wifredo
Pérez Roque, Felipe R.
Pérez Róspide, Luis
Pérez Villavicencio, Pablo
Pérez, Pedro M.
Piñeiro Lozada, Manuel
Portal León, Marcos Javier
Prieto Jiménez, Abel Enrique
Proenza Sánchez, Lizardo
Puebla Viltre, Delsa Ester
Quevedo Pérez., José
Quinta Solás, Joaquín
Quintana, Gilda G.
Rafael Rodríguez, Carlos
Ramírez Cruz, José
Ramos Pereira, Fidel
Regueiro, Tomás V. C.
Retamo, Ydalmiro

Reyes Castillo, Miriam
Riera Nelson, Eloy
Risquet Valdés, Jorge
Roa García, Raúl
Robinson Agramonte, Juan C.
Roca Calderío, Blas
Rocas Iglesias, Alejandro
Rodiles Planas, Samuel C.
Rodríguez González, Humberto
Rodríguez Puerta, Orlando
Rodríguez Rodríguez, Basilio
RodríguezFernández, Rafael
Rojas Santiesteban, Ursinio
Ross Leal, Pedro
Sánchez Cabrera, Osvaldo
Sánchez Díaz, Antonio
Sánchez Manduley, Celia

Santamaría Cuadrado, Haydée
Serguer, Paco
Serra Robledo, Clementina
Shuég Colás, Víctor
Silva Berroa, José R.
Sio Wong, Moisés
Solar Hernández, José
Soto Prieto, Leonel
Torena Danger, Alberto J.
Torralba González, Diocles
Torres Pérez, Nelson
Valdés Menéndez, Ramiro
Valdés Saldaña, Jorge R.
Vecino Alegret, Fernando
Viera Estrada, Roberto T.
Villegas Tamayo, Harry
Yabur Maluf, Alfredo

A WORLD OF TERROR

The officials of the G-2 with hate, horror and cruelty used to impress with the psychological torture in their interrogations to the detainee night and day by crimes against powers State. I spent several months in the cell which uses the G-2 with all kinds of tortures to the detainees to confess their guilt or not, the facts alleged. The Cuban State officers employ hundreds of hours of interrogation against the detainees and to plead guilty to charges that accuse him.

The months were filled with threats and interrogations. The lieutenant said that could carry me to the firing squads, trying to intimidate me and showing pictures of men that had been firing squads in the prison of The Cabaña, trying to impress me and to will confess everything I knew. The lieutenant each day was more violent when he saw that I had not anything to say.

One day a captain said to the interrogator. He has his ideology, not bother more. The lieutenant was furious and said: Brave men have spoken. He is not an exception. The Captain moved his head and left.

The interrogator calls the soldier and said: He cannot sleep in the cell. Thus was, all the militaries hit the metal door and I not could sleep with tranquility in the dungeon.

The day wore on and seeing that the strategy had not worked tries to use the soldiers hitting the metal doors with words threatening that I would be executed in the firing squads. I had followed the advice of my grandfather Tomas Batista veteran of the War of Independence 1895. He said: If you are prisoner, not open your mouth for nothing. Because, if you talk, you not go to be with quiet, is better to be deaf and dumb. Do not forget that. I appreciate the words of my grandfather. Maybe I could not make this story of what happened. I knew many people that the lieutenant showed me in the photography against the regime of Fidel Castro were known. I think if it were not for the words of my grandfather, my life would have ended in the firing squads.

Tomas Batista, my grandfather and veteran of the War of Independence of 1895 he repeated: If your enemy is surrender, never humiliate him. Perhaps, he was confused. The man in the battle is where you have to give him their merits.

The months passed with those tortures and me with the fear that they were going to torture me in that dark cell in the G-2. Two months later there is a silence of about two days. They took me to the barber shop. I had few hairs in the beard, because at that time I was beardless.

The barber told me sit. I sat down. He began to cut my hair with a razor. I told the barber, not shave me more, you are tearing me the skin. He laughed and grabbed another razor he had in the drawer. He told me, when he finished, you are very rebel. I said: Here are committing much injustice and nothing good this goes to end, because I am innocent victim. Here not there is pity for men who love the fatherland. He looked at me and no said nothing.

The lieutenant entered several minutes after to the barber shop and he said: I have a surprise for you. I did not answer. From the barber shop we headed to the office. The Lieutenant called the guard and said: Bring the man. The guard retired and minutes later he appeared with an informant, and, political prisoner sentenced to 30 years of privation of freedom. The lieutenant told me. "You know him." I did not respond to the word of the lieutenant. The interrogator said again. Now, you do not know who is Ferguson? The interrogator had taken him to accuse me in the G-2.

The lieutenant turns to where it was Leonel Ferguson and said: Do you know him? Ferguson said: yes. "How long have you known him?" Ferguson replied, "A year and a half." The lieutenant looked at me and said. By all the explosives you had in your power, we go to carry you to the firing squads.

For the first time I answered: "I am a racist, fascist, and I do not like blacks." I had to say these words by the seriousness of the problem, because in my real life is not like that. I have always had good friends of the black races, from my childhood, when we played baseball. Inclusive my receiver was of the black races and we were all like brothers.

Lieutenant glared at me when was questioned his informant Leonel Ferguson in those difficult times for me.

Depended of my words, because could carry me to the firing squads by cause of a man who had been weak. At that time were assassinated in the firing squads 472 political prisoners in the Cause of the Navy of August 30, 1962.

That was the right time to impact the Lieutenant who was interrogating and says to the soldier violently. You go outside with Ferguson of here. The soldier led with Ferguson to the other office, perhaps to follow the questioning.

Leonel Ferguson was flinched and started to cooperate with the G-2. That is, he became an informant. The terror of Leonel was reflected on his face. He was powerless, defeated: he had no other alternative to go to the Rehabilitation Plan. He preferred to surrender unconditionally to his cause.

The lieutenant looked at me without saying a word, perhaps to see if I said anything of the crimes charged and to see that I said nothing, he called the military and took me to the punishment cell. The next day, lieutenant leads me to a room that had two tables and two chairs. There, he began to question me and said: You wanted to overthrow the Revolutionary Government through an armed uprising with explosive materials you had in your power to do all sorts of sabotages. We are going to carry you to the firing squads, by all those explosives."

The time elapsed between those torture cells in the G-2 and the endless interrogations at any time of day, night and morning, in that dark world where men were sentenced to death, 30 and 20 years of privation of liberty. In the G-2, the cruelty and knew no bounds with those wild terrorists.

That is a dangerous world of miserable and cowardly men who only think about the murder and torture. I have never in my life seen such cruelty and such evil to have to live that situation so horrible and dangerous of a system that does not respect the human being.

Several months after I was transferred with suffering to the prison of the fortress of The Cabaña where one has to live among men with different ideologies and opinions that do not solved the problems. So the days passed until they celebrated the trial with the petition of 30 years imprisonment, that monstrosity used by Communists. I always remembered the advice of my grandfather Tomas Batista, who never forgot me. He said: If you are in a situation dangerous, you need to remain with the mouth closed, never to speak with anybody. From the moment do you did, you are already defeated.

In 1963, I was transferred to the Prison of the Isle of Pines. All political prisoners were transferred of the Cause of August 30, 1962 where they had shot to 472 political prisoners in one night. Who committed murder, Satan will wait for him and for all the evil he did.

In the Isle of Pines we found that family visits were suspended for creating metal fences to separate the families of political prisoners. Yes, it was unacceptable situation of political prisoners in this prison. They carried more than eighteen months without visits. Cuba's communist government had committed this outrage. The political prisoners never accepted the metal fences. The government used that infamy to separate the political prisoners from the family. The Cowards always act with evil. They are miserable, cruel and scoundrels.

On October 18, 1963, began the Plan of Forced Labor that lasted seven months of tortures and slavery.

The political prisoners resisted to that atrocity in stone quarries of the Isle of Pines, where they had been forced to work against their will in the Rocky Mountains of Nueva Gerona.

These men were mostly humble soldiers, workers and peasants resisted the inclement sun, hunger, rain and cold. Many of them were barefoot among those rocks in the stone quarries of the Isle of Pines. They were brave men to the beginning that face the horror of Stalinist brutality of slavery. They were brave and with honor that during the years of torture in prison confronted the monster more known as Fidel Castro with his criminal, terrorists and murderers.

In this world, if you not known the criminals with the mind poisoned by hatred, to quench the anger that lead into the soul of vulture against humanity. They are despicable men that think in evil, with the poison in the eyes and without hope in a better future.

Who have not experienced what is the communist system cannot imagine what is in reality, the system that applies with all kind of torture and slavery to achieve their goals. They not think good and only make the bad things. That is the terror that lead in the blood, because their minds are empty and their eyes blending with hatred. Satan will give them the hell to live because they are diabolical.

THE SLAVERY

It had been several years since communist guerrillas seized power in the Republic of Cuba in 1959. Was one of the black epochs in the history of the Cuban people?

On October 18, 1963 began the experiment darkest of Cuban Political Prisoners in the Isle of Pines. The horror of slavery was in action, planned by government psychologists who run these plans mass annihilation.

The men were subjected to slave labor to mid-twentieth century. They use the brutality and savagery of the army forces and conscription. Cruelty with a little more two hundred men in the experimental fields of the stone quarries of Nueva Gerona, where subjected to perform slave labor by force of arms and bayonets.

The malnourished political prisoners were forced to perform slave labor so brutal with picks and shovels. They had to work in the lime kilns, mills to stones. The work was from dawn to dusk every day. They had bloody hands of the picks and a shovel to break the biggest atones. Actually it was an eyesore that was living a group of 217 political prisoners in the mountains and stone quarries of Nueva Gerona.

The savagery was horrible in the moments. The militaries obeyed orders they received from the central government led by Fidel Castro, the criminal and thief of the Republic of Cuba. In those moments survival in labor camps was nonexistent. However, the purpose was the surrender of the political prisoners to surrender to the fight against the tyrannical regimen Marxist-Leninist and scoundrels, cowards, terrorists and the corrupt of

Fidel Castro, Raul Castro, Ramiro Valdes, Jose Abrantes, Ernesto "Che" Guevara and Sergio Del Valle. The corruption was to the all levels and the murders of the political prisoners.

At hat time most of the nations around world cooperated with Cuban communists, supporting the most perverse system that exists on the Earth.

All nations that helped to slave the political prisoners that were subjected to savagery of the forced labor, titled Plan Experimental Morejon against the heroic men who were murdered throughout the Republic of Cuba in the forced labor.

The Marxist-Leninist when they came to power, with the exception of some honest men, began to commit crimes against humanity in the Cuban population disagreed with the policy of the dictatorial regime and his gang of internationalists military. Those who had taken power had much hatred in their hearts and enjoyed as the men were executed on the firing squads for to implement the terror between populations in Cuba.

The massacres of Ernesto "Che" Guevara in the fortress of The Cabaña when was head of the prison. Ernesto Guevara did not mind murdering innocent young men. Ernesto Guevara de la Serna was an internationalist foreign offender who committed all manner of barbarity against civilians and military men, simply because Guevara was a murderer. Whose responsibility lies with Fidel Castro and his brother Raul Castro best known for the "Duck"? They gave him all the power to commit the mass murder when he was made chief of the fortress of La Cabaña in 1959. Fidel Castro knew that Ernesto "Che" Guevara was a murderer.

Ernesto "Che" Guevara, being a native of Argentina, he had become one of the cruellest assassins of the Cuban people. To all this I have to add that Fidel did him Minister of the National Bank of the Republic of Cuba, for sign the national currency. So, had been a shame to the Cuban people that Ernesto "Che" Guevara will sign the National Currency. In reality, Felipe Pazo was a coward and Castro supported to Ernesto "Che" Guevara.

Fidel Castro Ruz has been a coward and miserable for that reason is that the governments never have counted with him for anything. Neither the Soviet Union neither the United States in the crisis of October of 1962. This means that Castro will die so frustrated and with much suffering by all the pain he has caused the Cuban people. They were and are murderers from before being in the Sierra Maestra. So was Huber Matos Benitez when was chief of Camaguey Province in 1959. He carried to the firing squads innocent men and without legal defense.

That is, for him there were no courts because he gave the order of execution, and not caring that men died in the firing squads by defend the motherland, guilty or not guilty, they were between all murderers more savage of the history of the human beings. Were blind of hate these bastards.

Those bastards created the Plan Morejon of Forced Labor in the Stone Quarries. The first men than had been carried Stone Quarries from the Isle of Pines. The political prisoners not accepted the Plan of Rehabilitation. In the circulars anybody spoke of the men that were in the Stone quarries in Nueva Gerona. The political prisoners in Isle of Pines not accept the Plan of Rehabilitation. In the circulars, the men were forced to go to the labor camps in stone quarries as Nueva Gerona.

All was silent and the organizations that were in the circulars in Isla of Pines. All of them not spoke of the political prisoners who were in forced labor. Nobody said anything and neither complained about anything, because the leaders were not interested in the fate of the political prisoners or the barbarism of the forced labor in the mountains of Nueva Gerona.

Furthermore, it is sad to think that the men have no compassion of the men, when had to risk the life by his homeland from slavery we were living. The Forced Labor Plan ended on May 20, 1964, after many months of slavery, where many political prisoners could not withstand the torture and surrendered to the enemy and surrendered to the enemy and of the struggle. They had sacrificed their lives for many years.

The men had not strength to continue the war. They were surrendered before of die by the country in this world of the cruelty, because the assassin's military killed with fury, with the savagery and cruelty. However, these are always known by the savagery and the cruelties. So, it was like the Forced Labor Plan had ended, known as Plan Morejon.

THE PLAN OF FORCED LABOR

Forced Labor Plan Camilo Cienfuegos in the Isle of Pines prison lasted 33 months of pain and suffering. We had to endure from 1964 to 1967, like slaves in the seventeenth and eighteenth centuries.

The leaders of organizations with thousands of members, as the M-30-11, MRP and MRR did not have the courage to face the military because they were afraid. However, let each of the militants who did the best they believe appropriate.

The leaders of all organizations in general were terrified and panic. They did not dare to talk with militancy that was the most rebellious against the Cuban state communism. Leaders trembled before their enemies implanted terror and death for political prisoners to force them to work against they will through force of arms, violence and killings in the forced labor camps.

The responsibility of the leaders of the anticommunist organizations, all generally had bowed to the barbarism, that had been submitted by the communist's forces so many thousands of political prisoners. They were guilty of all the failures of political imprisonment by the weaknesses that were never able to overcome.

At the beginning of Forced Labor Plan Camilo Cienfuegos in Prison on the Isle of Pines, the order came to the leaders of all organizations that whoever is found in labor camps not to eat, or accept food if they contained proteins, such as beef, pork, chicken or fish and we accept only flour, macaroni, rice, viand broth, beans and bread when they took him. "Actually these leaders were eaters of salcocho".

Thus began the infamy of the leaders of all organizations, the consequences were devastating political prisoner who had been subjected to Forced Labor Plan Camilo Cienfuegos for 10 and 12 hours a day for the forces of guns and bayonets to rigor horrible ordeal of forced labor to the concentration camps.

So here comes the fear and cowardice of the leaders of all organizations anticommunist. However, everything seemed that the leaders of the organizations were cooperating with the government to annihilate Marxist political prisoner. This happened in 1971, by the treachery of the leaders of the organizations in Guanajay prison.

The leaders were frustrated and did not open their mouths to say anything. All of them were below the militants of the organizations and the only alternative was left silent and to wait. That wait was massive betrayal of all leaders, were already abandoned. Years later he joined the ranks of their enemies as confidants, even cooperate with them until they were released in 1979. So, they spent 8 and 18 years at the Rehabilitation Plan and Progressive in voluntary work for their unconditional surrender-Leninist Communist system-fascist criminal government that exists on earth.

The massacres carried out by military conscription, the officers of the armed forces and the political police became murderers for the genocide of gigantic proportions across the country.

No, no only in the Plan of Forced Labor Camilo Cienfuegos where Antonio Llerena Andrades, Alfredo Gonzalez Barrabas, Diosdado Aquit Manrique, Danny Crespo Regino, Eddy Alvarez Molina, Ernesto Diaz Madruga, Jose Pascual Guerra, Geronimo Candina Betancourt, Julio Tang Taxier, Luis Nieves Cruz, Mario Diaz Gonzalez, Manuel Pardo, Pedro Gonzalez Perna, Paco Pico, Roberto Lopez Chavez and many thousand who were killed in the shooting walls of jails and prisons around the country. No ceased the massacres of the rafters leaving the country illegally, jumping into the sea in search of freedom in 1960 and 1970.

Those who were caught at sea were killed by soldiers of the Guard, which destroyed their rustic rafts with huge boats that used for the surveillance of the Cuban coast and what they did was massacring defenseless people. Thus, most horrible murders committed for Cubans fleeing the communist regime.

The barbarity was committed and was committed by a criminal regime and atheist falls on the shoulders of Fidel Castro and docile military without conscience who have slaughtered the Cuban population because they feel hatred in their hearts.

The military thugs savagely murdered mercilessly political Prisoners who had been taken by force of arms and bayonets to labor camps Camilo Cienfuegos on the Isla of Pines, where they were machine-gunned by young compulsory military service by army officers, on orders from Fidel Castro wretched.

The men died pierced by bayonets and bullets fired by drugged executioners of hatred and revenge on the orders of communist dictator Fidel Castro and his criminals and corrupt elite army terrorists. Political prisoners were killed after being unjustly sentenced to death penalty, 30 and 20 years of imprisonment.

It was impressive to see how thousands of men were subjected to forced labor in the Isla of Pines by the military communists who came down from the Sierra Maestra and other provinces across the country. They were a communist plague that devoured everything in its path. Political prisoners died murdered by the mob whose had seized power by force of arms and terrorism.

On august 9, 1964 was a dark day for the Presidio Politico, where words do not flow from the throat of men hardened by fighting communist savagery of the executioners.

The silence was deathly throughout the prison. Ernesto Diaz Madruga had been killed by a bayonet that pierced from side to side that stomach, only a few days into the Plan Camilo Cienfuegos Forced Labor in the Isle of Pines. The thugs had killed Ernesto Diaz Madruga with such brutality and savagery that characterizes Marxist-Leninists and atheists Leninists-Fascist murderers on the Isle of Pines,

The Presidio Politico was not a prison organized and every man did what he thought he should do. However, the heads of the organizations were very afraid and never tried to join the membership so that everyone could agree and joined at critical moments.

The Presidio Politico was dismayed with the murder of Ernesto Diaz Madruga. In those crucial moments the brave men were forced to leave the camps Forced Labor Plan Camilo Cienfuegos.

The massacres continued through the months, the killings did not stop in those difficult times that we had been abandoned by all countries of the world.

The murders committed by the military in Forced Labor Plan Camilo Cienfuegos, were by guns or bayonets on defenseless prisoners, with merciless ferocity and brutality used by the military. Cruelty knew no bounds at the time of the Presidio Politico Cubano.

You had to see political Prisoners as blood gushed of his wounds when bayonets penetrated their bodies. What I am saying is almost indescribable, as the heads of forced labor brigades persecuted political prisoner to the liked and surrounded him with bayonets. Bayonets sharpened if they were hunting a wild animal.

I do not want to leave unmentioned Tariche. Two ends of the brigade, the Big-Headed Ant and Elio out, surrounded Tariche and he began to jump from place to place, but not luck for having fallen into a mattress Cuzu planting. That was when these two criminals took advantage and introduced the bayonet in the gluteus. Was used by those wild terrorists? Only God will is the judge of these criminals.

If was horrible to see a man being chased him to commit crime so savage. It was an eyesore which these miserable Communists committed against defenseless men. However, the cowardly act that way because they are murderers as the terrorist and criminal Fidel Castro and the plague of cowardly and docile military.

The fields of the Isle of Pines were covered with blood of constant beatings of those savages who had no scruples military to commit many crimes unforgivable.

In Forced Labor Plan Camilo Cienfuegos few thousand men suffered heavy beatings. They with their bodies full of blood in the labor camps, the military's ideological savagery without awareness of the oppressive regime of Fidel Castro and despicable "gangster".

Actually, everyone is miserable for the following reason: Many of them bowed to the regime after the horror lived in filthy jails and prisons, without food, without medicine, without medical care, cut off from the outside world like wild animal without access to their families and subjected to all kinds of torture. In the prisons were they consumed their lives and hard labor to which were subjected for their executioners. So, it was like they betrayed the cause for which they fought for decades.

These men have to have him scarier than the devil himself. We all know that Plan Camilo Cienfuegos Forced Labor in the Isle of Pines was criminal for Presidio Politico Cubano with the brutality that the murders used by military forces weapons to subdue political prisoners, vile and brutal.

We all know that the Isle of Pines prison arrive daily dozens of wounded men from the Forced Labor Plan Camilo Cienfuegos. I had never in my life seen so much horror as I saw in the prisons of death throughout my years in prison. The military used guns and bayonets to physically and psychologically torturing political prisoners to surrender through terror and murder.

Most political prisoners benefited from reeducation plan created in 1961. So, it was like fighting deserted. On the Isle of Pines prison had passed 14,000 political prisoners, civilian and military. At the end of the work plan forced Camilo Cienfuegos, only 4,000 inmates were without surrendering to communist enemies. The reeducated trembled with fear and no longer had the strength or courage to continue the fight because they had lost faith and hope of release.

That way it was disintegrating political imprisonment Isle of Pines after many months of hard labor, and with dozens of political prisoners killed by army officers and military conscription. Military who committed those massacres against the heroics men. Those martyrs gave their lives with patriotism for an ideal. We can never forget that were killed by so many scoundrels and coward's communist military army.

The blood shed by the military because they did not respect the lives of so many martyrs executed by the firing orders executions Fidel Castro more than half a century ago. But all this dilemma develops over most cruel sufferings of men in the history of the Cuban people is slowly consuming for having enslaved a generous and good people. So, it's like these wretches die full of pain and suffering for all the atrocities he committed so many brave men. Today he is paying all the evil he did and Satan is waiting in his final days of his death for reward in the Caldera of Hell.

No, we cannot forget our martyrs who were killed in jails and prisons, Forced Labor Plan Camilo Cienfuegos on the Isle of Pines. The henchman Communists murdered in cold blood the political prisoners who had been forced into slave labor in the stone quarries of Nueva Gerona, in rocky fields covered by thorny vegetation, and see how the political prisoners killed fell on the fields of forced labor in the Isle of Pines.

The pain had to endure our mothers in their hearts for so many men killed crimes that took the lives of its best sons in the firing squads in Forced Labor Plan Camilo Cienfuegos, in the hunger strikes, machine-gunned in the jails and persons without preceded in history, with this savagery used to murder defenseless brave men.

The Odyssey Forced Labor Plan Camilo Cienfuegos was cruel. That plan started in June 23, 1964. Slavery began in the Isle of Pines with more than 5,000 political prisoners compelled by forced of arms and bayonets to do slave labor in store quarries in the mountains of Nueva Gerona.

Nueva Gerona is a small town on the shores of the sea on the north coast of the Isle of Pines, south of the Isle of Cuba. The conditions for such work were subhuman by malnutrition and diseases that were suffering political prisoners. The rain, hunger and the sun lacerated skin of prisoners we were forced to do work against our will, but in those days began unexpected. The heads of the organizations did not know what they would do with the Plan Camilo Cienfuegos Forced Labor in the Isle of Pines.

A head of organizations in their most never removed than to work in forced labor schemes and lent themselves to such horrible cruelty to men who trusted them, without knowing the wickedness of evil men who were planning to destroy the Presidio Politico, and years later they succeeded.

The political prisoners accepted the provisions of the needs of the organizations and every day it became more difficult life for political prisoners who were in the labor camps Camilo Cienfuegos, by food shortages that existed and the rejection them by the inmates themselves to such foods.

Foods were essential for survival in those times of great political incapacity of the leaders of the organizations that they knew how much evil perpetrated against defenseless men were subjected to barbarism and terror. They with evil intentions, plans developed with the communist's system helping them in their purposes to demoralize political prisoner for their surrender.

The months went by and the government was still taking the right food for political prisoners in the labor camp. But the arbitrariness of the leaders led to the government, to see that we did not accept food, then suddenly changed strategy and began to make macaroni, flour, broth, eggs and bread. They changed all kinds of proteins leading to political prisoners. Since that time we started giving the salcocho that organization leaders wanted, because they were pigs. Since then started giving broths tanks not know that they were with some macaroni and a stalk of shark that tested urine and iodine.

10B.That was what they wanted the leaders of the organizations that were responsible for so vile cruelty to men who gave their lives in the firing squad daily. However, heads of organizations committed these atrocities in cooperation with the communist government that had like pigs in a pen. The wines of crimes that one could hardly eat it by than bad taste they had. Actually these leaders were greedy pig of Salcocho. They were docile and cowards.

So, time passed and began to kill political prisoners. And these cowardly leaders did not address the situation and because servile and submissive men because they were afraid. But the saddest thing never took the Plan Camilo Cienfuegos Forced Labor in Isla of pines.

This it took 33 months of torture in labor camps Isle of Pines. At that time, all nations of the world ignored the Prisoners who were in jail. While the Communist government was still in the walls by shooting men in the fortress of La Cabaña and all the other provinces of the Republic of Cuba. The violence grew and terror was implanted in all levels of the prisons of the Cuban nation.

The 33 months of uncertainty were of intrigue and murder. However, many men surrendered and accepted the perks they offered the military in Forced Labor Plan Camilo Cienfuegos. These men mostly had no alternative but to take the wrong path of reeducation plan in 1966 when we met with little hope of surviving the barbarism that was committing the communist dictatorship of Fidel Castro. But governments around the world were blind, deaf and dumb to the pain of the men who died defending democracy and freedom of the Cuban people, the horrors he was living since 1959. Not knowing if living in the Republic of Cuba.

In the sixties there was only faith and hope that God put his hands on the tens of thousands of political prisoners who were dying in labor camps in the Isle of Pines. Yes, only the divine power to save us from those who stayed with life massacres and savagery of a fascist regime and atheist. Men behind bars, diseases and misery, torture and suffering and not feel hungry, just felt the love of God because we were starving for an ideal that we had left the country, although it was our life.

We had hard times, but always with faith and hope someday to get out of that horrible prison where the military had turned into criminals against defenseless men defending the homeland and freedom, because we had not started hope and heart faith in God one day to get out of that fearful prison to defend what we had been robbed by the forces.

The 1960s were very difficult for the Presidio Politico. Forced Labor Plan Camilo Cienfuegos was the most horrible barbarity had been committed in the twentieth century. The men were killed in the buildings, and mostly circular in Forced Labor Plan Camilo Cienfuegos, in those moments where the men had to work through the terror, guns and bayonets of the military subservient and docile who obeyed the orders of their bosses.

About this I can add that military conscription became forced labor camps in the Isle of Pines in rivers of blood with those horrible murders of innocent men and victims of despicable regime of Fidel Castro and the military cowards and murderers.

Yes, was the slaughter of so many heroes who gave their lives for the freedom of an enslaved people? It was horrible what was happening in those labor camps in the Isle of Pines.

But the thing of all was that no nation in the Americas and Europe were interested in what was happening in the Isle of Pines and the Republic of Cuba. All nations had closed eyes and the rulers did not care that the youth was killed and died in prisons and labor camps that the communist system had been implemented on the Isle of Pines.

These wild communists were cruel and miserable murderers, knowing the blood of thousands of Cubans executed in firing squads and Plan Camilo Cienfuegos Forced Labor in the Isle of Pines.

THE POWER OF GOD

On April 28, 1965 was a day of contrast, the day cloudy like if the rain would fall, with all those black thunderheads reflecting the sun's heat.

I have always been a believing in God. Because it is actually the only thing I believe. However, in many occasions one finds people of good feelings whom like to do good thing with that compassion to help another without with knowing who is.

That day the lieutenant and chief of the Block #12 called us very early to labor camps Camilo Cienfuegos. The hours passed in this demanding and dangerous work, without much hope that everything would end without any tragedy in the Block of 200 men subjected to such brutal forced labor and cruel where one does not know whether returns alive or dead to the prison.

Each Brigade was composed of a corporal with 50 political prisoners and each was responsible for his Brigade. I was of Brigade #12 and Corporal Ernesto was responsible for it. He is best known for Black Dog. The day passed without much trouble in the four brigades. Suddenly Pastrana approached me and says: "You are going to be hit until die." The reason was that I was separated from the others. I saw the intentions in his eyes that sparkled with fury.

All day was of contrast with the black clouds to all hours, because the sky was for the sad for the massacres committed by the corporals in the forced labor. The chief block Brigades who were in the conscription become in executioners and assassins Marxists-Leninists. The killed the political prisoners in rebelliousness without any kind of pity.

The corporals were every day more violent forcing the political prisoners to work as slave labor in the concentration camps. The forced labor was very difficult, because we were surrounded of assassins. The political prisoners lived critical moment in Isle of Pines. Pastrana told me, I go to dismember will dismember your body today.

As was my habit I said nothing. I only watched the behavior and provocations without to have the corporal the reason for what I was doing. Of course, I do not like to work and let alone being a slave. I took the machete and buried it in the palm tree. The Corporal was behind the palm tree that supports the metallic fence. I did not mean, but, could have me cost the life. But if ne not low the head, would have split in two parts.

Pastrana called Lieutenant William, head of Block #12 of 200 political prisoners, who often smoked tobacco and began to explain what had happened. What I had done.

The Lieutenant William Block and head told me, 144 release the machete or sword. I not obeyed the orders of Lieutenant. Something powerful was happening around me at that moment that made me see things with indifference. Coldly watch all political prisoners in the Block. They were still making their slave labor.

Ernesto came, head of Brigade #12 with another corporal called the Golden Arm and Ernesto heard what he said Pastrana. Lieutenant William explains what had happened. Corporal Ernesto told, Lieutenant William with hoarse words to let me keep doing my job.

Lieutenant William hears what he said Corporal Ernesto and told me: "144 join your classmates and something." At that time I was of them about 5 meter away and without moving the place where I was. Corporal Ernesto turned to me and said: 144 still doing your job.

I started to walk slowly without knowing they thought. What they would want to do in the Forced Labor? I thought I had escaped death and reflected on what I had done. Actually, I find was among them in that world of men unforeseeable.

Minutes later the truck, with lunch and stayed. All political prisoners were gathered in about 900 square feet outdoors. Which incidentally was cloudy that day? So, was spending the day with no more problems until it was time to return to the circulars. We boarded the trucks without comments of what had happened in the morning, as was the custom among the political prisoners that we were in the Forced Labor Camilo Cienfuegos.

One hour later we arrived at the prison and the officers had begun the inspection. When we arrival, Lt. William separated me of other inmates. For now, and under great tension, I was only among those soldiers who looked me without comment.

Luis, chief of Internal Order arrived with the political delegate of the Isle of Pines. Luis Marihuana drew his bayonet violently. The Lieutenant William, head of Block #12, Ernest, Brigade #12, Golden Arm, Brigade #11, Pastrana, Brigade #10, Elio, Brigade #9, the chief of the Circular #3 and the soldiers guarding the prison. They observe the chief of Internal Order is going where I was with bayonet in hand.

The political delegate, who was of the black races, about 250 pounds, came between Luis and me to avoid a bayonet wound, or perhaps mortally.

Luis Marihuana said: "This is the man they say that is brave. I am going to see if it is true, because I am going to knocking." William and Ernesto also sided with the political delegate. But Luis Marihuana was violent. Ernesto and William watched that I was very quiet, as if nothing were happening in those crucial moments for me. But when you are actually in the battle not feel afraid. I do not care about what was happening, or that said the head of Internal Order. But Luis Marihuana tries to hurt me with his bayonet and political delegate opens his arms to protect me of the man furious. I looked in all directions and all was quiet.

The Delegate said: Does not touch him, I know him in difficult times. I know him and he will die before backing a centimeter". Delegates Political Instructor, with no military rank in his shirt opened his arms against the violent chief Luis Marihuana Internal Order. The political Officer said. "Let's take him to the punishment cells."

William, hear of the Block #12, and Ernest, head of Brigade #12. They could see me very quiet. The situation was not easy. Luis Chief Interior Order not reasoned. But the political delegate with his size do not left that the chief of Interior Order will injury me. Ernesto was passed his hand over his face and looked at Lieutenant William, head of the Block #12 without comment.

The instructor objected to injure or kill me off of the Circular #3. The Delegate said repeatedly in occasions to the chief of Interior Order will rise up to the jeep and took me to the to the punishment cells.

Luis, head of Internal Order moved his head and started walking toward the jeep he was driving. He sat at the wheel and mounted the political delegate, Lieutenant William, Ernesto, Golden Arm, Elio and Pastrana.

The instructor told me. You sit down here beside me, as if trying to protect me from the Chief Internal Order not knocks me out with his bayonet. We started traveling to the punishment cells and arrived in a few minutes and we got off the jeep. We entered to the office of the military responsible for the dungeon. Luis Marihuana, he said, to the military takes me to the punishment cell.

The officer said, "Take off your clothes? I did not pay attention, and he said again: take off your clothes? When I did not respond to what he said: he told me. Are you deaf? I was without moving a step from where I was.

The Deputy political Instructor said: Luis, I will take him to the cell. The officer gave him the key of the jail and headed for the pavilion cell. The Instructor opened the door to the punishment room and said: You know the consequences or you need to learn the lesson? Today you are lucky. The Delegate told a great truth. Ugh! Finally you are done. I just had a hard time. I was literally, crazy to believe that I would be rid. The Delegate Political was very wise and generous with his enemy.

I never went back to see the Instructor in my long years in prison. I also cannot forget what he did for me in those difficult and crucial moments, where life was uncertain for the political prisoners. Maybe God put him at the right time to protect me from such savagery and cruelty. Actually, must of the soldiers are cowards and only think about the cruelty and hatred. In the dungeon I spent 180 days in a wet cell where I had to sleep on the floor and warm the cold floor with my body. My health had damaged in that loathsome dungeon with no sanitation or water to bathe.

In this dungeon were next to my cell, Pedro Luis Boitel, Piloto Mora, Ernesto Toledo, Orlando Molina, Juan Jose Flores (Panama), Alfredo Izaguirre, Lincoln best known for the Prince and also Sosa was assassinated in the firing squads in the mountains of the Isle of Pines for absconding from prison. All confined in the dungeons of the prison of the Isle of Pines. The punishments applied sternly, monstrosity and cruelty by the Communists.

I lived for 60 per cent of my imprisonment in dungeons totally dark cell with bars and metal plates, hunger strokes, isolation, nudity and food negation by the authorities, without to see my parents, brothers and other family for 9 years lived in inhuman conditions and more than 12 years in total in the dungeons of punishment.

The other 40 per cent I spent in the forced labor Camilo Cienfuegos, and some of our private family visits. Our mothers fought against the Communists so that we see. The punishment was brutal in jails and prisons where thousands of men were killed in the firing squads. Each human being or animal, we have to respect the life. No one has absolute power to commit many crimes and massacres against political prisoners by hate. The Political Prisoners enslaved, tortured and massacred by their executioners. The barbarism and ostracism were criminal in jails and prisons of the communist regime.

I claim that in my prison and though that faith, hope and belief in God is what gave me strength in times of tragedy, in the tensions and dangers facing death, when I was in hunger strike on November 14 1959 in an uncertain situation behind of the bars of the prison and on hunger strike in the Combined of the Est. The Havana, God, faith and hope were part of my life now so difficult in jails and prisons. My belief in God, faith and hope made me free from this world of torture and suffering.

The pain caused to our family that was pending the horror that I was living in the last days of my isolation. Faith hope and my belief in God, I could to leave of this hell, where human life is an unimaginable ordeal. My out of jails and prisons I can be attributed to the intervention of a higher power. In the power of God, I put my life in his hands, faith and hope strengthened my spirit. God only could get me out of that hell where cruelty has no limits.

The real faith, hope and my belief in God moved beyond human understanding. In my opinion, the Holy Spirit careful guides of faith and hope, but both faith and hope in God as the Supreme Court, rewards good and punishes evil and hate.

The different ways of understanding and practicing the faith and hope can be complementary, not have to necessarily exclude each other. It takes a willingness to see that the various interpretations and practices of faith and hope can be integrated.

The usefulness or faith and hope are not comparable to any good, even with the blessings of nature. Nonetheless, it can be said that the fundamental usefulness of faith and hope are in the very fact of believing and trusting in God.

Faith and hope in me was stronger than the horrors that I lived in that world of shame and suffering. My belief in God strengthened my spirit. Faith and hope grew in me because God put wisdom in my thoughts and wisdom in my soul, giving me much peace on cold nights and each new dawn.

Why man, created by God, it is so difficult to return to the faith and hope? Man should not allow it lacks the grace of God, and so find faith, hope and the strength to overcome the obstacle and solitude where you live.

Tens of years passed and my firmness with faith and hope in God gave me more confidence to get out of this hell where I was captive. Yes, there were many years of pain and suffering. But God was watching me and put behavior, prudence and wisdom in my thoughts to come out stronger from all the horror of so cruel ordeal, only faith and hope to achieve freedom and love for humanity.

So, I leave this cruel oppression and aged for years and for all the suffering in this world of loneliness and sadness, where you love your best friends and breaking your heart in pain. Let no one doubt that faith and hope in God were part of my life, and my heart there is only generosity and virtue to all who love God and humanity.

I was living many years in captivity and ostracism the cruelty of the prison. I was able to reach the United States, where I study Business Administration at Miami Dade Community College, Arts and Sciences at Florida International University and Business Administration and Management at St Thomas University. For all these reasons that I have stated in my prison and thought only by the power of God, faith and hope which never left me in difficult times of confinement until the last day that I was free of that cruelty and oppression, where men die by their ideals.

Today I am an elderly man and I love God, the humanity, the freedom of the free and democratic world. God is love and happiness. You need think in these wonderful things of the life.

THE NAKEDNESS

Nudity was one of the most dangerous events in the struggle against the communist dictatorship. The conditions we were treated by the military mostly just think of the murder and torture. No, I am not lying, that's the reality that I had to live in punishment cells and dungeons, where you almost suffocated by the heat of the evens and stoves military used as torture for you to die suffocated by the heat of the furnaces at temperatures extreme. That was what did the military to political prisoners in rebelliousness.

In February 1967 began the nakedness of the political prisoners. The military used the force of arms to remove the Yellow Khaki Uniform. The military used the revenge by the force to change by the uniform by another blue. The Jean used by prisoner commons and inmates of the reeducation plan. There were men who deserted the struggle after taking several years in jails and prisons and joined the ranks of the enemy.

Thus began the nakedness of Cuban Political Prisoners with hundreds of political prisoners who were completely naked. The days passed quickly and we did not see a solution to the problem. The cold month went by without one to be protected from inclement weather. It was cruel to have so many naked men for over a month without any clothing, until we got underpants and a towel for us to cover part of our body.

That was depressing to see so many political prisoners completely naked. That was the revenge that used the Marxist-Leninist regime against Cuban Political Prisoners were naked until August 6, 1968 as a first step in subhuman condition, totally isolated unable to see our families. This savagery was created to force us to accept the blue uniform.

Thirty per cent of political prisoners, especially who were in the fortress of The Cabaña were disappointment of the struggle and the verge of a massive flight to the Plan of Rehabilitation.

The political Prisoners naked were separated in different provinces. In the cells closed and the tortures in different the positions we were in rebelliousness. The political prisoners were in a state of dehydration without feed and sick. We were 17 months in torture cells and dark we suffered political prisoners Semi-naked. The criminal's communists tried to break the resistance of Cuban Political Prisoners Semi-naked.

The whole process was because in February 1967 the political prisoners we have been moved from the Isle of Pines to the Island of Cuba and subjected to the most brutal nakedness of the history of Cuban Political Prisoners. Thousands and thousands of political prisoners were subjected to the savage humiliation. We were stripped of the uniform, creating a situation of confrontation between the communist authorities and political prisoner in 1867. The men had suffered tortures and massacres in the Plan of Forced Labor Camilo Cienfuegos from 1964 to 1967.

The Marxist-Leninist government never ceased in his crimes, starting a new plan with nakedness for all who did not accept the blue uniform, who only used in the Plan of Rehabilitation and ordinary prisoners. Thus began the process of nakedness in 1967, was humiliating to the Presidio Politico Cubano. Many of them died in huger strikes and malnutrition.

The epidermis of the men was as channels that stuck to the bones. It was depressing and painful to see so many thousands of political prisoners subjected to such brutal savagery of torture and suffering, only by refusing to accept the blue uniform that they wanted to impose by force against their will.

No, it was not easy for political prisoners who had spent more than 30 days completely naked. The body not resisted the cold in moisture and sleeping on the floors of the galleys and the punishment cells. The days passed and our bodies start to deteriorate during for many years in Forced Labor Plan Camilo Cienfuegos.

After more than a month of being completely naked, the Communists gave to each one of us the underpants and a towel for us to cover our most intimate parts. So spent 17 months with underpants, torture in closed cells and isolated. We not could to sleep in the wet and cold floor in dark cells of the death of the jails and prisons of the Communists.

Many men suffered paralysis for many years because of the time that spent locked up in the cells of death without accepting the purpose of the communist system in the Republic of Cuba.

Men malnourished, sick and the skin attached to the bones were willing to sacrifice their lives for not accepting the infamy by the executioner Marxist-Leninist and its supporters in such barbarisms that have had in the Republic of Cuba.

We had passed the odyssey of the Cuban Political Prisoners and the cowardly infamy in the Twenty Century. The communist System offender and murderer Fidel Castro decides to give us the uniform. Marxist-Leninist decides to transfer again all political prisoners naked to the prison of the Cabaña on August 5, 1968.

All political prisoners naked were in different provinces were transferred to the prison of The Cabaña. And to our surprise, we were accustomed to be transferred to different provinces and we not knew what was happening in the prison of The Cabaña. The surprise was when we received on August 6, 1968 at 8 am, after breakfast with bread and sugar water. The military began to arrive with truckloads of clothing. The same clothes that during 17 months we had were naked by the government. The same light-yellow clothes that we had been stripped to almost year and half.

That sacrifice consecrates all political prisoners the Yellow Uniform using violence, the guns, the bayonets, the tortures with Judokas and in total isolation. After all this time of suffering, the government refunded our uniform. The uniform we cost us many months of fighting in inhumane conditions, where dozens of men suffered paralysis for several years. However, the situation was complicated at the time of the delivered of the yellow Khaki Uniform.

On August 6, 1968 was our second win. The first was when we were in the Forced Labor Plan Camilo Cienfuegos, where the men were malnourished and many of them with paralysis.

However, the situation was complicated at the time of delivered of the yellow Khaki Uniform.

The political prisoners we were in the communist government's plan for everything that had happened in punishment cells and dungeons infested with insects. The most of political prisoners naked accepted the uniform that had been stripped by the force and violence that characterized the communist system. But in every battle there is always discrepancy, and certainly not more than two hundreds men not accept the uniform because we saw no transparency.

The political prisoners with the yellow Khaki Uniform transferred to the galleys 7, 8, 9, 10, 11, 14, 15, 16 and 17. While that the political prisoners Naked in underpants were transferred to the galley 12 and 13. Thus days of August passed and most of September, 1968

On September 28, 1968 there was an agreement between the political prisoners dressed in Khaki uniform and the underpants to begin a hunger strike to demand the government general medical consultations, our family visits, improvements in food, medicine and water sufficient to bath in the prison of The Cabaña.

The day passed quickly and weakened political prisoners were weakened. I saw many people throwing up and dehydrated, but with a great spirit of self-assurance, and an incredible desire risking their lives to get what we needed for subsistence in prison.

Brave men with honor as characterized the Cuban political prisoners when he fights for his ideals, sacrificing their lives for the struggle to enjoy freedom and peace.

Twenty days after the communist dictatorship accepted the points we had demanded. At that strike that we titled "Hunger Strike of the Centennial, for having turned 100 years of the War of Independence of 1858 in Cuba."

Our families spent twenty days of the hunger strike of the Centenary killing the political prisoners with impunity by demand our right that we corresponded.

Our families were heroes who fought valiantly against the communist criminals and without abandoning a minute their sons. Mothers were brave, with the value that characterizes every mother when she sees her son in danger.

Mothers had to travel hundreds of miles and in the sun, the nights and days claiming rights of their sons who were on the verge of death. They with heroism knew defend and patriotism, with the suffering for years. Now with value, shame, honor, dignity, courage, patriotism and firmness; defending her own sons. Mothers sacrificed their youth traveling to jails and prisons for decades to see relatives. There are no women on earth braver than Cuban mothers, for their dedication to her sons.

The hunger strike of 1968 was a triumph of our long struggle claiming rights and duties as we corresponded and freedom and struggle of a people enslaved by the communist hordes. For the first time the political prisoners had a period quiets of 11 months, but the good hard thing very few. Men evil and cowardly destroy all.

On September 1, 1969 everything was normal in a prison of men with different ideas. As the Cuban Political Prisoners with different ideologies in jails and prisons where there were many chiefs and not enough Indians but none sacrificed himself for his country. But many of them led to disaster for the Island of Cuba with its destructive communism to enslave their own people not deserved so horrible barbarity of these men little political vision.

In late 1969, at the beginning of September, the leaders of a group of organizations such as the CID, MRR, MRP, M-30-11, MID, MUR, MDM, M-20-05, AAA, MRB, MDC, OA, MRRC and others, which were under the Political disintegration, proclaimed a hunger strike at 9 pm without any kind of objectives, to favor the Presidio Politico Cubano who was in the prison of The Cabaña.

The political prisoners naked we opposed to as outlandish given by men who had no political power and that they had shown over the years in jails and prisons across the country. These men are always inventing how to divide the political prison in rebelliousness.

Intellectuals for his cowardice, were leading the Presidio Politico the more absurd object the company to achieve the most vile and shameful division of politics more miserable in the history of Cuban Political Prisoners.

These men were already frustrated from the Forced Labor Camilo Cienfuegos in the Isla of Pines in 1964 and the nakedness of 1967 and 1968.

Opposition to the hunger strike on September 1, 1969 was unequivocal on the part of political prisoners in difficult times, and we jump in a hunger strike to 35 days. Many prisoners were on the verge of death, risking their lives by a people enslaved and subjected to hunger, poverty, misery, in imprisonment recover their freedom and dignity.

The days passed and the political prisoners began to desert of the hunger strike that had begun with the arbitrariness of a group of men who wanted to divide the Presidio Politico Cubano.

At 30 days after starting the hunger strike on 40 percent of the political prisoners of the prison had deserted of the hunger strike. That was an embarrassment to the Presidio Politico. Professionals, intellectuals and other groups were the first to abandon the hunger strike. They leave their best friends and many men who risked their lives without being able to defend from certain death, but slowly they desert of the hunger strike. That was a big error to exchange for the three points that we had already obtained in the hunger strike of 1968.

Brave men through history Presidio Politico hung their heads and were integrated to Reeducation Plan and Progressive, while others were sent to different prison by the irresponsibility of the leaders of the organizations had defected filled with panic, the jaws trembled and cracked teeth.

Commanders, captains, intellectuals and professionals abandoned their teammates, after many years of struggle. They left defeated, demoralized, exhausted and there is no return.

At 35 days of having been on a hunger strike came the most humiliating and painful loss of political prisoners. We lost the hunger strike after 35 days where men were near death. We lost everything and did not recover in the long years in captivity.

Health problems had sharpened and never could recover from impact so strong that we receive. However, we lost the hunger strike but not the war. All the sacrifice of previous years we had lost because of the heads of the organizations mentioned above, when intellectuals and professionals capitulated fully.

Naked political prisoners knew that the hunger strike of 35 days was madness caused by the inability of intellectuals and professionals. As explained above. Commanders and captains were leading to the political prisoners for the Plan of Rehabilitation. We lost all the benefits that we had won in the Hunger Strike in 1968. The consequence was catastrophic for the political imprisonment in rebelliousness. They began to create division among political prisoners across the country.

However, the political prisoners naked in rebelliousness had paid a high price for over 9 years, without being able to see our families.

To all this I have to add the transfer to Puerto Boniato prison in Santiago of Cuba, Oriente in 1970, unable to see our mothers for more than nine years of total isolation in sealed cells in subhuman conditions, without adequate food, where men starved and murdered by the military henchmen. Nine years living in squalid conditions by in the absence of essential medicines. Yes, for 43 years had not been told the truth of so many scoundrels who destroyed the Presidio Politico Cubano.

The naked political prisoners lived in filthy cells without any hygiene; walled with iron doors and windows where you did not know when is in the morning. The cell had no artificial light or daylight. Only Knew it was daytime when we were counting the political prisoners. Minutes with the of cornstarch breakfast, lunch and dinner with flavored macaronis that just could not eat.

Of the 239 political prisoners were left naked only 150, as some of them had gone to the Rehabilitation Plan and others were dressed in the Yellow Khaki Uniform after surrender of the hunger strike in 1969.

I passed in the cell 35 with metal door in the building 4B. I spent several years only with faith in God, in that completely dark cell with the pupil dilated to see in the darkness of that gloomy cell hermetically sealed with metal plates. That was torture, as if you were a monster locked in that filthy cell that I will never forget. Cell without any water or without hygienic enough for personal toilet, because even that we refused.

The political prisoners were naked and started getting sick and nobody to hear our pain and suffering. Only God was the one who helped us bear in that time peace without and without any communication in 1970. The exile did not know what was happening with naked political prisoners who were dying in prison of Puerto Boniato. Men died of starvation and without medical assistance, murdered by communist thugs.

In Puerto Boniato prison were murdered Esteban Ramos Kessel, Ibrahim Torres Martinez, Olegario Charlotte Espileta, Jose Ramon Castillo del Pozo and Gerardo Gonzalez Alvarez. They were massacred by henchmen communist. Thus, in these inhumane conditions were murdered Enrique Garcia Cuevas Reynaldo Cordero Izquierdo, Carmelo Cuadras Hernandez, Pedro Luis Boitel, and many martyrs who were assassinated. So, many of them lost the life in the struggle against the communism.

We had to live in darkness many years and the brain does not get the energy of light. Nevertheless, the faith and hope in God are wonderful, because there no is nothing more beautiful than light and the faith in God. That is the more important in our lives of human being. Men love freedom and sacrificed their lives so that others live in peace without slavery and without fear.

To all this we must add that the political prisoners in rebelliousness have positions, well-defined, the reason why we were not agreed with the Hunger Strike in 1969. That hunger strike orchestrated by crazy men who had no ideas of was doing with the Political Prison and the mistake their lives. They were leading the political prison to suicide, as the 3 points were not necessary because we already had the points of the hunger strike of the 20 days of September 28, 1968."

The consequences were catastrophic for the political prisoners naked for so many years in the prison cells of Puerto Boniato guilt of organizations Hunger Strike of 1969. So the years passed when the March 28, 1972 the Communist government transferred the first mountain range in Rebelliousness of the 25 political prisoners from prison Boniato to Santa Clara, Matanzas and Pinar del Rio. In the second on April 16, 1972 was transferred to 47 political prisoners from Puerto Boniato prison. These groups of Semi-naked political prisoners were taken to the 23A and 23B. Galleys were full with soot from the military kitchen. Soot was unbearable night and day.

The political prisoners naked were led to the galleys 23A and 23B of The Cabaña, and the galleys were cover of soot of the military kitchen and the hot was worse. Soot was unbearable night and day. The bedding was covered with soot. With all that cruelty we had to live for years.

The political prisoners were transferred to the prisons of all the provinces of Cuba on 1970, when the prison of The Cabaña was closed. The years passed and on 1972 a group of 47 were transferred from the prison of Puerto Boniato to the prison of The Cabaña again.

Pedro Luis Boitel passed 53 days of agony in a hunger strike. He was separated of the rest of the political prisoners. He was committed to men of ideals. Pedro Luis Boitel will always be remembered by all political prisoners in rebelliousness by the value that always showed and heroism in the fight against communism. So they killed him, without water to die of thirsty in the filthy prison cell in the Castile of the Prince.

Pedro Luis was a man who never bowed and will always be faced with all kinds of torture in his long years of captivity. Against those hate the real heroes of the Fatherland. Those who did not surrender and risked their lives for a people enslaved and subjected to hunger, poverty, misery, murder, enslavement, imprisonment, repression, torture, the scoundrel's communist, the vicious and evil of the human being.

Pedro Luis Boitel in 1972 was re-launched in a hunger strike demanding the rights they were entitled to all political prisoners. Pedro Luis Boitel not rest to their fight against the communist system of the Castro dictatorship and all criminal's communists.

The days were adverse to Pedro Luis Boitel in inhumane conditions he was subjected. Were so cruel that the barely he had air to breathe. Men like Pedro Luis Boitel and many thousands of martyrs who gave their lives fighting for the freedom of the country live in the history of the Cuban nation forever.

About this say we had many brave men who gave their lives for the humanity would not suffer the evil communists that they have in the soul the poison and hate. However, we also had many men cowards and traitors who joined the ranks of the enemy in the most difficult of the moments of the Cuban Political Prisoners. Yes, we had many traitors, informers, defeated men who left on the battlefields to their best friends, to join the ranks of the enemy.

These men humiliated and towards and to see the worthless men facing Pedro Luis Boitel and many thousands of martyrs who gave their lives in hunger strike, firing squads in the labor camp Camilo Cienfuegos and on the battlefield. They were men who loved their fatherland.

Thus, prisoners died with a bunch of bullets in the chest, hunger strikes men struggling for the freedom and without slavery against the hordes of international communism Marxist-Leninist and dictatorship, hatred against the population of the country, the destruction of the Republic of Cuba and the separation of the family.

There is just miserable without consciousness and crime full of hate. They are skeletons awaiting death for Satan. The cowards destroyed the Cuban homeland with their misdeed and resentfully.

All of these crimes we can add that the March 19, 1971 by dawn, the machines guns opened fire in the hallways of Puerto Boniato prison and murdering four men inside the prison, murders we have been not forgo.

With machine gun seemed just were taking by assault the fortress, the amount of gunfire and soldiers running in the halls of Puerto Boniato Prison. There, to that hour of the morning they had killed four men completely unarmed and defenseless to be able to defend against the barbarism that were committed by the communist thugs. Four men had lost life in minutes. The savagery was used by criminals and miserable of the communist dictatorship, brutal and savage in the twentieth century.

Where were dead: Armando Rodriguez Somellan, Raul Balmaseda, Mario Fernandez Rico and Rafael Torres were assassinated by bullets from communist criminals?

This is the horrible reality of Cuban Political Prisoners. Truth of the fact as had occurred. The men defenseless were killed by the communist system men with impunity so tragically. So we had to live daily with the terror imposed after day and night. Terror and crimes that we had in our destination with these savages without scruples, because to kill was like drinking a grass of water. There, not ended the slaughter of political prisoners. The murders were across the notion every day.

On November 12, 1966, Lopez Chaves died of starvation, August 9, 1967, Luis Alvarez Rios died of starvation, July 21, 1969 died on hunger strike Carmelo Cuadras Hernandez, August 8, 1970, Jose Oriol was shot and killed, September 4, 1972, Ibraim Torres Martinez died of starvation, February 7, 1972, Esteban Ramos Kessel died of starvation, May 25, 1972 Pedro Luis Boitel, died of hunger strike. The soldiers left to die of thirsty. January 15, 1973, Olegario Charlotte Espileta died of starvation, February 2, 1973, Jose Ramon Castillo Del Pozo died of starvation, June 26, 1973, and Enrique Garcia Cuevas died in hunger strike. So the months passed. On September 1, 1975, Gerardo Gonzalez Alvarez was killed in prison in Puerto Boniato, with a spray of bullets in the chest fired by Communist thugs, and May 21, 1975, Reynaldo Cordero Izquierdo died in hunger strike.

So, were killing all these martyrs, with heroism and bravery that gave their lives for the freedom of the nation they had taken the criminals and offenders communists. Thus, tens of thousands were murdered by the communist criminals. Men were tortured by the violence of the Marxist-Leninist by the thugs Fidel Castro. However, they give asylum in democratic countries, only for the information that bring from the communist system and protect them as Ronald Reagan did with Rafael Del Pino and Hubert Matos Benitez. Knowing they were murderers these men live in the United States, Central America, South America, Europe, Africa and Asia. All of these murderers live protected by all governments and essentially live hidden in many countries worldwide.

However, the political prisoners were living nakedness in very sad moments of isolation in jails and prisons with the steel cells. So has been the criminal regime of the Castro brothers. But more sad part was that these criminals were responsible for the massacres of many heroes who are not gave the chance to live free.

The heroism and bravery of these men was such that shook his enemies and that's why they let them die without a glass of water to wet his parched lips. Because, even that was denied to so many martyrs for they feared terror at seeing so many brave men.

That was the cruelty of the criminal communist against the political prisoners that die of thirst. That tragedy was done there. At 6 pm on April 16, 1972 left 47 political prisoners come from the prison of Puerto Boniato to the fortress of The Cabaña. A trip that took 18 hours to arrive to The Cabaña prison on April 17, 1972 at 1 pm. Political prisoners were brought naked to the galley 23A and 23B.

Several hours after arriving from Puerto Boniato prison. Gerardo Batista decided to join the Reeducation Plan. That same day Kiki Salas goes to the Plan of Rehabilitation.

Of the 47 political prisoners naked of the group of 47 only remained in rebelliousness 45. We had come from prison of Puerto Boniato. The time had passed in those galleys 23A and 23B we were 13 months and 12 days. The time had passed and Juan went for the Plan of forced by circumstances adverse to his will and the coward and miserable Manuel Romeou Fernandez. This man had been repatriated from the United States in the 1950 by performing duties in favor of international communism of Fidel Castro and his communist gang.

In the prison, Pepe Vazquez, Jose Saura, Armando Valladares Perez and Enrique Vazquez Rosales were always inventing diseases that they not had. In that form they had the opportunity to see the families in the hospitals? Months after Israel Dominguez joined to them. These five gendarmes of the armed forces and deserters from the regime of Fidel Castro spent the days inventing diseases. Until some of them died of diseases dubious. So, we passed 13 months and 12 days in these galleys #23A and 23B. On May 29, 1973, we were transferred to the yard #1. And locked us in the galleys #13, few days of being in that galley was released Jose "Pepe" Vazquez after spending many months in hospital of Castle of the Prince where he was integrated to the Communist system.

In this galley #13 remained over one year until on June 23, 1974. In this galley #13 we were all the time, but us given not our family visits. We received the Physical and psychological tortures from communist regime of Fidel Castro and the gang of criminals from the Ministry of Internal Order let by Sergio Del Valle and Fidel Castro "the terrorist". The treatment was brutal with political prisoners naked for 9 years isolated in sealed cells without light, without enough water for our basic needs and we could not see our families.

The political prisoners Semi-naked spent over a year in the galley #13. To be more exact one year and 24 days. The June 23, 1974, the militaries made a general transfer of all political prisoners of the Yard #1 for the #2. We had established us in galley #1. And at 4 pm we had not lunched. Minutes after all political prisoners naked, the political prisoners with uniform of Khaki and Blue dresses were in the galleys in the Yard #2. The soldiers opened the gates of the galley #1, and they told us that we had to go to eat at dining room, that was at the end of the prison.

The political prisoner naked got along seven years without leave the galleys for lunch and the dinner. For that reason we refuse to go eat at the dining room, in the conditions that the political prisoners were in the Semi-nakedness since 1967.

The military to see our reaction denied food. That same day without lunch, except for Pedro Rodriguez, Gery Salas is going for the Plan of Reeducation and Enrique Vazquez Rosales accept to eat in the Dining. These three persons were very cowards. They have not value to continue the Struggle.

The group of 47 political prisoners naked we came to Puerto Boniato had fallen to 38. In addition, we added four who had come from other prisons and the behavior heroically of Cleto Perez Barrios, Santiago Diaz Bouza, Luis Bicet Thoreau and also Pablo Castellanos Caballero. Unsung heroes never mentioned because they are men of honor and patriots.

The government denied us food and on June 24, 1974 at 7 am we were transferred to the galleys 23A. There we slept all night of June 24, 1974.

On June 25, 1974 at 8 am we were transferred of the galley 23A for 24, next to the offices of the prison. We spent the day in the galleys, when suddenly Israel Torres Martinez sick with asthma the brother of Ibrahim Torres Martinez who had died of Starvation in prison of Puerto Boniato. Israel Torres Martinez deposes of the denial of food that we had refused. Cruelty was brutal and the military continued committing all kinds of crimes.

Better to depose the denial of food imposed by militaries suffocated asthma and lifesaving to die in such horrible conditions such as asthma attack. A few days later he decked to wear the Yellow Khaki Uniform. I think that was the best decision he made in his life and his brother's memory

Naked political prisoners had been reduced to 41 with the four who had come from other prisons. However, the Marxist-Leninist government was refusing the food by arbitrariness of communist thugs.

The unity of political prisoners naked was a monolithic block. The responsibility for what was happening was of the Communist who had refused us food only because the naked political prisoners did not want to eat in the dining room they had built.

Political prisoners dressed had not support the naked prisoners. The political prisoners with the Blue Uniform could not count with them, because they were the Ping Pong ball of the government. The Blue dresses never participated in any act of rebelliousness and when there was a problem in the political prison. The government collects all who were dressed in blue and took them out of the prison that was in conflict. That is, they were political prisoners extremely weak and docile and the government made them what they wanted.

The day passed and the only who supported us against the denial of food by the government were our mothers and sisters who spent the day in the sun and rain, demanding the militaries barbarism that was being committed with political prisoners naked with denial of food. Our family showed such courage during the difficult days that we were without to eat. Our mothers were the heroines of the twenty century. The mothers rested not until see us free from prison more fearful of the Cuban nation.

The mothers deserve all the honor of the world for their heroism and bravery. Mothers did not rest a day, because they were the heroic women who gave their all to see us free. Dear mother I thank you for all the love you gave me in the difficult moments of my life.

We arrived at 40 days in solitary confinement, in a state of almost total dehydration near death. We had already passed the hunger strike of 35 days. With the exception of the 40 days had been because the communist government we had refused food to the political prisoners naked. We were hours of death and all political prisoners were willing to die or succeed.

At 40 days, at 7 pm the government told us that everything was solved. That same day we returned to the galleys #1. The political prisoners Semi-naked that were in better conditions. We were taken on stretchers to the galleys and the rest for the doctor's office from prison; it did not have the necessary hygienic conditions. The place was horror. I think it was better to die than to be there.

The galley #1 began giving medical care to the political prisoners determined that were in a delicate condition. They spent 12 hours crucial ion that agony. The unexpected happened after that by the militaries made the counts of the political prisoners.

After of the 6 am the soldiers opened the door of the galleys #1 for that we to go to the dining room for breakfast. Pablo "Paco" Arenal told the militaries that was not what it had agreed with us. That was a disgrace said, Pablo "Paco" Arenal.

The director of Internal Order said they had not agreed to anything. We have to go breakfast, lunch and eat in the dining room, no in the galleys. This time the military were wrong again with political prisoners naked. They thought that we could accept such monstrous infamy as they had planned.

The decision was taken, the political prisoners naked in absentia were not going to the dining room for breakfast. If you can call it breakfast some water with sugar and bread.

The militaries saw that naked political prisoners were determined not go to the dining room. They at 8 am on day 41, we were transferred of the galleys #1 to the galleys #24 where were we had spent 40 days in solitary confinement without food.

In the gallery #24 the days were overwhelming in that lonely place. No one tried to help us in this inhuman situation we were living. In fact, as in all systems, there are conservatives and liberals, looking from different points of view, and which is best to get the better part. But only remain as observers without getting into anything.

However, they have success. They join them. That's what happened with the struggle, and most expected to see that they could grab lion's share after that will fix the problem. I know that in every war there are all kinds of brave men, cowards and deserters.

At that time the militaries had been wrong. The communist and oppressive regime after six days they accepted and acknowledge their mistakes with barbarism that had committed to deny food for 46 days. The monstrosity committed all these miserable Marxist-Leninists led by Fidel Castro was interfering in our affairs. The political prisoners with the Uniform of Khaki Yellow have not a direct participation although they would benefit from what we are achieving with the high cost of sacrifice. However, you cannot live only for viewer because damages the human being.

That is how we won the battle against the imposition of the militaries, villains and cowards, who only think about violence to satiate his lust crimes.

The soldiers saw that all political prisoners had returned to the same position. They realized that we were willing to die.

The military after 46 days are agreed that our galley can receive the foods without having to go to the dining rooms. The militaries never again spoke of the eaters. That was a great battle against the communism and I will remember all my life with my brave partners against the evil and cowardice of the militaries. The men die for the Fatherland and never are surrender to the enemies.

Everyone had left us alone, but God and our family who supported us all the time until that finished that horror. The Catholic Church was silent around the world. Nobody said anything because the Church was not interested that dozens of men would die of Starvation. Besides, I have always thought that the Catholic Church is used as a market and not in reality as God and Jesus Christ wanted.

However, the priests love the mercantilism. Not only used mercantilism, but also Psychology against the parishioners to fill their churches and their pockets with the gold and the silver. That is what I think about the entire bad thing by that I have lived in my life.

When humans are in a difficult situation is when you have to help them, not when you have great wealth. Yes, all of us were abandoned by the Catholic Church, businessmen, capitalists and governments around the world. These ambitious do not realize that humanity must live without suffering in a world better than we live.

The family and God were the one who raised their arms to prevent the mass extermination that slowly be approaching to our captivity where Cuban political prisoners are skeletons walking in the galley of death without a sheet and blanket to cover us.

We had experienced critical moments in the past, but this was the most difficult test for us and to consecrate the History of the political prisoners naked. Men who did not surrender the enemy during the whole struggle against communism that destroys everything of a people enslaved across the Republic of Cuba.

The victory is sweet, but also is very bitter in our lives when you have to leave in the battlefield thousands of martyrs who gave their lives so that others would not suffer the genocide of thousands of Cubans murdered, imprisonment, ostracism and oppression of a people generous and good.

THE MOTHERS

In the history of Cuba never had women Cuban the value and courage as our mothers and I think if it was not for hers with their courage to face the communist executioners all of us. Not exist in this earthly world woman as the Cuban mothers who were able to face their enemies for decades. In the sixty and seventy they were the heroines with extraordinary value. So were our mothers.

Through the years our mothers suffered the pain of not being able to see their children for 9 years. They were totally isolated in the punishment cells. The mothers had sacrificed all their life to see her children and give her a hug as every mother does with the son and the love of their lives.

Mothers were very heroines and face the savage and criminal communist system. The Courage characterizes to Cuban mother without retreating an inch demanding to the minions that they wanted to see their children isolated and dying in punishment cells.

So, were our mothers never yielded to those torture and murderers? Mothers gave their sons to defend the homeland that had been contaminated by communist thugs.

The braves mothers and daughters of veterans of the Independence War of 1895. Who can deny that these women were brave? Who can deny their sacrifice and

struggle for their children? Yes, they were brave and heroines. Our mothers with the heart destroyed of pain and suffering by the delinquent's criminals and murderers communists

Mothers age quickly and feeling in their hearts the suffering of the sons. The sons die in terrible prisons and punishment cells without light or water sufficient for their personal needs. Our mothers suffered for many years. Mothers can never forget his devotion and sacrifice for many years of massive massacres throughout the country.

The saddest part is that our mothers died without seeing the freedom of their homeland and the triumph of his sons who gave their all so that others would not suffer the ordeal of a slow but sure death. I understand who does not love his dear mother is unaware of all the pain they went through by decades defending their sons in jails and prisons.

The suffering of our mothers had to endure all the crimes committed by the savage criminals who do not respect the lives of their sons. The sacrifices of our mothers who now dwell on God's side watching her sons as were murdered by men hateful and atheists.

Mothers never left us alone in the difficult moments of our lives with that courage and heroism demonstrated by all mothers defending their sons until the last day of their lives. So, they were brave and heroics, the mothers who faced barbarism and horror implanted by the terrorist regime, bastards of Fidel Castro.

I am proud to have had an extraordinary and wonderful mother with her words. I left strengthened with her optimism among those walls where the men are living. She inspired me every day more rebelliousness and firmness in my ideals against barbarism and murder in the oppressive system. Yes, my mother was a heroine and never surrendered to the enemy. Of course, the enemy used psychological methods to humiliate our mothers that never left us alone in the most critical moments of our lives.

Mothers were the bastion of rebellion against all the injustice done on a system of oppression and shame. Mothers were brave with that value unsurpassed by any human being. They had been characterized as mother's patriot. So they were and never failed us because they were brave. So, they were steel, because never in history will be women like them.

THE HONESTY

In 1963 I met Roberto Torres in Prison in the Isle of Pines when he began the Plan of the Forced Labor. That Plan was called Morejon and months later the Plan of Forced Labor Camilo Cienfuegos from 1964 to 1967 was ended of the Plan Forced Labor Camilo Cienfuegos. I talked with him of all that had passed on the Isle of Pines in the same Block of Force Labor. The nakedness, the hunger strikes we had done from 1967 to 1970, the epics sadder of the political prisoners. I had just arrived from the Prison of Moron, Province of Camaguey. Because, the prison of The Cabaña had been closed since 1970 when we were transferred to different Province of Cuba. But two weeks later I was transferred from prison of Guanajay to the prison of Puerto Boniato, Santiago of Cuba, Oriente. However, in the two weeks that I was in Guanajay I can talk with Roberto Torres about what were planning the organizations in the prison of Guanajay.

Pedro: What do you think of the governments that have never wanted to help liberate our country?

Roberto: The Government will not do anything for us. They only defend their interests and we have nothing to offer in change for our freedom from slavery that we are living. They use the manipulation of the people when they need something. The governments worldwide are similar and none wants to help our country.

Pedro: Maybe you are right in what you say. Nevertheless, we struggle for democracy for the people can live in freedom and not slaves of the brutal system as is the international communism that not respects the life of the human beings.

Roberto: Yes, it is true that we give the life for see a world without oppression, where human beings can develop and grow in the freedom. Without anyone in this world can forbid the liberty of the human beings. We have to live the reality of the government processes that use the people by force of arms to slavery the human beings.

Pedro: You had faced to this ignominy of the communism for many years. What is happening?

Roberto: I have only struggled for the liberty for many years. You have suffered as me the horror of this system of cruelty, torture, crime, the deaths, the impunity and the firing squads against our best friends, the revenge and hate. That is not important for governments around the world. They are powerful and they not think that a day they can be in a war and lose all.

Pedro: We have many Americans that suffering as us in the jails and the prisons that suffering that and some of them were abandoned by their own government. The ambassadors said that the best way was the Plan of Rehabilitation. So they can be free and return to their country. I think that is not fair and to treat to humiliate his veterans and agents of the government.

Roberto: That was what I wanted to say. They were abandoned and not take care for them. Behold Frank Emmick, Larry Kirby Long, Evere D. Jackson, Richard Poyle and many more were agents of the Intelligence of the American Government and did nothing for them. That is cruel to abandon them to their fate without interest for the life of its citizens, who gave their all in World War II. I believe that when one sacrifices as have made the Americans who are in prison for our country. We are all obliged and grateful for all they have done for our fatherland. Men struggle for freedom of the people that live with opposed by communist dictatorships in many nations.

Pedro: We for many years that know us and we have experienced all the savagery of our communist executioners and criminals. Why did you decide to go to the Progressive Plan of Reeducation and give up the fight?

Roberto: We have all lived with the hope of overthrowing Castro's communist government and from the prison cannot. The reason I have changed the strategy, does not mean I will not continue the fight against these systems that stifle the people. Meanwhile, I will be fighting for democracy in my country. Besides, life in prison is hard with much suffering and inhumane living conditions. But the country is above our sacrifice

Pedro: From the moment you left your best friends to move into the world of the enemy, one must feel frustrated.

Roberto: Part yes and part no, if you wear a goal. All know that in life everything has risks in the jail and to die as they have done with thousands of men gave their lives in the firing squads, Forced Labor Camilo Cienfuegos, nakedness, hunger Strikes, isolation and torture in the dungeons of punishment.

Pedro: Explain to me why if you get a goal after you have met more than a decade behind bars?

Roberto: Listen to me, when you have to complete mission no matter which way you go, long as you will be honest with yourself and make what you have in your mind.

Pedro: We have been in all the battles and we have come out of it, but with great sacrifice and pain to see many of our compatriots who have been murdered with a nosegay of bullets in the chest or a bayonet in his stomach from side to side.

Roberto: That is true, for that reason I have come to tell you I am going for the Progressive Plan or Reeducation Plan. I think that is the best choice I ever made. I do not go to die in jail Communists murdered by henchmen, or die in a hunger strike and without right to defend myself.

Pedro: That is a decision that I respect although I disagree with the humiliation. I have not the courage to leave my comrades who gave their lives for their ideals.

Roberto: I think it is not easy making a decision like this. You and I have suffered very much in the Plan Camilo Cienfuegos Forced Labor, Nakedness and hunger strikes. We are marked for life with the wounds that we carry in our bodies by the bayonets of our enemies, criminals and cowards.

Pedro: You know like me the list of martyrs who were killed in the Plan of Forced Labor Camilo Cienfuegos in Isle of Pines with the brutality and savagery that were massacred political prisoners. I'd rather die than fail to the martyrs.

Roberto: No, I am not failed to go to the concentration camps, or the Progressive Plan for slave labor that the communist imposes me. I want to continue the fight our anywhere in the world.

Pedro: Do you think is fair and worthy of a man wearing the skin lacerated by the bayonets of your enemies to surrender to the enemy communist?

Roberto: I had never thought to make a decision like this, let alone leave prison with a government communist. The Forced Labor had been created by Reynold Gonzalez. Pedro Azcarate, Lino Bernabe Fernandez, Pelayo Torres, Alberto Souer, Juan Souer, Alberto Muller, Juan Muller, Pedro Fraginals, Pruna Beltot, Manuel Suarez Mata, Juan Falcon, Alberto Bayolo, Juan Bayolo, Julio Hernandez Rojo, Raul Falcon, Santo Soto, Luis Fernandez Plana, Jose Fernandez, Pablo Palmiere, Laureano Pequeño Velo, Vladimir Ramirez, Armando A. Zaldivar. Mario Simon, Paco Almoina, Piloto Mora, Agustin Perez Medina, Rolando De Veras, Raul Trujillo Pelaez, Jose Saura, Jery Salas, Kiki Salas, Gerardo Batista, Miguel Perez, Eduardo Perez, Victor Ortiz, Fernando Fonseca, Mario Fajardo, Santiago Echemendia, Ignacio Segurola, Atilano Gamez, Miguel Martinez, Andres Cao Mendigury, Pedro Perez Castro, Salvador Subira, Alberto Walsh Rios, Alfrerto Elias, Pedro Forcades, Roberto Nuñez, Ramon Mestre, Leonel Ferguson, Manuel Romeou, Vikin Meso Llada, Rowaldo Calero Sosa, Domingo Sanchez Costa and Roberto Torres.

Organizations with thousands of political prisoners joined him to create this infamy Progressive Plan. I know this create this eyesore to our friends with this betrayal. Was being planned from the Isle of Pines, where the heads of organizations and their leaders who were working to divide the Presidio Politico several years ago. That was the vilest infamy of movements in the prison. As the MRP, MRR, M-30-11, MDM, MRB, MUR, MID, AAA, MCD, M-20-05 and other minor organizations were making many damage the political prisoner in rebelliousness. While the communist tyranny takes advantage of these divisions.

Pedro: You know that it has happened since the Invasion of Playa Giron when surrendered in 1961. Because no could agree and will always had different viewpoints.

Roberto: that is true. Look, the only people who took to the fight overthrow the communist government were the workers and Vicente Mendez in 1970 with 23 men landed in Santiago of Cuba, Oriente Province and as you see they were killed all except one who remains alive. Those are brave men that love their country.

You know that there are many informants in the organizations working with the Communists and I do believe that others are against Marxist-Leninist dictatorship. Looking at these men you are going to hospitals in Havana frequently. While those are truly sick never they go them out because they do not work for them. For all we know, there are many men are not faithful and are committed with the government to blackmail the political prisoners with the visits to the hospital.

Pedro: That has always existed and it even seems that they are conspiring against the government, they are punished in prison.

Roberto: I after being in prison a so many years as we, I have noticed that not all men are sincere and open to everything. They are wrong in their lives because they have not force to struggle. If we see what happened with the government of Fulgencio Batista in 1957 and 1958 we realize the wickedness of men.

This you know when you were a student at the School of Commerce and knew those who were conspiring against the government of Fulgencio Batista and now you look like the Generals, Colonels, Ministers, Senators, Representatives, Journalists, Lawyer, Engineers, Captains and men business were to blame for this disaster we are living. We have no blame for what they did. Men inside the Government who were Communist of the Party, as Carlos Rafael Rodriguez, Blas Roca Calderio, Lazaro Peña Gonzalez and other as the capitalists were those who supported Fidel Castro "the rustler" with large sums of money and officials who were in the dictatorship of Fulgencio Batista. You do not want to forget the communist system of Fidel Castro. This system became in a monstrous against the Cuban people. Today are paying the crimes of others. The same was when Miguel Angel Quevedo said the Batista government had killed 20,000 Cubans. For that reason he committed suicide like a coward and liar.

Pedro: what will you do after you get out of the jails and prisons where we have been over a decade?

Roberto: First, I go to travel to Venezuela and then to France where I have some friends to continue the struggle until the complete overthrow of the communist's dictatorship. That is what I go to do when I get to those countries of the free world.

Pedro: Why do not you go to the United States where you have more security?

Roberto: To go to the United States is going to be more difficult for the relations of the United States and Cuba that are in conflict and that I will remain many years.

Pedro: What can you tell me of the capitalists, intellectuals, professionals and all high society who supported the communist guerrillas in the Sierra Maestra?

Roberto: They mostly have destroyed the country next to Castro. This species is full of malice and evil against the people who suffer the betrayal of capitalist and the bitterly. The intellectuals were the responsible and the professionals, when the guerrillas were in the Sierra Maestra and other parts of the country.

Pedro: What you are saying is extremely hard and cruel to men who may mistake or were blind and deaf of what they did.

Roberto: No, in this life there are many who are deaf, blind and dumb. They are like the bad grass that is full of thorns and when you the plucked root has been again when out. However, we must cultivate good grass to grow and not die.

Pedro: I have heard that in this prison of Guanajay things are not going well. What is happening?

Roberto: I will tell you the errors of the organizations that are doing the heads of the organizations could go to where they want, without intervene of the political prisoners who are in closed prisons in inhuman conditions. I do not agree with them to make agreements as embarrassing as they are doing the heads of the organizations that created the Progressive Plan of Reeducation. That is an infamous project. The Covenant is embarrassing for the following Reason:

First: All political Prisoners who are in Rebelliousness in jails and prisons and closed will not be able to go free if not welcome Progressive Plan benefits.

Second: All political Prisoners who have completed their sanction should not be released until his full Rehabilitation unconditionally.

Third: The Political Prisoners who do not accept the Progressive Plan must be punished until full Rehabilitation.

Fourth: If the political prisoners in Rebelliousness do not accept the Progressive Plan in prisons will have to remain completely in jails and prisons closed at all times until they decide to join the Progressive Plan.

Fifth: The day that political prisoners decide to join the Progressive Plan will be taken into account if they are released unconditionally or not.

This was the most brutal and despicable in the history of the political prisoners by the traitors Reynold Gonzalez and the organizations of the Progressive Plan. I ask you please that if you someday out of these dark prisons where men die for their ideals. I want that you try to write the truth with the intelligence that you always have had in difficult time without flaunting courage and heroism. You have lived so many years of torture, isolation, and forced labor, punished in dungeons and many hungers strikes without giving an inch.

Pedro: We have spent many strikes together risked our lives. However, I have the pain of having lost in 1969 the Hunger Strike. The losses of hundreds of men that not fight because are spectators.

Roberto: The Hunger Strike of 1969 was planned by Huber Matos Benitez with other leaders of political prison to claim the same points that we already had from 1968. That strike was a trap infamous and despicable that the political prisoner fell. However, the only one that will give count was the political prisoners that were naked. They were the one who did not agree in the hunger strike to claim three points that already had. You know we had those points from the hunger strike in 1968, which for the first time the political prisoner during the 20 days were together. As we all know, Huber Matos had many privileges. Perhaps by all the murders he had committed in the prison of Camaguey. Huber Matos was a miserable assassin and coward like the Che Guevara. The communist government has had it separate a group of rebel officers of the army forced to not bother the rest of the political prisoners naked that were living in inhumane conditions without medical care without food adequate in the cells closed in Puerto Boniato prison. Where were dying many of Inanition in the cell close in the jail of death in Puerto Boniato?

Pedro: I understand that Hubert Matos was a criminal and never fought for the freedom of Cuba. He was a coward assassin in the prison of Camaguey. He was an active military in the Province of Camaguey when was arrested by order of Fidel Castro.

Roberto: I will never forget the brave men and the people live enslaved by a disgraceful regime without mercy and the massacres committed by the monstrous dictatorship of Fidel Castro and the mob of soldiers, cowards and scoundrels. I will never forget our ancestors and men of good will who want to be free. I wish you good luck and may God protect you in the place that you are, because you know as I do that the prison is a cemetery of living men.

Pedro: In this way was Robert Torres with his sincerity and his fighting against the Communists in those years of 1964 and 1967. Roberto was covered in blood for the beatings of the bayonets that lacerated your body and bleed until death in the forced labor camps in Isle of Pines. The scorching sun and rain covered the skin with crying the crime that he was living in torture camps in Isle of Pines. I recognize that Roberto Torres was a brave man to say the truth of what had happened in the jails and prisons, recognizing that political prisoners with buggy made for many years. So, Roberto Torres was so humble and simple that I will never forget his words in this uncertain world where life is a ray of light that comes and goes in a second.

THE INVINCIBLE

Agustin Robaina was jailed in 1963, accused of crimes of conspiracy against the State authorities to overthrow the government through armed struggle, and to promote uprisings to remove from power the communist system Fidel Castro and the gang of terrorists.

Agustin became an opponent of the communist regime since January 28, 1959. At that time the firing began shooting, places where massacres were committed that humans have never see in the history of the Republic of Cuba. It can be said that these killings were the first bells that awakened consciousness of rebellion among created hypnosis foe alleged fraudulent victory of the messianic revolution. Conspiracies and began guerrilla outbreaks against Revolution. The fight did not take long to show to around the country, becoming more intense and bitter.

For years, Agustin was directly integrated into this process through participation in the armed anticommunist guerrillas, as were the White Rose Movement (WRM), the Revolutionary of Recovery Movement (RRM) and the Western United Front (WUF). This organization was renamed the May 20, Movement (M-20-05). And Agustin Robaina is one of those men who have not forgotten his homeland. Fatherland has been destroyed by the violence of an oppressive regime, the killings, terrorism, massacres, torture, misery, slavery and the holocaust of men, women, elderly and children.

Pedro: How many were you born and where in the Republic of Cuba?

Agustin: I was born on August 28, 1936 in the Municipality of Consolation of the South. Pinar Del Rio, Cuba. I cursed my education in public school. We were a family we were working around the clock to bring home a few cents at that time did not earn almost nothing. The technology had not progressed much and we had to do the work manually and with rudimentary tools.

Pedro: How many were family and they called each?

Agustin: We were 11 children of whom have already died several. Esperanza, Ana Maria, Asteria, Maria, Ada, Natalia, Rodriguez, Narcisa, Mateo Pedro, Jose, Reynaldo, Agustin Jr. And I, Agustin Robaina. As you can see, we were a close-knit extended family. I never knew my grandfather because I was very young when he died.

Pedro: What were the reasons that led him to conspire against Castro's communist dictatorship?

Agustin: I started wrestling when I get Castro to power in January 1, 1959. From day began to assassinate the military without celebrate them. Those crimes never accepted. I did not with these daily murders innocent men across the country and with the destruction of the Cuban nation.

Pedro: What happened in 1959 and 1960 that the population was sympathetic to the Marxist-Leninist regime of Castro?

Agustin: In 1950 and 1960 we began the struggle to remove Castro and military power. At that time the fighting had begun against the Castro regime for all the injustices being committed against the population, and mass murder throughout the Island of Cuba.

Castro's communist regime could not manipulate the farmers while in the Sierra Maestra in 1957 and 1958. For that reason they were caught was so much hatred the peasants, being the visionaries of the wickedness of the communists.

The peasants could not read or write in their majority, bur they were very smart and knew the evil of communist criminals. That is the true who wanted to hide in all media of television, radio and press write. Without, but they do not say that the landowner's intellectuals, capitalists and professionals were those supported the communist government.

We know that the people had a lot of discontent against the regime of the communist dictatorship of Castro since he took power. Besides, we all know that people are struggle in silence, doing resistance in all workplaces, resulting in poor performance of the production, as if waiting for the system to collapse only by the destruction of our nation's infrastructure. In reality, the government is not interested in the economy, agriculture, transport and communication. That is the way to control people so they do not move in the country.

Pedro: What experiences have had from prison led you upright positions you currently have?

Agustin: I was sentence to 15 years imprisonment and this was my second and final arrest. From that moment I knew that I was expecting a prison full of difficulty and danger of death. I knew that the communist prison system is slowly eliminate his political opponents, destroying them physically and psychologically through isolation, malnutrition, dietary experiments, torture, beatings and forced labor. That we suffered in the Isle of Pines.

Forced Labor Plan Camilo Cienfuegos was so brutal and monstrous, with all those murders committed by the military and the individual and collective beatings, inflicted with machetes and bayonets. We see so many men wounded, covered with blood and frequent murders, at that savagery of communist criminals. That was terrible. Do not think I can banish the memory. And do not say because I was the victim of several such beating and because I almost killed on more than one occasion, but because the guards were not human beings, they were killing monsters and machines powered by the sadistic murderous hatred of communism.

Looking at all the atrocities that occurred in the Camilo Cienfuegos Forced Labor in Isle of Pines and Throughout the Isla of Cuba, we realize that our civilization still exists in the brutality and savagery of cruel and savage men. I put my life at the disposal of the country to avoid causing the whole ordeal and suffering that has been suffering from since January 1, 1959. Today with 76 years and older and pulverized crushed by that prison, did not hesitate to put my life back at the disposal of the nation and participate in any military operation aimed at freeing.

Yes, I am willing to give my life for my country to be free and that terrorism is over the system of the Castro dictatorship has remained for over half a century.

Pedro: What was the development of Guanajay prison in 1970 and 1971, and what were the problems that existed since the end of the 1969 hunger strike?

Agustin: To my Guanajay prison was the destruction of political imprisonment. The leaders of the organizations made a pact with the government to create the Progressive Plan. We agreed we had colleagues who leave for Progressive Plan earning a salary of $190 pesos monthly. These political prisoners took between 10 and 12 years in prison. Unfortunately, they chose to follow very of these bad leaders and humiliated, invoking Progressive Plan, which was the same Reeducation Plan 1962 in the Isle of Pines.

The Progressive Plan was a disaster for the Presidio Politico. Those who reject this ignominious step us were transferred to prison in Pinar del Rio to force us to savagery punishing desert. The cells militaries we flooded with contaminated water, and so we were about 45 days in the sewage coming out of the toilets in the cells. That punishment was one of the most brutal prisons live in Pinar del Rio was the result of the creation of Progressive Plan. The physical and psychological torture they did to us, I repeat, was the fault of the group's treachery deserted the battle for his country to join the enemy to go Progressive Plan.

I went through many hardships. In Guanajay prison because of these embarrassing circumstances, the behavior of men who have no ideology in the heart and consciousness. They not respect thousands of martyrs who gave their lives for their country.

Pedro: What happened in the Black September in Guanajay prison?

Agustin: The Black September was a day that did not count for political prisoner. That day had come not a delegation of country and a group of us started screaming. The day was so unusual because there was no violent retaliation in response to our protest. At night arrived, a crowd of soldiers and began a vandal requisition of our cells and our bodies. At about 9 pm unbridled military swarming down on us. Three and four for each of us and proceeded to undress to the forces. We were supplied with bayonets and other blunt objects, leaving us naked and then we rode bumped and thumps in transport crates and were transferred the prison of The Cabaña. We fell to blow a transport crates and taken to the galleys of Patio #1. That was the process of Black September.

Pedro: Do you remember what year the Black September was when were transferred the prison of The Cabaña.

Agustin: The Black September in 1972. We had hard times because of the men who betrayed us and went to the Progressive Plan. Men that had to the beginning a good behavior. But second time went by, they and their leaders went softening Progressive Plan as chocolate and no more be resisted where life imprisonment behind bars was highly uncertain.

Pedro: What happened to the political prisoners, few days after when they were transferred, on June 23, 1974, and wounded many political prisoners in the fortress of The Cabaña?

Agustin: On June 23, 1974 we moved to Patio #2 and they placed us in the galley #5, in the galley has passed 3 days and have led to the firing squad a prisoner who we did not know who was. Immediately we began to protest for the firing squads. The garrison enters the galley #5 with gas tear where wounded in the head to Curiel Perez, Bruno Salas, Servando Infante and several more were hit. Days later the fingers of the hand of Eduardo Capote were amputated with one bayonet. That was the violence used by the militaries oppressor of Fidel Castro, the terrorist, mother fucker.

Then Patio #2 also shot Daniel Escalona, a good friend of mine. And another that was several years he had been sentenced to death and had him working on the Reeducation Plan. He did not think he would be shot.

Pedro: What do think will happen when that infamous dictatorship is gone and the country has a new generation?

Agustin: I think we will have many years of democracy and peace we need. Our people have had to under terror, massacres in the firing squads, torture, slavery and famine is going on since 1959. Besides, we all know that there are thousands of soldiers who volunteered to commit murder in the walls shooting and many of them are alive yet and several in the United States. As we as other terrorists who have been internationalists and have many murders, not only in Cuba but also in others countries where criminals were guerrillas as was Che Guevara, Jorge Massiti, Alarcon Ramirez (Benigno), Rafael del Pino, Alvaro Prende, Arnaldo T. Ochoa Sanchez, Fautino Perez Hernandez, Manuel Piñeiro Losada, Huber Matos Benitez, Raul Castro, Fidel Castro, Ramiro Valdes, Jose Abrantes, Abelardo Colome Ibarra, Raul Menendez Tomassevich, Rolando Kindeland Bles, Enrique Lusson Battles, Pedro Perez Betancourt, Silvino Colas Sanchez, Diocles Torralba Gonzalez, Rigoberto Garcia Fernandez, Leopordo Cintra Frias, Filiberto Olivera Moya, Fernando Vecino Alegret, Jose Ramon Fernandez Alvarez, Nestor Lopez Cuba, Ulises Rosales del Toro, Julio Casas Regueiro, Juam Almeida Bosque, Sergio del Valle Jimenez, Jaime Vega, Victor Mora and many others who committed crimes. Some of these men are in exile in various parts of the world and many others have died and are with Satan.

Pedro: I understand that democratic governments have not been fair to the political prisoners who suffered and suffer the tortures of the communist bastards who spend all their time talking about freedom. What do think of them?

Agustin: Look, no see these governments who talk a lot and do not interested in any political prisoners in the world. However, we see many cowards who murdered dozens of men and aspire to be president in the democratic world, despite having committed many crimes and governments help them. However, the Cuban people will never forgive them for the chain carrying dead behind them. These men will live the rest of their lives full of terror and justice will take care of them for all the monstrosities committed. Actually people do not forget the torture and deaths caused these evil murders.

Pedro: There are many who think only militarism knowing that the military is very abusive to citizens and often abuse them. In Cuba there are thousands of men killed by the military and you cannot trust them because they become evil criminals.

Agustin: If we analyze the thousands of brave and heroic men who were executed on the walls of shootings by these criminals.

I think the only one who can forgive is Satan. Because the law of men there is no forgiveness, let alone the holocaust of thousands of Cubans who were tortured and massacred by these soldiers.

Pedro: Tell me something of your sister Ada Robaina died after a long illness. What can you can say about her?

Agustin: I can tell you that my sister Ada lived in Havana and I in Pinar del Rio when I fell prisoner for conspiring against the state power to overthrow the communist government. She took the reins of the family and took care of me to go to prison where I was. She never failed a visit and was always pending what was happening to me in prison, the inhuman condition I had. She was a remarkable woman and very courageous, facing the Communists so that I can see. When my beloved mother died she occupied that place and went to visit prisons with my wife and I took my son who was practically a child of months for me to see. So, years passed and she was my right arm.

I spent 23 months without being able to know anything about my family in prison in Pinar del Rio, where I had isolated and punished savagely cell flooded with sister. When I heard my sister Ada again was when I was transferred to the prison at Guanajay.

Ada was the one I was going to see when I gave the prison visiting. Took care of me all the time I spent in jail, forced labor, isolation and hunger strike until I pardoned in 1979.

She was my sister, my mother, my friend and partner in all the secrets of the fight. She was everything to me. When I got out of the prison went to live in his house, 5 days I was there with her until I left my country indefinitely.

Times passed and I brought my sister Ada visiting several times. The last time she came to see me was to say goodbye to me indefinitely. I will never forget when received at the airport and I said, "my sister Ana has come to say goodbye forever. She forever kept the secrets of our childhood and my long years in prison and tortures". I spend as much time with her in the days she was with me.

Ada wanted to spend the last days of his life with me, but luck did not accompany the 18 days and be with me, she had a terminal illness and had a few days of life. She would not tell me not to worry about anything with his long illness. When we left from the hospital told me she wanted to die in Cuba. I would have preferred that she had stayed here, but she wanted to go to his country and few days later she died in Cuba.

Pedro: I have understood that you had a good friend, who was shot at the beginning of the communist system. What can you say about this great man and hero of the Fatherland?

... comrades in prison. This fri... onately called him "Pupo". H... the system anticommunist or... s very religious in prison I t... urch. Then the day before gc... on and the day before we lei... o bring a change of clothes m... owever, he refused to take it... d thought that you could co...

... couragement, if they take me... ission on Earth is finished an... altar. Yes you will release very happy, but will continue to suffer and suffer in this world of horrors and shame which will be living, therefore I am going to the firing squad without concern because it is over for me on earth, thus be sentenced to death.

I never will understand how Osvaldo Gil Carril spent the day singing hymns they brought it to the death cells to shoot. He came out singing religious hymns. He was convinced that he would live in eternal life in Paradise. With Osvaldo Gil Carril has led to Juan Valdes Cansio come out singing the National Anthem. That is the story of our comrades who with courage and heroism knew at that time faced with faith and courage to the horror of the genocide of Cuban Political Prisoners. These are the men who knew how to defend with horror and shame the country had been enslaved and defiled by these Marxism-Leninist military criminals.

Pedro: What do you think now of what is happening in Cuba and as you see that situation?

Agustin: I have faith that the Cuba issue is resolved soon because there is nothing eternal on earth and the last days of tyranny are numbered.

I want to be freedom in my country and Cuba will be free as we have all dreamed. We know that Fidel Castro is sick. It is an old man walking limp that I have to wear sustained by the arms to keep from falling. And actually we do not know whether to die Castro and his brother have a civil war in Cuba. The people must do justice to eradicate all those murderers who are in the country.

I want communism in Cuba disappears and there is a dawn of peace and freedom. That has been our struggle for many years. I want freedom for the People of Cuba, in a democracy representative worldwide.

Pedro: Every man's duty to defend his country where he was born and there have been thousands of men who have given their lives so that an enslaved people live without oppression, without slavery, without shame, with tranquility and freedom. The man loves the country lives or dies by it. Those are the freedom of others who do not fight because they are spectators, without faith in God, without honor and conformist.

MAN OF HONOR

The man of honor, as Aldo Cabrera was always aware of his friends and never forgot them. On May 18, 1992 came to see me. Because, towards several months that he not saw me and wanted to talk to me about those times that we knew in Havana in 1957. In 1959 I had begun the fight against communism with several students and I go to see to Also Cabrera to the Confederation of Workers of Cuba (CTC). Aldo was on the desk in his office and when he saw me said: How long time I not saw you? I respond, is that things are not going well. He replied and said: not walk here. I understood and said: I came to see you and to talk with you. We started walking towards the exit door and when we were on the sidewalk he said: this is full of communists. I replied: That I do not like and Aldo said: to me either.

Months passed and in 1960, I went to see Jose Antonio Llerena Andrades and by chance I met Aldo Cabrera, Javier Gonzalez, Miguel Rodriguez, Felix La Guardia, Norberto Abreu and Rufino Sierra talking what we were going to do to join the militancy disagreed with the communist regime. So, time passed and Jose Francisco Lamas had come to speak with me. He was a Student Movement of November and Coordinator of the same Movement 30 of November (M-30-11). Alejandro Moreno Maya, Public Relation, Coordinator Student of Finance, Jose Antonio Miranda Castell, Coordinator Student Action and Sabotage, Jose Sanchez Carpente, a Student leader, Luis Carlos Sanchez Carpente, (FEU), Student leader, he was assassinated in the firing squads of The Cabaña, Nieve Illobre Abraham, Coordinator student of Finance, Lucia Sanchez, Coordinator Student and

Eddy O. Sanchez, Coordinator Student, Advertising, Movement Thirty of November (M-30-11).

Aldo was an exceptional man and respected by all leaders of organizations that fought to topple the communist dictatorship. We were fiends and had a good friendship until the day of his death from a long illness against both struggled to escape. Aldo was of strong ideals and never forgot his friends. Friend knew before the struggle against the communist system Fidel Castro and terrorist thief.

Pedro: We would have been able to overthrow the government have gotten weapons in the early years we started fighting the communist system that was massacring the best sons of the fatherland.

Aldo: The weapons were very hard to come by a lack of capital which organizations did not have and was hard to fight when we started to struggle to overthrow the communist system.

Pedro: If actually to overthrow the system against the Marxist-Leninist dictatorship of Castro failed for lack of resources we did not have in the opening moments of the fight.

Aldo: We did not have money and much fewer weapons. If we analyze every detail you can see that we were alone and nobody helped us.

Pedro: What happened to the leaders of organizations that did not join?

Aldo: We have many chiefs and not enough Indians. Everyone wanted to be the executive of the Cuban nation and none of them had the ability to lead government. We talked a lot but did not anything.

Pedro: Why failures overthrow the communist government, if organizations had thousands of members?

Aldo: The lack of unity among the leaders of the organizations, the division that existed between them. You know the ranchers, setters, businessmen, capitalists, professionals and intellectuals did not agree among them. Something similar happened in exile and cannot have succeeded alone. They were uncompromising with the other organizations and without ideology, with thousands of political prisoners in the jails and prisons.

Pedro: Do you think the lack of resources could not succeed, or was for the divisions of political imprisonment?

Aldo: I am glad you touched that point. I can tell you that both things. However, we did not have capital to buy weapons. Remember the problems of the peasants who were in the Escambray Mountains had no resources and no one helped. With all the capitalists who are in the Cuban nation. Thousands of Cuban had left the country toward the exile to rush out of the Cuban nation. Because they had abandoned their companies and they had supported to Castro in the Sierra Maestra.

Pedro: I think you have touched on a very important point regarding the Cuban exile and his hasty departure from the country before joining the fight. What happened to the capitalists, blacks and farmers?

Aldo: You know perfectly the problems of the Cuban people. The white population began to leave Cuba. But the most curious case was that blacks did not join the emigration and the country remained totally silent. The white capitalist went out massively with their family.

Pedro: That is important what you said of the white population and the black's population. Why the silence of the black if they can do it too?

Aldo: The black actually at 99.9 percent does not interfere in the affairs of government and they are easily manipulated by those evil systems that exist in the world.

The black in if you are afraid to fight for their country and not linked to politics. For that reason is where governments take advantage of them. If the black people would have fought, as white would have been different. However, if we observe that the prison population was entirely of white with 99.9 percent, while the black's population was practically nonexistent. That is to say almost zero.

If the black population had joined the white population in the fight against communism turned around. Political prisoners were 120,000 whites and blacks only 120 political prisoners. That is, 0.1 percent of those in prison. I am black and I acknowledge the mistake of my races black. However, the few who were in prison were mostly faithful to the fight all the time. That was what happened with the political prisoners in the jails and prisons.

The black did not fight in Cuba and not treats to leave from the Island and simply see what was happening in the country. That was what happened and the people become spectators when they are massacred, killed, tortured, in the misery, hunger, slavery and isolation with the people in the country.

A starving people without medical resources and trembling with fear, all age and die deeming and looking skyward. The generation of the twentieth century have disappeared and asking clemency for something better. And those remain almost at the end of the road, without the strength to move your feel and facial skin hanging because nature overcame suffering and full of bitterness. This is how people die when they are not fighting for their fatherland.

Pedro: What can you tell me of the twentieth century Cuban capitalists?

Aldo: I can tell you that none of them fought to overthrow the government that had taken power. Therefore, they are guilty of all the horror that has lived the Cuban people. I think are very few capitalists that are with life, because they have been overcome by time and some are at the end of their lives with their children and grandchildren do not really know what their parents and grandparent did. Grandparents never explained to their grandchildren what they had done. Perhaps for that reason is that those grandchildren think their grandparents and parents left everything because of communism, partly yes and partly no.

They were responsible when Castro was in the Sierra Maestra. They gave many millions of dollars in those days of 1957 and 1958, when the Cuban peso had the same value as the dollar. But what they do not say is that when Castro took to power brought $48 million dollars with him to the presidential palace. Castro had to hire accountants to account of the $48 million he had brought from the Sierra Maestra. However, I can say that the Cuban capitalist were the ones who gave the money to overthrow the Government unconstitutional of Fulgencio Batista. That is what happened and nobody talks about the mistakes, thinking that the guerrillas would bring something better for the country. Yes, what was brought slavery, misery, murder, torture, terrorism, isolation, persecution, imprisonment and the holocaust of thousands of Cubans People?

What happens is that these men have hidden the truth that hurts like a whip which lacerate the skin and prefer to silence political the irresponsibility that took to the Communist Party came to power. Trying disability policy or by personal emotions of those capitalists who did not think what they were doing.

Pedro: You fought and participated in the overthrow of the government of the Republic of Cuba. Want can me say about those years of struggle of 1957 and 1958?

Aldo: I was part of that barbarism for having participated in the overthrow of Fulgencio Batista. I repent and regret all my life. I thought you were going to live in a better world. I was wrong and I apologize to my Cuban people, which he had always struggled to have a better salary. However, my help had been to destroy everything, because we rely on many occasions of evil men who pose as humanitarians and what they carry in their soul is a volcano of hatred and horror.

Pedro: What do you think of the organizations of political imprisonment in absentia?

Aldo: I can tell you that in the prison had brave men who ate the pineapple with the rind and betrayed us all. That is, they were not brave. All of them have been like the façade of a residence; that when you enter, is full of frets that never uses.

Time proved us right, because while brave a man is, also is a man coward. That was the case in 70 percent of Cuba's political prisoners. The example we have had throughout the Presidio Politico Cubano history. The men who were killed and the men who have carried the weight of political imprisonment have been able to fight for the cause and die for it, and as heroes brave they are. Others are not mention, as scrap in a landfill that nobody cares.

Yes, we were betrayed. Because were not all that are thrown to die or succeed. In war we see many soldiers desert and they are passed into the ranks of the enemy, because they are not men consistent. That will not be the slightest doubt I am going to give you an example. There are two men in battle field fighting heroically, one is humble and the other is capitalist. The battle is fierce and the capitalist tells to humble that he goes to surrender to the enemy. The humble told him not, because, the enemies could kill them both.

The capitalist does not stand over the bloody battle. The humble said: Resists a few more until reinforcements arrive. However, the capitalist not think of the consequences that can cause to the friend. The humble fought valiantly against the enemy, protecting the capitalist for that he not died. However, the capitalist surrendered and let to humble in the battlefield to defend the interest of the capitalist.

That was what happened in the Presidio Politico Cubano. The betrayal of thousands of men and others who were waiting by they were in rebelliousness with for better dividend for every one of them. The price the brave and humble heroes they had to pay dearly the ordeal. Of course, they sacrificed their youth and their lives for the freedom. That was what happened in the Presidio Politico Cubano with the heroes of the Fatherland.

I have the honor of having fulfilled the sacred right to have fought for all those who did not have the value to continue for being fore and cannot arrive to your destination. Because has capitulated to the struggle.

They could not see the soldiers with tears in their eyes and sadness in the soul. The could not see the brave warriors returning from the battlefield with dignity, honor and shame, especially, with a handful of earth would covered the bodies of the heroes of the Fatherland who had fought for the freedom of those were tired. Freedom can only reach those who struggle for it. Meanwhile, others look to the sky for a miracle, because they were the indifferent, liberals and conservatives.

Pedro: Who is Reynold Gonzalez and he did in 1962 against Castro communists system

Aldo: Reynold fought against Fulgencio Batista and was then foreign secretary of the Confederation of Workers of Cuba (CTC). Time passed and Reynold began to oppose communism, although Reynold had no concrete ideas come from the Catholic Church.

At that time existed the November 30 Movement (M-30-11), the Revolutionary Movement of Recovery (MRR), the Christian Democratic Movement (MDC), Martiano Democratic Movement (MDM) and other movements. But Reynold Gonzalez never agreed with organizations that started the fight. Reynold was actually very pragmatic and with little vision for the future. This means that his ideas were not unclear and confusing.

Pedro: How did you think of the People's Revolutionary Movement (MRP) whose were leaders' men professionals?

Aldo: The Movement MRP was created with all the items that belonged to the Communist government. These men were from the Castro regime. Some of them were leaders of the communist government.

The ideas of these men were opposed to the ideas of the other organizations who wanted to overthrow to the Communists that were in power. The contradictions of Reynold Gonzalez were controversial because he had no specific ideas. The political prisoners knew that the MRP was very different from the other organization.

Pedro: How Reynold Gonzalez knows your activities against the communist system that had seized power?

Aldo: Actually Reynold Gonzalez did not know my activities. Reynold imagined something, but he cannot prove, because he knew the truth. Reynold flinch when he saw me and that's the problem. He was trying to save his life.

Reynold was leaving Cuba when he was arrested. With Reynold could not you trust? He had the weakness of terror on the face and it really could not trust, reliable, justly that. When was taken prisoner come forward to cooperate with the communist system as an informant.

A near cost me my life where Reynold Gonzalez was ready to betray his friends. I had never seen a man with such terror as that Reynold Gonzalez showed.

God alone can forgive him for everything he did. I cannot make because as you see I have lost my two legs and is uncontrollable hypertension, headaches and I cannot remove. All this I owe to Reynold Gonzalez for torture I received in the

G-2. Reynold looked like a ragdoll on TV talking like a parrot. As Eloy Gutierrez Menoyo did and Doctor Ralando Cubelas Secades, "Dr, Rolando Cubelas Secades said on TV that he was Homosexual". I am going to let God of that pardon, because I cannot forgive for all that did in the G-2.

Pedro: How Reynold Gonzalez was projected in the business world and capitalist?

Aldo: Reynold did not see capitalism as a system that could help the social system of the nation. That is, Reynold was against capitalism. He wanted a political, economic and social more progressive than existed in the Batista regime. Reynold Gonzalez was a man of socialist ideas did not want anything good for the country. The only he interested him was the job and the rest that can sink it with the Republic of Cuba. So, the people humble and hardworking were not important for him.

Reynold was anti-imperialist, as political prisoners were afraid for his economics and social benefits. For these reasons Reynold had not within the Presidio Politico Cubano much relevance. But Reynold Gonzalez was an opponent of all organizations that were against the communist-system. Reynold had no control. Despite there was a minority of opposed systematically to almost everything the organizations had agreed in the Presidio Politico. Those who were not of agreement were the minority. Reynold was the socialist left and a danger to the political organizations.

Reynold had had a systematic opposition against freedom and the organizations that were fighting against communist. He had a trauma personal and without ideology defined. He was a coward, only sought in the asylum in an embassy to leave the country. He went to throw to the sea by the fear he had and to leave from the country to escape and was arrested by State Security. So did some who were elevations in the Escambray. As Evelio Duque Millar that abandoned the patriots in the battlefields in the Escambray. These men are never dependable because they always betray the patriots in the battlefield.

These leaders had abandoned the patriots that were at the fighting to overthrow Castro's communist dictatorship "offender" in the Cuban nation. We know that Evelio Duque Millar had abandoned the veterans that were fighting heroically against communist militias, in the moment that Reynold Gonzalez was arrested by State Security trying to leave the country. If you see a leader running, he goes always to betray you. You cannot trust these men because they are not men ideals nor dependable.

In 1959 Reynold Gonzalez supported the Marxist-Leninist Fidel Castro. At that time had several organizations fighting the Communist system. Reynold disagreed with these movements seeking to overthrow Castro's totalitarian system.

Then came the Movement Revolutionary of the People as I said, men and women had come from of the Communist Party. But we have to wait several more years. Young women will be into the streets and will be the detonating the overthrow of the regimen, because the woman has always been the one that has not been afraid.

Reynold Gonzalez in the prison seemed a man sent to destroy all organizations and years later in 1970 and 1971 achieved its goal when he creates the Progressive Plan with other organizations. Reynold was a frustrated man since he began the fight against communism. He was against the American government. But, he saw all very dark. Reynold felt hate by the Intelligence Department of United States

Reynold's opposition was very weak, so much so that this man had a total blindness to what was happening in the in the country. Reynold really did not want anything good for Cuba. Reynold just wanted some basic changes regardless of the workers, peasants and the very people who had not resources for their livelihoods. Reynold not want anything good for the people and saw Castro's communist system as a social system where the working people are going to benefit. Of course, Reynold was blind, deaf and dumb because he knew nothing about what the government was doing. These men pragmatists have no ideas if what they are doing is good or bad.

Pedro: What did Reynold Gonzalez of the November 30th Movement and which was his concern?

Aldo: Reynold Gonzalez respected the November 30 Movement (M-30-11), because that organization was not created by professionals. The November 30 Movement was led by trade unionists, workers, peasants, students and people who did not have sufficient resources to be able to move easily in the country, because of economic problems. But it was the most powerful organization in the entire country. Maybe that's why there was it was so jealous and want to destroy it, maybe because had the most powerful union leadership and deeper knowledge in the working class and business. That's why he could not speak Reynold Gonzalez of the November 30 Movement. Although, I try by all means to destroy the organization through the years.

Pedro: You had told me that Reynold was leaving the country when he was arrested by the G-2. What happened with him?

Aldo: I told you Reynold was leaving the country when he was arrested. Also, from that moment began the imprisonment of the leaders of the organizations. I mean imprisonment because when he went arrested, he began cooperating with State Security G-2, and members of organizations began to fall across the country.

A few years later, the G-2 led to Reynold Television. Something similar happened with Eloy Gutierrez Menoyo and Dr. Rolando Cubelas Secades. These men spoke as parrots. And one of them said he was gay. In that press conference against Reynold Gonzalez explained his view television. That interview had a negative impact among the political prisoners, who regarded him as an infiltrated in the ranks insurrectionary fighting to overthrow the Castro dictatorship and communist elite will all around him. That was a crushing blow for organizations in the country.

At that time the Presidio Politico was very strict and when a person becomes in a confident, as with Reynold Gonzalez, Eloy Gutierrez Menoyo and Ralando Cubales Secades the homosexual began to distrust all leaders of each organization. The political prisoners began to distrust all leaders of each organization. Those were difficult moments for the Presidio Politico, where were killing to men in the firing squads every day and you had to listen to downloads of the military rifles killing too many brave men. Heroes did not deserve to be murdered just because he disagreed with the Communists. The executions hurt us in the soul and the heart. When the brave youths were arrested in action and were killed they began to live their youth.

Pedro: What happened when you were arrested by State Security G-2?

Aldo: In 1962, I was arrested by the State Security, which was infiltrated organizations November 30 Movement, the People's Revolutionary Movement and the Revolutionary Movement of Recovery. The big surprise was when I brought Reynold Gonzalez trying to justify fighting against Castro that made no sense. It was all a mistake of the men that were struggling against Castro's socialist government.

Pedro: So Reynold Gonzalez started telling you the cooperating with the bodies of intelligence of Marxist-Leninist dictatorship?

Aldo: Yes, Reynold started telling me that all was become in confidants of his own organizations and all those who were working to overthrow the system of communist dictatorship of Fidel Castro.

Pedro: What happened to Reynold Gonzalez in those months that you passed in cells of the State Security of the G-2?

Aldo: Reynold Gonzalez followed informing the intelligence of the G-2 all I knew of organizations and were gradually falling massively members of all organizations that were fighting in secret to overthrow the communist regime through armed struggle.

Pedro: What happened to you in the G-2 at the time of interrogation and imprisonment?

Aldo: I was taken to a cell in the same G-2 where I had to stand the 24 hours. In the cell I could not sit, had been to stand still all the time in that vault with leg pain due to lack of blood circulation. I could not move; the fever had invaded my body. In addition, blood pressure went up so much that I was on the verge of a heart attack. I had swollen legs and the blood accumulated in my legs. So, I passed 24 hours in critical conditions.

You now I never can get that problem and when I arrived to the United States, years later, I had to amputate both legs, with harsh consequences for me. Not only the amputation of both legs, bur also hypertension that I have never cured. All those problems I have are due to Reynold Gonzalez and communist henchmen of the G-2.

The torture applied almost cost me my life in that bault on the wall vertical where I could not move and unable to sleep.

That's how I torture the criminal communist of the G-2. Moreover, with the help of Reynold Gonzalez ready to cooperate with them. Actually there are times in the life of human being immediate death means nothing with these murderers and criminals' communists. That is not done nor with wild animals. However, the one in power becomes a murder without mercilessly.

Pedro: What did Reynold Gonzalez after his cowardly betrayal in the G-2?

Aldo: Reynold in prison was an opponent all the time. He was envious of the organizations stronger and more militants across the country and that to Reynold never liked.

That was the justification for creating the Progressive Plan and to destroy organizations. Reynold was a frustrated man, not only by informant G-2. Never could overcome his betrayal and was devoted to ideological proselytism against organization, M-30-11, MRR and MRP. Definitely he wants to break fight against the tyranny of Castro communist that used the traitor and the infamy of Reynold Gonzalez.

Reynold was the founder of Progressive Plan in Guanajay prison in 1970 and 1971. This man joined almost all the leaders of other militant organizations as: Lino Benabe Fernandez, Andres Cao Mendigury, Pedro Azcarate Santiago Echemendia, Alberto Muller, Juan Muller, Pedro Fraginals, Alfredo Elias, Jorge Gutierrez Izaguirre, Eduardo Perez, Carlos Sotolongo, Alfredo Gamez, Alberto Souer, Juan Souer, Juan Falcon, Pelayo Torres, Raul Falcon, Manuel Suarez Mata, Pedro Forcades, Mario Fajardo, Mario Simon, Pruna Beltot, Julio Hernandez Rojo, Atilano Gomez, Miguel Martinez, Alberto Bayolo, Juan Bayolo, Piloto Mora, Roberto Torres and many more with the leaders who surrendered unconditionally to do volunteer work in agriculture, construction and livestock farms with a salary of $190 pesos monthly and periodic visit to relatives and friends in the street.

In 1970 and 1971 we were alone and the process that we lived all our nakedness, hunger strikes, isolation, forced labor, dozens of political prisoners starved and murdered by the henchmen communist in the jails and prisons.

The monstrosity of Fidel Castro the motherfucker, with the surrender of the leaders of the organizations had contributed to all these killings by the minions of the Communist tyranny of Castro and his henchmen unconditional.

Reynold Gonzalez manipulated through proselytizing organizations and went to the Progressive Plan or Reeducations Plan massively betraying thousands of martyrs who were killed in the firing squads.

Pedro: The dissidents are opponents of the communist government. What do you think of them?

Aldo: Of that group of dissidents we can trust in a 60 percent, but you have to give him the benefit of the doubt for the following reason: Perhaps, many of them have been disappointed of the regime that has ruled for half a century. Moreover, the communist leaders are in the last days of their lives and the only thing they go to leave is only the nation's total destruction. To all this I would say that the Castro government will use paramilitary mobs to hit civilian dissidents. Furthermore, the police forces, men and women will launch against who march peacefully. However, many of the leaders of the organization of the ladies with the white dress will be murdered to frighten all dissident. That is the tragedy of our people enslaved.

All these things can happen in Castro's communist regime to contain the demonstrations against the Government. But The Catholic Church is projecting with ideas acceptable to groups within the dissidents, not in all its totality with exception of The Cardinal Jaime Ortega that is not agreeing with the dissidents. That is what will happen between them that are linked to the Catholic Church, and they think totally different from the truth of the dissidents because they are blind. There will come a time when the Cuban women will be the main protagonist of change toward democracy. No matter if we have to wait several years where young women will throw definitively to the streets and will be the trigger for the overthrow of the regime, because, the woman has never had afraid against the regime.

And hopefully we can see the development the overthrow this system immoral and torture. The women were the heroines and demonstrated the heroism when her children were in jails and prisons. The women fought for many years to see their children freedom. The sons were living in the horror and the death. I hope all this generation of young women will do the call for men to wake from hypnosis. That earthquake cannot be to stop. Because, Cuban women carry in their heart the patriotism and they have shown across the history of the Republic of Cuba their heroism. But the most important thing is that everything is developing in a civil war, because governments want to remain in power until the last day of the death.

Pedro: You knew that for the Progressive Plan, thousands of political prisoners had gone? What could be done to stop the mass escape to Progressive Plan and Rehabilitation Plan?

Aldo: You could not do anything. They are not warriors and we know that intellectuals, professionals and capitalists don't have strong ideals and without patriotism and homeless. I had many friends before we stripped the Yellow Khaki Uniform and punished several months of isolation and torture without being able to know where they were. And they went massively to Progressive Plan. They are men who lose faith and hope. They are not fighter. Were men frustrated and defeated.

Pedro: Also and I were remembering all the times we had spent in prison and torture so horrible that we had spend the Communists to die of starvation and dehydration in the cells, completely isolated to eliminate us physically in such horrible conditions and also remembered everything that had passed in prison. Those have not experienced our experiences in cell of punishment. They don't know what is communism and the cruelty of the cowards men.

Aldo: I had great faith that we would leave that hell where we had been locked in those inhuman conditions we were experiencing political prisoners in communist prisons. Life was miserable, full of illnesses and without powerless have a pain relieving medicine. One has to experience to know the suffering. You know that I had many friends and most of them died of starvation and killed in prison by the militaries. We spent behind bars 13 years naked, since 1967 until 1969. I never in my life see such cruelty and savagery as we have lived.

Pedro: Why did they suffer so much for the Political division that did not lead to anything good in the historic moments that were living in prison?

Aldo: On August 6, 1968 came the division of the Presidio Politico where the government we returned the clothes that we cost us very dearly in the 17 months we were Simi-naked. That day in 1968, most of the political prisoners accepted the Yellow Khaki Uniform which we had fought for almost a year and a half.

However, a majority of those who did not accept the Uniform Yellow Khaki was because we did not see transparency at the time. The things were not clear and is created the division between Semi-naked, the Khaki yellow Uniform in rebelliousness, the Blue Uniform that was not in rebelliousness. But we had four positions in total including the Reeducation Plan. But these two last never participated in the rebellious because they were very conservative and liberals.

On September 28, 1968 we declare hunger strike claiming better benefits for all political prisoners. The hunger strike of the Centenary of the War of the Independence, of 1868, and 1878, hunger strike in that we had won all the points that were demanded to the communist government. So, 11 months passed of relative calm. But on September I, 1969, a group of leaders of the organizations had agreed, without count with the militants of all organizations for declare a hunger strike, with the same points, similar to the Hunger Strike of 1968. The responsibility fell over the leaders who had been transferred to the galleys #23A and 23B. Most of these leaders capitulated in the hunger strike and we lost all the benefits won in 1968.

I was in the prison hospital in the Prince with other groups of political prisoners and when we learn that in the prison of The Cabaña were in hunger strike. We returned immediately. However, I have understood that the political prisoner that were in the galleys 12 and 13 Semi-naked of the prison of The Cabaña were not agreed with the hunger strike because that did not make sense to claim the same points of the of 1968 hunger strike. On September 1, 1969, the political prisoners of the galleys in underpants 12 and 13 we set agreed in solidarity with the rest of the Presidio Politico. But, we were not agreeing with the hunger strike.

That mistake we pay dearly the political prisoners Semi-naked. You and I know that the leaders who had proclaimed the huger strike after 35 days of suffering in the hunger strike capitulated and went to work voluntarily in the Progressive Plan with a salary of $190 pesos a month. That was the betrayal of the leaders of the political organizations.

The men Semi-naked were in critical conditions, due to the irresponsibility of the leaders of almost all organizations, as if they were working with the government to destroy the political imprisonment. We lost everything. The Hunger Strike in 1969 was a big error in the history of the political prisoners. The tragedy began and betrayal of the leaders of organizations of Cuban Political Prisoners. They surrendered and capitulated from the struggle.

We never recovered us from the devastating blow. The naked political prisoners Semi-naked were isolated for more than nine years in the prison in the Port of Sweet Potato, Oriente. The saddest part was that we were naked. We were paying all the mistakes they made the leaders of the organizations of political imprisonment. Since the strike of 1969, we did not get family visits until 1979, in the prison of the Combined of the East, The Havana.

The political prisoners Semi-naked had lost all the benefits that had with family visits, food, water in the showers in the Yard #1, the sun and bath that we caught, the humiliating defeat that we had suffered in the hunger strike of 1969, knowing the behavior of the communists.

Most of the disabled heads of the organizations of political imprisonment in 1970 and 1971 created the Progressive Work plan and they all joined the Communist system. Actually the plan was the same Progressive and Rehabilitation Plan with the name changed. We know that the communists have changed the name of everything. That's what happened with all these traitors who joined that ranks of his enemies. These men were tired, defeated, frustrated and capitulated.

I had said most of these leaders had come from the ranks of government and Marxist-Leninist they did was go back to the same place they came from, that's what they did these wretches.

Pedro: Why Hubert Matos made the mistake of planning the 1969 Hunger Strike as Roberto Torres said?

Aldo: We know that the MRP and its leaders humiliated to Huber Matos at The Cabaña prison when unveiled the secret meeting with the leaders of the movement of the MRP. At that meeting Huber Matos acknowledged that he was a socialist and agreed to nationalize monopolies in Cuba. That demonstration was not well between the leaders of the Movement MRR decided to inform the Presidio Politico ideas of Huber Matos.

That's when the problem started with the three letters that Huber Matos did to the leaders of the MRP. These letters were read in all galleys for political prisoners knew the ides of Huber Matos. For that reason Huber Matos planned the 1969 hunger strike in revenge with the leadership of the MRP. Fell into that trap the political prisoners. However, Huber Matos deserted Hunger Strike in 1969. That was another humiliation suffered Huber Matos a murderer, of the left communist, scoundrel and coward as the Che Guevara de la Serna.

We all know that Huber Matos is a dangerous and violent man. We know the crimes he committed in the prison of Camaguey. Huber carried the political prisoners the firing squads without celebrate a just trial without take to court. Huber Matos became a murderer like Che Guevara. They were what the liked to see how die innocent in the firing squads in the Fortress of The Cabaña. The story of these men is the darkness and despicable. Huber Matos thought he was Adolf Hitler or Joseph Stalin and could do anything he wanted.

On October 1970 we moved to all provinces of Cuba. The majority of political prisoners naked were transferred to the prison of Sweet Potato, Oriente. In this prison we isolated wildly in sealed cells of the prison of the dead in the Port of Sweet Potato.

On that prison, the communist government of Fidel Castro made many psychological and biological experiments with political prisoner naked, food shortages and the malnutrition method and the elimination through starvation, without medical care, without enough water for our basic needs, without detergents to clean the Turkish bath full of germs and feces. So, we had to live for many years in cells dirty.

Completely the dark cells where political prisoners languished slowly by the communists and all those soldiers who fulfilled the orders of Fidel Castro murder. So we had to live in the death cells of Puerto Boniato prison, where many men died of starvation and savagely murdered by communist thugs.

Pedro: Huber Matos was your friends. What happened through the years?

Aldo: No, nor really, Huber Matos is not nobody's friend. He is much like Fidel Castro watching us all as enemies. If you remember that captain Roberto Cruzamora was his assistant in the Province of Camaguey when Huber Matos put as military commander of the province. When was deposed the commander Victor Mora. Then Huber Matos began with the firing squads without knowing who they were, and many of them were shot without trial by the courts. Not the courts had any guarantees of the prisoners. So were assassinated the men who perhaps had no crimes. But Huber Matos was the chief and gave the order to kill the young people.

Pedro: What happened with Roberto Cruzamora in the Isle of Pines?

Aldo: Like I said, Huber Matos is not nobody's friend. Roberto did not support the imposition of Huber Matos. He believed that everyone had to make him reverence. But Roberto Cruzamora not supported this imposition and others things that are depressing to say them. Huber Matos is a man unforeseeable, and he likes men who are his side be docile and subservient as the army of Fidel Castro.

That was what happened with Tony Lamas in Combined of East in Havana. Huber Matos believed he could manipulate to Tony Lamas and was his big mistake. Huber Matos did not realize that Tony Lamas is a man with more embarrassment that him. Huber did not take in the consideration the years that Tony Lamas helped him in the jails and prisons, and when he was released after serving 20 years. Huber Matos was annoying with Tony Lamas and he not wanted to talk more with Tony, definitely a man carrying hatred and evil in the heart. However, Tony Lamas is a sincere, honest, without hatred or rancor because Tony is heroic and especially generous. So are men who do not look the good that do because they are humanitarian and patriots.

I believe that if Huber Matos is elected president of the Republic of Cuba. I am sure would have been the same or worse than Fidel Castro. Those men are worse than Satan because they are diabolic.

Huber Matos and Fidel Castro are two monsters and dangerous and we cannot lose sight these assassins. They committed many crimes and you cannot trust them because they are scoundrels and cowards.

Huber Matos thought in his mind atrophied he would be president of the Republic of Cuba. That it did when created the Organization Independent and Democratic Cuba (CID), with it's proselytizing in Guanajay prison in Havana province, formerly province of Pinar Del Rio. This man wanted to nationalize monopolies and confiscate the entire the Cuban nation. The same that did Fidel Castro when came to power. Huber wanted to be the chief of all the armed forces, air, sea and earth. So, Huber Matos thought with the absolute power. That monstrosity they have these murderers in the brain.

Huber Matos is a cynical man and a liar as has been Castro. Huber Matos flaunts of the star that Fidel Castro gave him and carrying on the lapel of his jacket. That to me would be embarrassed with so much blood that was shed in the Uvero, Eastern Province when he was a guerrilla and in the prison in the Province of Camaguey when Castro put him as commander. When deposed to Victor Mora as commander.

I told you earlier that this Province of Camaguey, Huber Matos with his arrogance and cowardice had killed innocent men without trial in court. All these atrocities committed by Huber Matos and his arrogance, assassinating men innocents. For the reason, Huber Matos killed them, because he knew that they were innocent's victims. This man is a criminal as the Che Guevara, Fidel Castro, Raul Castro, Ramiro Valdes, Ydalmiro Retano, Guillermo Garcia Frias, Rafael Del Pino, Arnaldo T. Ochoa and Juan Escalona Reguera, because they are motherfucker, cowards and miserable assassins. Yes, we have to wait many years, but many have died and others in the last days of their lives of these delinquent terrorists and thieves of the century XX and XXI.

THE REASON

Orlado Molina Contreras was born on November 12, 1932 in Ciego de Avila. Camaguey, Cuba. He attended public and private schools of Ciego de Avila. Orlando spent his childhoods in a family of veterans of the War of Independence of 1895. Aquilino's grandson and Josefa, two veterans of the War of Independence. They fought in the Mambi Army led by Jose Marti Perez, Maximo Gomez and Antonio Maceo. Maximo Gomez and Antonio Meceo fought in the War of Independence of 1868 and 1895. The captain Aquilino Molina was very strict and the lieutenant Josefa Gallardo fought in the Mambi Army under the orders of Maximo Gomez. She was strong willed and never to boasted of her exploits on the battlefield. They were outstanding and courageous fighters without ambition and without discrimination with those who had not fought for the freedom of our country. The motherland is love of the brave men and women. The others are spectators watching the sky and hopeless.

Juan Molina and Epifania Contreras had a family of six children; Orlando, Alcides, Emma, Lydia, Elida and Eladio. They were sons of veterans of the War of Independence of 1895. They had the pride of being grandchildren of those who gave their youth in the battlefields with the insurrection against the Spanish Army. All of them have been able to defend the homeland, when the country is in danger, because they carry in their blood of their ancestors the value who gave their all for their country. That is the reason why the man sacrifices his life so that those who are not consistent with their duties may to live in a world of hope and a brighter future, without denial of their rights to live in peace and freedom.

Orlando Molina has been a fighter since childhood and has to live through many stages in his life happy, but also sad at losing the freedom of the nation, always expecting as a mother to her child that never forgot. That's the dream that every human beings carry in their heart, because there is nothing more beautiful than freedom and all right and daylight.

Pedro: Why the communists are submissive and approve everything?

Orlando: Everybody knew in Cuba there were many communists. But they were very submissive and obeyed everything. Nevertheless, all work that they did in the shadows. So were these miserable bastards and delinquents. For that reason the communists took the power in our country. They are: Fidel Castro, Raul Castro, Aracelio Iglesias, Carlos Boliños, Alejandro Castro, Julio Cuevas, Faustino Perez, Fernando Gonzalez Llort, Celia Hart, Ada Kouri Barreto, Carlos Rafael Rodriguez, Blas Roca Carderio, Lazaro Peña Gonzalez, Rene Gonzalez, Antonio Guerrero Rodriguez, Aleida Guevara, Nicolas Guillen, ramón Labañino Salazar, Carlos Lage Avila, Esteban Lazo Hernandez, Jose Ramon Machado Ventura, Julio Antonio Mella, Rene Ramos Latour, Fructroso Rodriguez, Edith Garcia Buchaca, Ordoqui, Sergio del Valle, Sergio Corniere, Abelardo Colome Ibarra, AbelaRDO Alvarez Gil, Armando Diaz Garcia, Jose Ramon Fernandez Alvarez, Ricardo Alarcon de Quesada, Juan Almeida Bosque, Antonio Evidio Hernandez Lopez, Pedro Saez Montejo, Melba Hernandez Rodriguez, Abel Santamaria, Carlos Fernandez Gondin, Ramiro Valdes Menendez, Jaime Crombet Hernandez, Baquero, Jesus Antonio Infante Lopez, Julio Martinez Ramirez, Armando Tamayo Mendez, Orlando Lugo Fonte, Tubal Paez hernandez, Lazaro Fernando Exposito Canto, Pedro Alcantara Ross Leal, Pastorita Nuñez, Marcos Rodriguez, Osmany Cienfuegos, Julio Casas Regueiro, Ernesto Che Guebara de, Jorge Massetti, Ydalmiro Retano, la Serna Huber Matos Benitez, Eloy Gutierrez Menoyo, Rafael del Pino Arnaldo Ochoa, Ricardo Kindelan Bles, Victor E Drecke Cruz, Diocle Torralbe Gonzalez, Silvino Colas Sanchez and more.

Pedro: Why many people are confused with the organizations that fought to overthrow the government of the Republic of Cuba?

Orlando: People are confused, because only there is talk of the guerrillas who were in the Sierra Maestra. That is an error because there were several organizations that disagreed with the government of the Republic of Cuba. At that time the Organization (OA), Orthodox Organization (OO), Student Movement (SM) and other who disagreed with the government. I belonged to the Orthodox Organization. But that Organization was not only, as was also the Student Organization at the time. People have been very confused with the process of the struggle to overthrow the dictator Fulgencio Batista.

These organizations did not agree with the corruption that existed in the country. The Army was not acting correctly and corruption grew and grew and could hot continue with that system of government unconstitutional. We had to put another to fulfill the Republic of Cuba, 1940. If it would have made choices Fulgencio Batista had not happened what happened. And for that reason was that we had to act to remove Batista from power, because he did not respect the constitutional laws of the country. But was worse the cure than the illness.

Organizations were in the Sierra Maestra, the Minas of the Cold, the Mountains of Camaguey, Las Villas and Pinar del Rio, which became guerrilla groups, as well as other parts of Cuba. That's what is said and only speaking of the Sierra Maestra. That is a stupid.

Pedro: I have understood that the guerrilla's commandants committed many murders with the peasants that served as practical or guidelines in the conflict zone. What in the conflict zone. What happened to them when they wanted to return home?

Orlando: War is cruel and the guerrillas had had serious mistakes that you cannot forget. I can tell you that the leaders of the guerrillas were almost all commanders and the farmers needed to serve us in the area as guide in the zone were we would operate the guerrillas. Those peasants were required to take us to a place safety and the army not fought us. The peasants are catching as guide in the area of conflict

When we got to camp, the peasants wanted to return home. Of course, it was logical for them to return with their families. However, the farmer was followed by some members of the guerrillas with the orders of commanders to kill the peasants to two or three kilometers of where the camp was.

Raul Castro and Che Guevara killed the peasants. In that form the peasants could not say anything to the army operating of certain areas of the mountains. Of course, they were assassinated. That was a cruel crime, but in the war be committed many abuses and killings of innocent people.

Pedro: Who are these commanders were so miserable to commit such crimes?

Orlando: All commanders committed crimes and killed the peasants, especially Fidel Castro Ruz, Raul Castro Ruz, Ramiro Valdes Menendez, Ernesto Guevara de la Serna, Efigenio Almejeira, Ulises Rosales del Toro, Juan Almeida Bosque, Abelardo Colome Ibarra, Julio Casas Regueiro, Juan Escalona Rwequera, Jose Ramon Machado Ventura, Joaquin Quinta Solas, Antonio Nuñez Jimenez, Sergio del Valle, Silvino Colas Sanchez, Manuel Piñeiro Losada, Fautino Perez Fernandez, Victor E Drecke Cruz, Jesus Montane Oropesa, Raul Menendez Tomasevich, Manuel Losada Garcia, Rolando Kindelan Bles, Diocle Torralba Gonzalez, Rolando Cubelas Secades, Alvaro Lopez Miera, Rogelio Acevedo Gonzalez, Enrique Carreras Rojas, Antonio Enrique Lusson, Victor Shueg Colas, Filiberto Olivara Moya, Jose Ramon Fernandez Alvarez, Fernando Vecino Alegret, Leopoldo Cintas Frias Tapes, Hubert Matos Benitez, Eloy Gutierrez Menoyo, Rafael del Pino, and others who were not as Daniel Alarcon Ramirez, Arnaldo T Ochoa Sanchez, Alvaro Prende. They were cruel murderers of the peasants.

They were criminals and have no mercy on anyone. We can say that the commanders were a murderer because they had much hatred to those who helped them. That happened in Bolivia with Che Guevara that peasants did not accept it. For that reason they ware killed because he had a phobia against the peasant who had not guilty of cruelty committed by their hatred, only killing many thousand of heroic men in the firing squads by hatred. But the Che Guevara had to pay the crimes.

We all know that to the military give the degrees of commanders, colonels, generals, to all who have been wounded in combat. Do not think they give degrees to lawyers, doctors, engineers, educators and economists for being professionals only. No, that's not true. These degrees are earned killing what they find along the way.

In the war against Fulgencio Batista had died in ambushes and about 900 combat soldiers, peasants and guerrillas. However, do not talk about them, because most are afraid to open the mouth. Also, when say the truth everyone tries to deny what you say.

We speak in all levels and nobody says anything. It is painful to live believing that only those who were convicted were unconstitutional government of the Republic of Cuba. That is false; we all know that many crimes were committed unjustly. So we must all tell the truth of those murders. There were almost 900 people died in the fight against Batista. Then who were those who killed them? This means that in six years there was an average of 150 deaths per year. Insignificant figures across a country at war subversive. That is the problems of the irresponsibility of not doing things properly. So, all of us have suffered the brutal savagery of that mob of commanders when they came to power in 1959. The most of the crimes were committed for them. Nevertheless, that is not said.

Pedro: Why Raul Castro and Ernesto Guevara the "Che" were disagreed with Camilo Cienfuegos? As I have understood Camilo opposed the executions of former military unconstitutional government of the Republic of Cuba. Was that the cause for which Camilo was killed.

Orlando: As we know, through history Fidel Castro systematically eliminated thousands of men who gave their lives for the country. Heroes who wanted a representative democracy worldwide for Cuba and all were killed by the tyranny of Fidel Castro and his military docile.

We do not accept Raul nor to Ernesto Guevara the "Che". They did not want that Camilo be chief of the armed forces as second in the nation after of Fidel Castro, Che Guevara and as the third and Raul Castro as four. That was the reason for his murder and had to be eliminated, as they did thousand of heroes who fought for democracy and freedom.

We all know that Raul Castro killed 55 soldiers in Santiago de Cuba, the Che Guevara Murderer to 14 rebel fighters of his troops. After, he assassinated 23 in Santa Clara, Las Villas. In the fortress of The Cabaña murderer in firing squads to 175 men, making a total of 212, However, we realize that all statements of the firing squads are signed by Fidel Castro and executed by Che Guevara who was always a murderer and criminal internationalist, as they have been Fidel Castro, Raul Castro, Ramiro Valdes and most commanders and captains who had had a phobia against the Cubans. Nevertheless, to Camilo Cienfuegos did not like to kill the men, although he participated in some trials where the military condemned to death, as did most of the commanders across the Island of Cuba.

I was of the invading column of Camilo Cienfuegos with 109 men from Camaguey to Yaguajay in Las Villas, Santa Clara. Days after, Fulgencio Batista was fleeing of Cuba, seeking asylum in Santo Domingo, Dominican Republic. On January 2, 1959 we arrived in Havana with 16 men and journalist Agustin Alles to the Camp Columbia. The doors were opened by Colonel Barquin that was charge of the armed forces and the camp of Columbia, welcoming the troops of Camilo Cienfuegos. While at the other end of the north of Havana the Che Guevara took the fortress of The Cabaña.

Of course, Fidel had sent the Che Guevara to take the Fortress of The Cabaña to control the city of Havana. Fidel Castro knowing that Guevara was a murder ruthless, terrorist communist from the Sierra Maestra, when he was a guerrilla, who liked to kill soldiers of the Batista regime and those who disagreed with rebels. Che Guevara was a rogue terrorist murderer who massacred hundred of men by the hatred and revenge that they had in the soul of vulture.

You know that when Huber Matos was arrested by Camilo Cienfuegos and he sent to Havana with a special escort. However, Camilo Goes out of Camaguey to Oriente Province. Eight days after Camilo came back to Camaguey on a technical scale. Fidel Castro calls to Camilo to will return to Matanzas, where he was

Raul, Almeida, Aragones, Dorticos and of course Fidel Castro. All were complicit in the murder of Camilo Cienfuegos as a man of ideas contrary to those of Raul and Che Guevara. They thought only in murder, international terrorism and subversion in all countries of Central America, The America of South and the Caribbean.

Everything had been planed to kill to Camilo. So it was as Raul Castro held the post of Camilo Cienfuegos as chief of the army. This happened because Raul and Che Guevara did not want at Camilo as head of the armed forces because Camilo as head of the armed forces because Camilo did not agree with the firing squads against the ex-military. In reality, Fidel Castro is a motherfucker and terrorist international with his brother Raul the "Duck".

Camilo had different ideas of Raul Castro and Che Guevara, therefore Camilo was opposed to what Raul and the Che Guevara said. Camilo was in total disagreement with the murders or any oppressive system that was not conform the individual and being in total disagreement with the murders or any oppressive system that did not conform to the individual rights of every citizen in any political system, economic and social.

He defended the absolute freedom and spontaneity of the individual. We all know that Camilo defended the private property, consumer goods and the individual freedom. Camilo thought so and that's why he was murdered. He did not believe what said Fidel Castro, Raul Castro and Ernesto Guevara. However, Camilo was pro-socialist, and anarchist. He wanted a society more open, anyone who said otherwise is lying.

Pedro: What happened to Antonio Perez Sanchez when you were in Columbia?

Orlando: When we were in Havana sent me to Columbia Camp, which was divided into two parts #1 and #2. In part #1 was Antonio Sanchez Perez who died in Bolivia and Waldo Reyna. I was in the company #1 with rank of captain. A discussion with Antonio Sanchez Perez sent me to military police with Ricardo Mario Toranza.

As of Police instructor sent me to the tank company #4 with Rodolfo Vazquez, for administrate the company. There, it was where the problem started. In November 1950 we steal part of the weapons with a military group and left to the Port of the Mosquito. But the boat broke and we cannot do anything on the ship with weapons we had. In the Port we were arrested and from the Port we led to the jail of Pinar del Rio, and a few days later to Havana.

That was the situation in which I had to suffer by carry out the subtraction of the arms shipment regimental. That was the reason for my imprisonment, with many years of suffering and many men who gave their lives to live in freedom.

Pedro: What did Alberto Walsh Rio when took the power and why he decided to take up arms against of the government?

Orlando: As we all know, Sinesio Walsh Rio, Alberto's brother was the leading cause of Escambray. Alberto began conspiring since 1960 and was arrested in 1962. He was in Pinar del Rio with the Martinez brothers who were commanders and captains. Alberto was in Pinar del Rio when I fall prisoner in late 1959. The commander Miguel and the Captains Vicente and Blanco Martinez sent me with the captain Alberto Walsh to Havana with a special escort to the General Staff of the Navy, where Raul Castro was waiting me.

Pedro: I know that you had passed through all the physical and psychological torture in jails and prisons across the length and breadth of the country. Why we had to make so brutal slave labor in the Isle of Pines?

Orlando: The Forced Labor we had to make in the political prison had been. Because, the political prisoners were not organized and every man did what he thought? All this was because the disabled leaders and no ability to pose the alternative to the political prisoners what they had to do, if you remember, when we began the Morejon Plan of Forced Labor in the prison. The leaders not say anything of the men that had been carried to the slave labor in the stone quarries of Nueva Gerona. The leaders were in silent and full of terror and fear.

The Plan Morejon was an experiment to see which the behavior of the political prisoners. The government realized that experiment had been a success in the stone quarries of Nueva Gerona. Of the 217 men who had carried as experiment deserted

136 political prisoners and military of the army of Fulgencio Batista and the army of Fidel Castro. The Rehabilitation Plan was the solution for them. The political prisoners are agreed with that infamy that the communist government had planned. They capitulated betrayed the cause of thousand of martyrs who had been killed in the firing squads.

Thus began the tragedy of Cuban Political Prisoners. We know that there are men in struggles docile and easy to handle. The Plan Morejon was the misfortune of the Presidio Politico Cubano by the irresponsibility of weak men who do not have exemplary behavior and sometimes struggling with emotional problems that had, and that is nothing good.

We must understand that not all men who die for their ideals. We had many men without fighting spirit that settled for anything. The Plan Morejon was devastating for political prisoners at the beginning of the fight, because they did not had an ideological formation. That was, and there was so many treachery in the ranks of insurgent.

We all know what happened in the Isle of Pines prison. We never expected the October 18, 1963 began the experiment of Morejon Plan, this plan of forced labor. I had very good friends who had exemplary behavior.

The Plan Morejon ended seven months later of to be suffering. The political prisoners went out to work without shoes in the stone quarries in kilns to make lime and mills for gravel. Thereby began the tragedy of political prisoners that we were in the Isle of Pines prison. The Plan Morejon ended on May 20, 1964.

On June 23, 1964 began the New Forced Labor Plan Camilo Cienfuegos. That was the most horrible national tragedy that has lived the Cuban Political Prisoners in the history of the Republic of Cuba.

The political prisoners received were savage kicked, injured and killed in the labor camp forced Camilo Cienfuegos, in the Isle of Pines. In the early years of this monstrous plan all political prisoners were united against this monstrosity that we had been subjected over 5,000 men in sweatshop.

The murderers and savagery cruelty massacred dozens of men in the camp on the Isle of Pines. The political prisoners we were left to our own. It seemed that the world had agreed with communist regime's criminal Stalinist Castro and his henchmen who wanted to eliminate us by means of forced labor to brave men in the most critical moments of Cuban Political Prisoners. Heroic men die for his county with honor and shame.

Our ranks were weakened and thousand of men went to the Reeducation Plan in the agriculture fields and the sugar harvest in 1966. Years later in 1970 and 1971, they created the Progressive Plan to work voluntary in the construction, agriculture, and dairy farms where they spent mostly eight years waiting for his freedom in 1979. These men had deserted, or capitulated of the struggle. For that reason was that they suffered the most devastating defeat of political imprisonment in rebelliousness, when they were integrated into the system voluntarily to the communism. In reality we have many men cowards and his struggle is in vain because they not love the motherland.

What I can say is that was a horrible plan. Those courts did not respect the dozens of men killed in the forced labor camps in the Isle of Pines. No, not all men have strong ideals and think of the country and family, only those who have died for the motherland. Neither are all that and sacrifice their lives defending freedom of the population.

We had I remember the year 1961 when we had to live on an arsenal of explosives. That is, we see the savagery of the military when were filled with dozens of tons of high explosives in the tunnels of the four circular Isle of Pines prison to remove the Presidio Politico Cubano. The military had called mass extermination with more than 5,000 political prisoners in the prison. This is terrorism, so, as the massacres committed in more than 50 years of terror, mass shootings, destruction and misery on a people who do not surrender for these criminals and communist executioners.

It is not easy to live with dozens of tons of explosives 24 hours a day and night without knowing when could detonate with thousand of kilos of explosives by fear and cowardice of the Communists.

Many truths lived in the 25 years and 6 months in those cemeteries of prison across the country of Republic of Cuba and with the violence try to eliminate us all historical political prisoners that we were facing criminal monstrosity of Fidel Castro, terrorist y coward.

Insignificant battles may be lost, but the Cuban people that are not going to miss, the final battle of the brave and heroic Cuban people who never surrendered to the savagery of the massacres of communists, the overwhelming advance of the Cuban people, as did the patriots of the War of the Independence of 1868 and 1895.

All subject people through slavery, murder, misery and torture have always been released from his tormentors and miserable scoundrels. They destroyed the Cuban nation with men and women who had provided with servility, cowardice and cruelty, to create terror, brutality and crimes by terrorism, with massacres against a people humble and hardworking.

In the first days of 1959 we started fighting against the government that I put in power. I was arrested and taken to the jail of government for many years.

Many officers we found that Castro was a terrorist astray and we through to fight that cost us many years in prison, forced labor, isolation, hunger strikes, nudity, murder where many were left to die by dehydration and massacres in the forced labor camps and prisons of the Cuban nation.

All that is terrorism and I could not make me complicit in many crimes by a regime whose achievements have been: poverty, hunger, slavery, destruction of the country and all the massacres committee by the evil regime and Fidel Castro's offender. That I do not accept. I thought that changing government was to stabilize the country and fight against a government that had given a coup with the help of the military. We know that the military had to blame for that Batista had given the coup d'état to government elected by the people through the direct and secret vote. So, it was that I rise against the administration in power at the time.

But there were others who thought differently and they wanted absolute power and that was unacceptable to me. I fought for democracy and social justice for my people, my nation and nobody can doubt because I sacrificed my youth for that our people can to live without slavery and without the suffering ago more than half a century.

I acknowledge that I made many mistakes, but I made many mistakes, and I could to see the destructive elements as those who sow hatred to take advantage of the lower classes. Yes, I was responsible for having failed my people and my nation. So I threw myself into the struggle to overthrow the tyranny that was in power. For these reason I spent many years in prison.

The political prisoners know that I fulfilled 25 years and 6 months behind the bars of the cell sacrificed my youth so that the people would not suffer the barbarism that are suffering many that belonged to that monstrosity and refuse to admit their mistakes. Perhaps not mean they are guilty.

I am wrong and I am feeling satisfied with having fought all my life, for democracy and without slavery. If, I have to go back again for my people that suffer the misery that is living.

Do not think that we were beside these murderers are as miserable as those who established the apartheid regime there is in Cuba. The history of these men is black and had to die with remorse for all the evil they did these scoundrels and cowards assassins.

Men have a long life carry with the suffering of our mothers that were aging quickly awaiting the beloved son of her heart that will never returned.

The men must be free as the wind, the light of the sun, moon and without anyone bothering him in his short years of life on earth. Man must live in peace and freedom from birth to death in the arms of God.

THE GLADIATORS

Miguel Hernandez Miranda has been a tireless fighter against the communist regimen throughout life. Miguel started the struggle with his uncle, Captain Clodomiro Miranda had launched in the field battle, the insurrection to overthrow the communist government that was in power. Clodomiro Miranda Captain of the Rebel Army, after have subtracted various weapons in the village of Cabañas, Pinar del Rio, he began the struggle in the mountains with a group of men at Finca Oliaga, Sierra of the Organs, municipality of Cabañas with the following results: Clodomiro Miranda Martinez and Gregorio Miranda Fonteciella hurt in the battle and taken prisoner.

Clodomiro Miranda's brother, Roberto Miranda Martinez was killed in combat alongside their brothers Miguel Hernandez Miranda, Antonio Hernandez Miranda, Jose M. Hernandez Miranda, Raul Hernandez Miranda, Gregorio Miranda Fonteciella and others over the Rebels who were in the struggle insurrectional in the mountains of Pinar del Rio.

Pedro: What can you tell of the struggle against the dictatorship of Fidel Castro?

Miguel: We started the struggle in the first few months that the communist system was installed in power in 1959. We started organizations on several fronts against the system that was in power. That struggle began against those who wanted to control the system of trade unions, associations of settlers in the northern part of the Central San Ramon and the Central Niagra. Settlers, Associations and all extraordinary union posts. For that reason we prepare with the Associations for elections in 1960.

The elections of 1960 won all. The Communists did not have any kind of victory the Settlers, nor the Associations and Unions.

We continue to struggle and we saw that we had no choice. The fight with weapons, we had no other choice. Clodomiro is realized that the revolution was not to be for the people and much less democratic. Fidel is a communist, and will break all Cuban institutions, enslaving the people, all companies would intervene and no one would be entitled to nothing. That was what was going to happen through the months. The communist revolution doesn't want anything good and we had to act immediately before it was too late.

We began to prepare for an armed uprising in the mountains of Pinar Del Rios hours later. Clodomiro told us, we had to leave because it's time we have planned and organized to strengthen us in the mountains against the Marxist-Leninist government of Castro. We are anti-communist and we will deliver life for our country. Furthermore, we know that we will have 50,000 soldiers and militiamen behind us. That was the reason that we carry us the weapons of the Township Cabañas and went into the mountains to struggle against the communism.

Pedro: Who were those who lift up in the arms in the mountains of Pinar del Rio?

Miguel: We were all like brothers: Clodomiro Miranda Martinez, Gregorio Miranda Fonteciella, Roberto Miranda Martinez, Antonio Hernandez Miranda, Jose Manuel Hernandez Miranda, Miguel Hernandez Miranda, Raul Hernandez Miranda, Ramon Hernandez Miranda, Bartolome Hernandez Miranda Sergio Hernandez Miranda, Armando Hernandez Miranda, Walfrido Hernandez Miranda and Ramon Hernandez Miranda of 66 years with other family members and friends who did not agree with the communist regime.

From there we started to come together with other people. Clodomiro Miranda Martinez told me that I see the others when the bell rings the phone and the conversation stops momentarily. Hours after we of the reunion and we rose up in the mountains of Pinar del Rio.

Pedro: What happened after the uprising and execution of your uncle and the rest who were arrested?

Miguel: All of us went sentenced to 20 and 30 years of deprivation of liberty in cause No. 215/60 by the Revolutionary Court of Pinar del Rio. The months passed and on April 11, 1961 we were transferred from prison of Pinar del Rio to the Prince Prison, Havana. In the Prince we were isolated in the cell. Hours later we were transferred to to Surgidero of Batabano and we were locked in the dungeons of the Tenure Marine until April 15, 1961. Of Batabano we went transferred to the Isle of Pines prison.

We arrived at the Isle of Pines on April 15, 1951. In Isle of Pines we were expecting the director Julio Tarrado with a Chinese plainclothes watched us all that had arrived. A few minutes later we were taken to the direction of prison and got the yellow clothes, they took photos and then we pulled punches to Circular No. 1. In Circular gave us numbers of political prisoners. Manolo Hernandez Miranda #27449, Antonio Hernandez Miranda #27450, Miguel Hernandez Miranda #27452 and Raul Hernandez Miranda #27453.

Pedro: What can you tell me when Gregorio was wounded in combat in the mountains of Pinar del Rio when was in the fight of the insurrection?

Miguel: Gregorio fell badly wounded in combat, almost unconscious, with several bullet holes in the side of the abdomen groin and leg had been shattered by the impact of bullets. They took him to hospital Military with Clodomiro Miranda. Gregorio Fonteciella when he fell in battle said: You continue until final victory against this plague that devours everything. No matter my conditions. The war must to be won. Although a lot of us will have to die in the battlefield. You have to fight until you have not ammunition. That is our duty to the Fatherland.

That reminds me of an anecdote of General Maximo Gomez. After the death of Antonio Maceo, in San Pedro, Punta Brava, Antonio Maceo, Gomez was substituted. Then Gomez designed to Calixto Garcia in a small ceremony at their camp for arming ten new soldiers, who toll them. These weapons are the property of the Republic of Cuba. I handed them with a warning that they can only give the price of life, on pain to be firing squads. Someone in the audience made a comment that reached the ears of General Maximo Gomez, who said: I made this warning to avoid more defections in our ranks, for he who comes to my camp without weapons that gave the Republic of Cuba, firing squads are prepared for him, a traitor, a coward or surrender, both deserve the same punishment.

Pedro: After you went through that ordeal in the mountains of Pinar del Rio fighting for the freedom of our country and taken to the Isle of Pines prison, what Happened?

Miguel: The Isle of Pines was for us all a great experience. There we met good friends through the pain and suffering of those who were confined for life in practically most fearsome prisons in the history of Cuban Political Prisoners in the Republic of Cuba in rebelliousness. We note as to the military used to hate, torture, killings and bayonets to hit thousands of men. View as vile communists murdered political prisoners, men heroic in the forced labor. We can never forget the cruelty of the military massacred mercilessly the political prisoners in the concentration camps in the Forced Labor in the Isle of Pines.

I remember when I started the plan of forced labor began on October 18, 1963 with a group of 217 men of the circulars and us taken to the Pavilions A and B. In the Pavilions of punishment, we did not know we were going to work in the Plan of Forced Labor Morejon. Those they us imposed with bayonets and firearms. Day after that we were transferred of the circular, the director Julio Tarrado with the garrison Chief, Lt. Morejon and the Chief Pomponio of Internal Order. They told us we had to go to work in the stone quarries of New Genona by order of Fidel Castro and Raul Castro. We told them we were not going to go to work, the head of Internal Order Pomponio, Julio Tarrado and Morejon. They told us. Let's get them out alive or dead, because you have to go to work.

Pedro: When did you start the Plan Forced Labor Morejon in the stone quarries on Nueva Gerona on Isle of Pines?

Miguel: Isle of Pines was a national tragedy when began the Forced Labor Plan Marejon, where men were subjected by guns and bayonets as punishment in jails and prisons. From that moment began the cruelty and savagery to force us to work in the camps of concentration of the stone quarries of Nueva Gerona, with corporals, soldiers and machine guns emplaced in vehicles. We were taken to the concentration camp. Forced labor and with the hot of the sun, the men fainted because they were malnourished at the prison.

Pedro: What you can say me about the men who began the work plan in the concentration camps of Nueva Gerona and the quarries stone in Isle of Pines?

Miguel: The Reeducation Plan on the Isle of Pines began after of Playa de Giron in 1981. On March political prisoners went carrying to the dining room. In the Dining room told that if they wanted to work as cooks. They returned to the circular. However, after that spent several months in the circular, the officials said that to those who have interviewed that, they go for the buildind#5 and #6. Then they began to carry the men to the buildings to work in the dining room. In buildings they began to prepare lists of everyone who wanted to go to work. The political prisoners and military believed that this was a good solution thinking that they were going to release them. So, many of them went to work voluntarily. They really are not imagined what the communists were planning against political imprisonment.

Pedro: You have to be very ingénues for not knowing how the communists act. The political prisoners and military all they did was give up the fight against the system that prevailed in the Cuban nation. They betrayed the memories of political prisoners who had been killed in the firing squads. What you think of them?

Miguel: The opinion of us at that time was a betrayal of the heroes who were in prison with bloodshed, wound of bayonets. They dishonestly knew the truth of what the Communists wanted. That faith a shame for political prisoners had accepted the Plan Reeducation. They knew that thousands of men were in rebellion defending their principles for which they fought. They will live a lifetime humiliated by what they did in bowing to a system that has no compassion for anyone and even kill themselves.

Pedro: We hear a lot of ex-military of both governments who have had many problems between them in prison for the resentment of losing power. What you can say about these military?

Miguel: I would say that the problems that happened in the Presidio Politico were due to lack of political vision in the moments that thousands were of men fighting in the battlefield to overthrow the communist government that was in power.

The soldiers who were in prison thought they had been betrayed by all world and we not us saw as allies. Through the years we fought to overthrow the system Marxism-Leninism system. Perhaps, they thought that we were to blame for the misfortune of the Cuban people, partly yes, and partly no. These were the problems of verbal and physical confrontation.

We had to live that moment. Because unfortunately, instead of facing to the enemy was killing us every day, the problems are more acute among us. In these conditions could not have unity to face the villainous system that was in power? I think that was a very serious mistake that had solution. All errors and reflect on these years. Later we had a more unified in the prison.

Pedro: The Forced Labor was for eliminate the Presidio Politico through the years with poor nutrition and brutal work through which we underwent during 33 months of slavery in the concentration camps of the Stalinist system of Fidel Castro as executioner and his brother Raul Castro, best known for the "Duck". What can you tell me the plan of forced labor?

Miguel: We had to resist all crimes in the Forced Labor Plan Camilo Cienfuegos during many months of suffering and murder against men who do not deserve the horror of the system. The military only thinks about the murders. You know that the communist could not destroy ideologically or physically the political prisoners because shame is stronger that evil. However, we saw as the Presidio Politico began to take consciousness between the classes with civilians and militaries in the jails and prisons. Men murdered and overcame that embarrassing situation that had been created in the Isle of Pines prison. The time passed and more rebellious groups were united and the communist system has to disintegrate the Forced Labor Plan, Camilo Cienfuegos on March 21, 1967.

Pedro: Who in your family were firing squads?

Miguel: I can tell you that Roberto Miranda Martinez died in combat on December 7, 1960 in the battlefield. In the firing squad were the captain Clodomiro Miranda Martinez and Jose Luis Laza Miranda on January 23, 1961.

I want to mention that when Gregorio Miranda Fonteciella fell seriously injured on the battlefield and his legs were shattered by impact of the bullets from the guns of the enemy. Heroic men who gave their lives fighting for the country they had taken the communists. Heroes that will live forever in the hearts of all Cubans by defend the Cuban nation, freedom and a people who had been subjected to the barbarism of slavery, misery and massacres in firing squads.

The Cuban people did not deserve that horrible savagery of the murderer Fidel Castro and his military Stalinists, in addition, we fell prisoners; not sentenced to death the followings: Manuel Reyes Hernandez, Ramon Hernandez Reyes, Armando Miranda Hernandez, Walfrido Hernandez Miranda, Raul Hernandez Miranda, Jose Manuel Hernandez Miranda, Antonio Hernandez Miranda, Miguel Hernandez Miranda, Bartolome Hernandez Reyes, Sergio Hernandez Ledesma, Gregorio Miranda Fonteciella and my father Manuel Hernandez, the military threw the vehicle against him and fractured to both legs, an arm and collarbone.

I also want to tell you that my cousins were taken prisoners. My father Manuel Hernandez was arrested a short time like my mother Maria Miranda Martinez in the moments that we were elevations in the mountains of Pinar del Rio.

When Manuel Hernandez was released, he went to prison on the Isle of Pines with crutches to see us with my dear mother Maria Miranda. However, my sister Maria Hernandez Miranda was not arrested by the State Security.

Pedro: There were many people who were willing to macabre plans as informers in the prison. For that reason many men who were shot were already sanctioned and killed because informants that told what they had done. That is a crime and when Cuba is free, what go to do those that were informants. What can you say about them?

Miguel: I can tell you that many of them were working of the same State Security. Men were trying to save the life for that their sentence were less severe were less severe. We know that they could activate the mountains of explosive. Do you remember when Circulars were dynamited with four tons of explosives on April 18, 1961? They started throwing their written messages that the authorities pick up. That was throwing through the bars of the prison window and the garrison took it to the prison management for them to read. They were compromised with the direction to work with them, with the condition that they not activated the explosives.

They started throwing their massagers written to the authorities pick up and taken to the prison administration of the prison. In these writes they were committed to working with the prison authorities if they no activate explosives of the circulars. These men cowered and over time went to the Reeducation Plan. They were nor sure of themselves to fight the communist system. Perhaps they believed that the government could capitulate immediately and they would not accept the sacrifice of risking their lives. Unfortunately these people have not been for nothing, let along to fight for the freedom of the Cuban people. Cuba has to keep waiting for a miracle for his people to be free.

Pedro: In Guanajay the proselytizing began with the Progressive Plan that had been created by the leaders of all organizations, the same leaders who capitulated in the hunger strikes because they not resisted more the hunger strike. Yes, they were eaten of salcocho and only thought in the stomach and not in the patriotic ideals of thousands of men who died in the firing squads.

We say there can extremely men who do give the face any kind of situation. They prefer to give up as they did in the Guanajay prison and join the ranks of the enemies not care that other men can be killed, as happened in the hunger strikes and then in Puerto Boniato prison where men died of starvation and killed in cell, knowing that the men who were in rebelliousness died for rights and duties that they did not defend. Why these men were so docile.

Miguel: The proselytizing began from the Isle of Pines, where a group of leaders had not very cleared those started to disintegrate. At first they were very brave in the Isle of Pines and possibly on the street. But at the end of the dismantling of the Isle of Pines prison have a very weak line in the final years of the Plan Camilo Cienfuegos Forced Labor in the Isle of Pines, but they were frustrated with many concerns. They had to find a solution in Guanajay and have not choice but to create the Progressive Plan. There began the ideological proselytizing phase with a majority of disabled leaders. They invented the Progressive Plan. That's what makes the leaders of the organizations Reeducated.

No, not the Progressive Plan was a work plan with a salary of $190 pesos a month. It was actually a work plan in agriculture, the dairy and the construction. Where, they had to work. So, they were taken to the camps concentration to do volunteer work. They received the benefits of the visit the families with the passport that they gave for several days. That was the plan of Rehabilitation. I do not know what is the difference in the Progressive Plan and Rehabilitation Plan or Reeducation Plan? the surrender, defeated without forces and unable to continue the fight.

They came to see us with the leaders of the organizations. I said before of my brothers and Armando Valdes Morejon. I believe what are doing is a betrayal of the dead, to Cuba and fight. I told him that I would regret forever with that step. They told me, I did not know what they were doing.

They response was, we'll use a new fighting strategy. I ask them, what is that strategy? The only thing I know is that all of them are defeated and they are joined the communist system with the organizations. That is all I think. All this is an embarrassing result for all those who planned the Progressive Plan which is the same Reeducation Plan. For all that reason, all of them not talk with us more in the jail of Guanajay.

Pedro: The prison of Guanajay had many irregularities in work proselytizing, was not acting responsibly with the disintegration of the organizations of the political prisoners. Why?

Miguel: In the Guanajay began volunteering Progressive Plan. The political prisoners had in the Organizations as: Reynold Gonzalez, Pedro Azcarate, Dr. Lino Bernabe Fernandez, Dr. Pelayo Torres, Dr. Santiago Echemendia, Dr. Andres Cao Mendigury, Dr. Rolando Cubelas, Dr. Vladimoro Ramirez, Dr. Jose Aguiar, Dr. Armando Zaldivar, Dr. Ignacio Segurola, Dr. Julio Abreu, Dr. Gazarian, Dr. Codinach, Dr. Portela, Dr. Manuel Romeu Fernandez, Pepito Fernandez Plana, Roberto Torres, Juan Muller, Alberto Muller, Santo Soto, Juan Souer, Tony Souer, Paco Almoina, Mario Simon, Mario Fajardo, Ricardo Bofill Pages,

Pruna Beltot, Jorge Gutierrez Izaguirre, Miguel Martinez, and leadership of November Thirty Movement (M-30-11) as: Pedro Fraginals, Pedro Forcades, Manuel Suarez Mata, Eduardo Perez, Carlos Sotolongo, Alfredo Elias and others that would make the list endless. Perhaps they thought that in this way they would have the political prisoners volunteer to work, but many men did not accept the Plan Progressive. Nevertheless, the leaders of the organizations were tired of the struggle and capitulated.

Pedro: At the end of 1979 put in freedom 300 hundred political prisoners in Rebellion and 3,300 from the Rehabilitation Plan and ex-political prisoners. They were in the Rehabilitation Plan and Progressive Plan. They were integrated and receive a salary of $190 pesos monthly and go to the homes every month. Of the 3,600, the 60 percent were Reeducation Plan and Progressive Plan. That is the same plan with different names. As we all know the communists changed the name to everything.

All were built, receiving a salary of $190 pesos per month and they visit their houses frequently. The other 30 percent of the rest of political prisoners were released in rebelliousness to the 20 percent and 10 percent of the rest of the political prisoner's historical remained in prison. The government strategy communist used leave in jails and prisons in Rebellion political prisoners who were in jail and prisons closed.

However, those in the Progressive and Reeducation Plan had released them in full. Meanwhile, the political prisoners in jails and prisons in absentia were released only 30 percent. The Communist Government used the strategy cheating to the United Stated. That was what happened in 1979 and 1080.

Miguel: We were pardoned in the prison Combined of the East, Havana, with U.S visas, a treaty of Jimmy Carter, President of the United States government and the Marxist-Leninist of Cuba, on November 14, 1979. Those same years we travel to Costa Rica, and months after we had to travel to the United States in February 27, 1980.

As we all know, were pardoned only 30 percent of the political prisoners who were in rebellion, in jails and prisons closed. We had been pardoned and we are in freedom, to reach the United States and continue with the same ideals of the struggle and return to Cuba to free from the communist system to the Cuban people. I believe God will give us the opportunity to live in our country. By which we have fought all life, and that our ancestors, of their graves are waiting for us to return to the homeland that awaits us with open arms as the mother when hug her son.

In the United States we have had many slaughtered men that spent many years in prison and have given part of their lives fighting for the freedom of our country.

We know that there are many discrepancies between the exile organizations that agree to take the fight to Cuba. In these conditions cannot succeed because of the lack of unity that we have, that is what happened with Political organizations that agreed to fight together. In exile is very difficult to find a capable leader who can unite the masses to take the war in Cuba. That only he could do and Jose Marti Perez that was able to unite the whole world in the war of Independence with Maximo Gomez, Antonio Maceo, Flor Crombet, Calixto Garcia, Bartolome Maso and all those veterans of the War of Independence, 1868 and 1895 that had discrepancies.

However, Marti fought because the country, to help Cuba become free. Unfortunately, has happened in over half a century we have been fighting to overthrow the system prevailing in the Republic of Cuba. We can assume you that this has been a very wealthy exile, with luxury cars, modern houses, and big businesses and practically are not fighting for their country. They talk a lot when are drunk, at a party or at a banquet. Meanwhile, there are not struggle against the communism in our country. But they speak much about their fortunes.

Pedro: Over the years I have not seen a unity among Cuban inside and outside the country. Do not know if it I apathy or fatigue. However, men and women of today are not like before. Today's societies are more submissive and without spiritless. Comparing the societies of today and before, we give realize, we are living without hope or faith. It is very sad to see the society that wears disposable clothes and seem destitute with dirty shoes. They fill the Bus and the Automobile with garbage. They enter to their houses with the shoes filled with grime without realizing that live in it. Besides, you see them with a hamburger, fries potatoes, a telephone in their ears and soda in their hands in all parts of the city. And when they finish eating throw the containers in any street pate of the street and be cleaning their hands with the clothes on their backs.

How sad to live in a society so depressing that when mounted in a car, bus, or train of passengers put their feet with dirty shoes over the seats and fill them with paper and waste instead of throwing them in a dumpster. No need that our generation has to live as destitute and dirty.

Every human being must understand no living just to have the houses littered around, and in many cases within them. If you look the mountains of waste that are around them and that they are not interested because they live without hope without faith, and without believe in God. I think is not good for a society.

If we start to observe the businessmen and workers we give account that we are living in a world of despair, as if asking for clemency by a miracle and I do not know why. No, Not I am talking about thing that are not true, I am telling you the reality of this world where we dwell like robots and not thinking that we can do to improve our lives.

How many truths can say about our society that does not understand the reality of an uncontrollable materialism ultimately die without hope and without faith in a world that may be better to live?

That is the truths that we are living in the XXI century, and if I am not mistaken this society will have to suffer what they destroyed when they could have everything you need, and when they realize that they had no life. Is late to reflect?

Miguel: I do not believe so. We will not see the unity we all need. The init has never existed between human's beings and each does what is correct or incorrect good and when it should be united, all are not disagree. That is a reality and we have to live with them all the time.

We are living in an individualistic society that must be faced daily. If, as you say, it is sad to have to live in a society that does not understand the pain of others. That pain must be the life as we lived us with hopeful and faith but with many sufferings.

Pedro: The brave mother Maria Miranda Martinez was arrested with her husband Manuel Hernandez, father of Hernandez Miranda brothers, uncles and cousins suffering political prison. They are sons heroic and patriotic defended the homeland that had fallen into the nets of the communists with Fidel Castro, Raul Castro, Ramiro Valdes, Ernesto Guevara, Carlos Rafael Rodriguez, Blas Roca Calderio, Antonio Nuñez Jimenez, Anibal Escalante, Raul Roa Garcia and Lazaro Peña.

However, there are always men as Clodomiro Miranda Martinez, Manuel Hernandez Miranda, Miguel Hernandez Miranda, Antonio Hernandez Miranda, Raul Hernandez Miranda, Gregorio Miranda Fonteciella and other braves men who took up arms to defend the country that had been enslaved by an oppressive system of assassins in 1959. The fighting was fierce in the mountains, prairies and plains of the province of Pinar Del Rio without ammunition, water and food, by the conditions unequal fight. The tired is exhausting for the men are mobilize in the rocks of the mountains, swamps and plains of places that are inaccessible to humans, 30,000 militia and army, in pursuit of a little more than 50 men fighting against communist troops.

The brave and heroic warriors left not overcome by the enemy that was released with all kinds of weapons against a group of seasoned fighter's veterans and almost without arms and ammunition. Men who fought tirelessly against this human invasion by land, air and sea to decimate and to assassinate a group of brave men who fought against the oppressive system that had taken power of force of arms, assassination and terror of a explosives in cities.

Never had been so much heroism in these men that gave their lives for freedom, peace and democracy of the motherland, the communist executioners of Castro and his elite of military Stalinist criminals and murders communists' executioner and his elite military Stalinist criminals and murders.

How many truths can say of these men that give their lives in the battlefields and prisons of the Island of Cuba? They were brave in the forced labor of Morejon and Camilo Cienfuegos. These are the true heroes of the struggle against communism in Cuba. Furthermore, we mention the Hernandez Miranda brothers as great fighters in the struggle against communism as: Antonio Hernandez Miranda, Jose Manuel Hernandez Miranda, Raul Hernandez Miranda, Miguel Hernandez Miranda and Gregorio Miranda Fonteciella.

Nor could forget to Maria Manuela Hernandez Miranda never abandoned her parents and brothers in the most difficult moments of the struggle against barbarism that communist Fidel Castro.

The greatness of this woman goes beyond of the limits of infinite. In the most moments of the fight insurrectional could say that had to travel thousands of miles across the Island of Cuba, without resting a second to see his brothers released. That's patriotism and love of country and family. Honor women who with the sacred duty to the fatherland she carries in hearts and never has forgotten for her country, family and freedom. So are Cuban women when are fighting for their country, family and freedom. That honor no one can take it off a Cuban woman, when are defending the homeland with honor by an enslaved people.

How can we say about the Cuban heroines to face the communist system in defense of his family? The Cuban patriots are stronger that a volcano in this earthly world. They are women of honor and have always fought for his country and family. That honor no one can take it away for Cuban women.

How can we say about the Cuban heroines to face the communist system in defense of her family? The patriot women are stronger that a volcano in this earthly world. They are women of honor and have always fought for the country and family. The honor cannot to remove off of the Cuban women. Women are pride of the nation who have given their best sons defend the people enslaved, subjected to the horror of the state terrorism, imprisonment, massacres in the firing squads, poverty, slavery and suffering of a people noble and generous. The Cuban heroines struggled with patriotism against the monstrosity of an oppressive system and criminal who tortures the people for revenge and hate. The women are giants in the battle, because are patriot heroines.

THE INFAMY

The infamy is cruel, of warped minds of men by the process that are living and cannot get out of trouble. If we analyze the behavior of Armando Valladares Perez (AVP) we see that since he was in the prison did not have a correct behavior. This man had many mental problems and acted like a psychopath, without analyzing what he did in his life since he was a military frustrated.

In 1975, in the prison of The Cabaña, in Havana, Valladares had to run and leave the wheelchair he used as a personal hobby. This man made many mistakes in jails and prisons. He was inventing things that were not of a normal person.

There began the ordeal of Valladares until 1975 that Enrique Vazquez Rosales (EVR) accused him of giving information about his personal life to the prison authorities.

That same day Enrique Vazquez Rosales took a coat rack to punish to Valladares. However, when Valladares saw to Enrique Vazquez that was going for where he was. He was lowered of the wheelchair and started to run nonstop. Valladares and Enrique ran so fast that in fractions of minutes Valladares arrived to the 100 meters unhindered. Armando Valladares became the fastest man in the world. That was the laughingstock of all political prisoners and the militaries that observed to Valladares and Enrique Vazquez Rosales with coat rack in the hand with good speed. But Valladares swift as a hare, escaped. Enrique with good speed was unable to reach him.

Valladares had broken all records of the world seeking asylum at the galley 8 during 15 days in the prison of The Cabaña, until the political prisoners resolved the problem he had with Enrique Vazquez Rosales.

Valladares and Enrique Vazquez apparently were good friends of their behavior in prison. They spent their days inventing diseases that they had not.

One day Enrique Vazquez Rosales started to mix the blood with urine for that the Dr. will carry to the laboratory the analysis and so, he could go to the hospital. I say hospital because it does not really knew where this guy had gone very mysterious.

I have understood that blood is not processed when it is extracted from the veins directly, was invent of Enrique Vazquez and Valladares with negative result. These two soldiers were inventing things without important in their life of pain and suffering in the jail.

Here I write of Valladares and is about the following: Valladares forgot that he was feigning an illness that not had. But Valladares Had committed a grave error with Enrique Vazquez Rosales for the information he had gave to the officers of the Ministry in the prison of The Cabaña. Valladares said to the chief of Internal Order the personal problems of Enrique Vazquez Rosales. That was a big problem to Valladares. Days passed and Enrique Vazquez was called to the direction of the prison to inform him of what Valladares said about him.

Enrique Vazquez Rosales came from the interview. Enrique informed all political prisoners, what Valladares had told the Ministry Officials. Enrique Vazquez Rosales then took a coat rack to hang to Valladares by what he had done to the officers. The situation worsened when Valladares saw that Enrique Vazquez took the coat rack to punish to Valladares by what he said to the officers of the prison. The situation worsened when Valladares saw that Enrique Vazquez took the coat rack to punish him. Valladares abandoned the wheelchair and began to run.

Was unforgettable the problem in the prison of The Cabaña. From that moment, Valladares was blackmailed by the intelligence and counter-intelligence of the Cuban State.

They made fun of Valladares and they came to question his illness frequently for the invention of Valladares.

The Secret Intelligence Service had made several videos of Valladares when was making workout in the cell of the hospital. That is the disease, disability, the lie and invention of Valladares until the last day he walked out of the airport Jose Marti walking until Europe.

We know that Valladares has never had diseases. Only thing that has is hoarseness from birth. That is not disease. He had no pathology that will note as a sick person.

Valladares was well fed by the authorities of the jails and prisons with a Special Diet rich in protein such as meat of chicken, meat beef, fish, eggs, bananas, salads, milk, bread and sweets every day.

All this I am saying, is wrote in the files and medical records of jails and prisons, where he spent almost 22 years of imprisonment of the 25 years that was sanctioned in Sate Establishment in the cause 5/61 of the Revolutionary Court of The Cabaña, in Havana.

The curious case is that Valladares had mixed the feces with membrane of chicken for go to hospital more frequently. So, Valladares mysteriously is going at the hospital and we did not know the place he was going really.

All this is in the records of jail and prisons of the Republic of Cuba. For this reason I am telling you the truth of the facts as they were and in particular in the medical records and the doctor writes all about the patient

Valladares was not in wheelchair. This man was used by the military intelligence and counter-intelligence of the government. The position to of blackmail by donning the Yellow Khaki Uniform against the position he was Semi-naked in rebelliousness.

The Communist system used docile men as useful information to their military, the position in rebelliousness in ranks insurgent. They believed they could to destroy the position Semi-naked with the Uniform Yellow Khaki. But the informant was humiliated all the time.

The reason of the lieutenant Adrian and Roberto were with the purpose to receive all kinds of information with Armando Valladares, like two friends who were known since childhood. The lieutenant promised that wanted to help with the purpose of knowing the truth of what was happening in his problem that he not knew. The lieutenant Adrian was a student of Law at the University in Havana, and every day he was interested more for the life of Valladares and the activities of his girlfriend Marta.

Lieutenant Adrian taught him the Medal of Playa Giron, the highest decoration that he had been awarded for his service in the Ministry of Interior. In addition, he said that he was going to get a job to his brother in law Ramiro Garcia in the construction, earning a salary of $190 pesos a month because he needed to work.

The time passed quickly as the race of Valladares and the questions began with the Lieutenant Adrian knowing that Valladares and his personal emotions were easy of manipulate. He started asking the question of interest about Valladares.

Adrian: What happened with Enrique Vazquez Rosales, to see his reaction psychologically?

Valladares: Me nothing, I get along with everyone. I have never had problems with Enrique Vazquez Rosales.

Adrian: Why he wanted to punish you with the coat rack in the prison of The Cabaña, if you were two inseparable friends?

Valladares: I have never had problems with Enrique Vazquez Rasales. He is my friend and we have never discussed our personal affairs. I think everything is a gossip.

Adrian: How you can to go out from the jails if they are closed with iron in the windows?

Valladares: We used military uniform in order to escape the vigilance of the military that are around prisons.

Adrian: How you had obtained the military uniform and as you could get out of prison?

Valladares: We used the tablets that brought us the family visits to make the drawings, and with these tablets we were painting the uniforms.

Adrian: How you getting the military uniform and as you could get out of the prison?

Valladares: We used the tablets that brought us the family visits for make drawings, and with these tablets we painted the uniforms.

Adrian: How could leave the cells if has bars and cannot be opened?

Valladares: We had companions in the Plan of Reeducation and brought us the hacksaw to cut the iron bars, and so we could go out, when the will pass the count from the political prisoners that they make it twice daily.

Adrian: What did when you were cutting the bars and to jump out of the prison, if the prison has fence around?

Valladares: Pedro Luis Boitel and I prepared the escape from the Isle of Pines prison. We easily mock of the soldiers who were monitoring and we went walking normally down for the street that goes to the hospital without medical assistance to the political prisoners that only could make dental extractions when piece ached. Across the Hospital there was a field of harvest of plantains which gave us the opportunity to jump the fence and no one could see us.

To jump the metal fence, we got into the woods, where no one could see us. So, we escaped from prison, that was completely closed and us we could not go out. However, how to escape was cutting the bars of the cell and later jump the fence of metal.

Adrian: Why were you arrested when you were out of the prison and in the forest?

Valladares: I had a broken leg and I could not walk in the wood. I had fractured my leg when jumping from the first floor to the outside of the prison. We surrender because the person was not in the boat to pick us up. In addition, Pedro Luis Boitel not abandoned me in the condition that was.

Adrian: Why you are in a wheelchair, if you have no pathology that that you are sick?

Valladares: I hope to help me out of this entire problem you caused me the negation of the foods by the authority of the prison.

Adrian: you worked in the government of Fulgencio Batista in the department at Fingerprints. What did you do?

Valladares: I did not question anyone about what he had done. That was not my job. I made fingerprints without any question. I want to tell something. I did not like as the Cuban nation had fallen with so many problems in the streets. I infiltrate between them to cooperate with the movements in fighting to overthrow dictatorial government we had in the country. That was justly.

"Of course, Valladares is a lot like Jose Quevedo Perez who betrayed his own government and spent 46 years supporting Communist murderers, because they are miserable and docile men."

Adrian: You were military policeman with Ventura. So time passed. But you began with Oliver Obregon Obregon to plotting to overthrow the government Revolutionary. For that reason, you are in prison?

Valladares: I have not hidden anything, because I have not conspired against government that I have helped to cooperate to put in power. I was accused of conspiring against the government that came to power. It is unfair my prison, because was in the National Institute of Tourism Industry (INIT) and will accused me of plotting to overthrow the government I had cooperated establish in the power.

Adrian: Why you are pale and nervous? I go to call a doctor for that you attend. Now when I leave, Olga Elena will come to see you. "Uf, Adrian took leave smiling." Valladares had had a hard time. So passed two weeks and Valladares was very nervous because Olga Elena had not come.

Olga Elena appeared with much kindness, as if everything were among family. She smiled frequently and observing to Valladares, as could grab the prey.

Olga Elena: What I can do for you and I can help you with your problems?

Valladares: Not, I believe that are very important because to me feel better

Olga Elena: Why you have not gone to see a doctor. You need a general recognition of your headaches?

Valladares: When you come here and what day are you working in this prison?

Olga Elena: I work the alternate days. That way I can see you more often. You do not hesitate to call me when you need me. I am here to attend your case. You can call me all the time.

Valladares: I have been waiting for two weeks and did not think you were coming.

Olga Elena: I could not come earlier because I had to make some adjustments to my office and did not have times available.

I knew that you had missed me. However, I thought a lot about you, but I was informed you were well. That was the most important thing.

Valladares: He imagined that Olga Elena goes to come as she had said, but Valladatres walked and paced back and forth in the cell waiting by Olga Elena. So, they spent 15 days and Olga Elena did not appear".

Olga Elena: Everybody knows you had a problem with Enrique Vazquez in the prison of The Cabaña.

Valladares: Who else are you talking about me and that incident so unpleasant that I do not want remembers.

Olga Elena: You know that Peter the Specialist of Physiotherapy knows you have nothing and he thinks you have mental problems. He says that you behavior is not normal and you are pretending.

Valladares: That is they talk of me and why they do it so often. If I am not going to Therapy were giving me?

Olga Elena: Of course, if you have not problems. Dr. Campos says that you have not any pathology that will indicate his disability. That means that you are in wheelchair because you want. Everyone knows that when you began running in The Cabaña prison and you left to galley 8, because, Enrique Vazquez wants to hit you with the coat rack.

Valladares: Please in the medicines of Pedro Santos Gallardo, add one tablet of Mepromabamate and Amitritiline to fall asleep and we will be quiet.

Olga Elena: She did what Valladares had told and left me in a plastic cup with the tablets. These tablets practically would cause me a state of coma with a deep sleep, perhaps forever in my condition of starvation.

"Maybe if I had taken those tables, I would not be writing this book and all my experiences in the jails and prisons in my real life. Nevertheless, they never could imagine that I not swallowed the tablets in prison. By the following reasons: You had no confidence in the government with the medicines and all the experiments done to political prisoners naked."

Olga Elena had to fulfill the mission entrusted to her by the Department of Intelligence. However, Olga Elena decided her future to fulfill the mission that have entrusted her to know the truth of the disability of Valladares. The time had come to take all necessary with precaution to make to sex planned by the Intelligence and contra-intelligence.

The dawn is expectation and the time was coming to an expected climax by Olga Elena. She had to complete his plan at her appropriate moments to know the reasons, why Armando Valladares Perez was in a wheelchair without to have Invalidity, or the pathology that prevented him from walking.

The intelligence department gave the crushing blow against Amando Valladares through sex. Olga Elena was played all in her life and fell into the arms of Valladares. Maybe, Valladares was in love with a beautiful woman as was Olga Elena with sweet words to convince Valladares for sex.

When I saw them at 2 am in the morning without to realize that I was in the bathroom, and when I turned on the light in the cell where we were Valladares, Israel and me. Olga Elena yelled terrified, because I had caught them in the sex act. She scared in the cell where she had accomplished the mission entrusted and to demoralize to Valladares and know the truth of this wretched man that had not invalidity.

The Cuban Intelligence Department used the first major blow against Valladares through sex. Valladares had fallen into the trap that had the Intelligence Cuban tended to destroy this man scoundrel and miserable.

That was the deadliest weapon used against Valladares. He was humiliated by miserable. The Cuban delegation presented the videos and demonstrated the falsity of Valladares in committing Gineva when Valladares was in the hospital pretending him his Invalidity. That suffering will carry until last day of his death, by scoundrel and miserable.

Sex was the method lethal used by State Security to demoralize to Valladares. The succeeded was in a few days using a beautiful woman from the Security of State to undertake such immorality.

Next day the doctor Edreira and Psychiatrist of jails and prisons comes to see to Valladares.

Dr Edreira: What happened with you that is in a wheelchair?

Valladares: I think everyone knows my problem. I have not need to be saying what happened.

Dr. Edreira: What happened to you that cannot walk? What is the problem if you walked for more than a month, when the hunger strike finished?

Valladares: I had Paraplegia in the 46 days I was no eating. That is the problem of my disability. That is the problem.

"I believe that Valladares wants to say a muscular distension. That is another thing by injury caused violently by a muscle of joint. Meanwhile, the paraplegia is the paralysis of the inner half of the body. Besides, said that he had muscular flaccidity. He could not escape of the problem that he had. Valladares was a psychopath out of control. Were invented diseases that he had not? For reason everybody questions him about his problem.

Dr. Edreira: How long you have not seen the family, asked him psychologically?

Valladares: I saw them a few days ago and they said they were prepared to leave the country with my brother in law Ramiro Garcia, who was a former political prisoner in the Plan of Reeducation.

Dr. Edreira: I have understood that you walk and I not understand why you are in wheelchairs. It is not very comfortable. Do you like?

Valladares: I cannot walk, for that reason I am in wheelchair from 1974 that affected me the muscular system.

Dr. Edreira: Do you know that if you have Paraplegia, I am sure you cost a lot of work to walk in your life? "Ah! Valladares was pale when the doctor Edreira said that word."

Valladares: I want to go the hospital as much as quickly possible to cure me soon.

Dr. Edreira: You feel very upset and you have to control your emotions. You are affecting with backlash.

Valladares: He said, I will carry you to the orthopedic hospital. That is what I said Lt. Adrian.

Dr. Edreira: He is not a doctor and he has to obey the order of his superiors as I, as a physician. The Lieutenant Adrian only has other safety issues.

Valladares: I need that carry me to the hospital as soon as possible for my recovery.

Dr. Edreira: you have much anxiety and I will send you the medicine you will take twice a day.

Valladares: Dr. I don't need those drugs, what I want is to cure me of my illness. That is it.

The Psychology of Psychiatrist Dr. Edreira had hit to Valladares strongly with the invention of his illness. Dr. Edreira went out knowing that Valladares was pretending an illness that had not.

The times elapsed between metal bars in that cell, distant from each other about two meters. Of that way, we could not to see what was happening on the other side, where was the rest of the political prisoners? The doctor Campos came to the cell where we were us. The doctor was very talkative and loved to talk to the political prisoners to discuss of the politics. The doctor noticed that the Neuropathy was affecting to Valladares and his behavior. Dr. Domingo Campos looked him very seriously.

Dr. Campos: What happens Valladares. I see you are worried these days?

Valladares: I am waiting to take me to the hospital to cure me of my illness. This is compounded every day more and then I will have no cure.

Dr. Campos: You are in wheelchair because you want, but that is your problem.

Valladares: I want to be a normal man like others and being able to move to wherever I want.

Dr. Campos: I think that there is no problem. I know that you have a behavior lately no very organized and you not know the reality. You not know the reality and you go to surprise.

Valladares: want to move me to another cell with my friend Eugenio Israel Dominguez by incompatibility of character with Pedro S. Gallardo.

Dr. Campos: You are worried. Why do you want to go to other cell and what is the other problem?

Valladares: He laughs bitterly and said: I am going to collect my personal belongings.

Dr. Campos: You seem very nervous. What happened with the medicines of Pedro Santos Gallardo? Do you know? "Valladares pales and he spoke with great incoherence and nervous".

Valladares: I do not know what you are taking about, I do not know about that.

Dr. Campos: You know what you are saying? I was sure you would have a great problem with the drugs. The Psychosis you led you to do thing that are not normal for a person. Dr. Campos went out. Valladares was on the brink of madness as a psychopath, whose monstrosity he had planned with Olga Elena that had reported what she had made in the words of Dr. Campos.

Two hours later lieutenant Soler had come to transfer to Valladares and Eugenio Israel Dominguez, his friend to another cell. Valladares with his psychosis says that he was a disabled, philatelic, poet and painter. But none of these four things conformed to reality, because they were totally false. That is the truth that you are not known about Valladares until today.

THE DUTY

Rodolfo Mazo Mazo was born in 1937 in Pinar del Rio, Cuba. He studies the course of at the Institute of Agronomy. When the situation in the country became in a chaos for the seizure of the power by the Marxist-Leninist guerrillas who were in the Sierra Maestra, was given the task to organize with other groups that did not agree with those who had come to power. That led him to establish contact with all those brave men who took up arms to defend his country that had fallen into the hands of unscrupulous men and could not let it take over power indefinitely.

Rodolfo Mazo Mazo was joined men began fighting alongside Bernardo Corrales with all those brave warriors who took up arms to defend the homeland with heroism because had fallen in the hands of the communists. The struggle was violent with the militia and the army force. The patriots Veterans fought all the time and not surrendered. They were overcome by the 20,000 men of the militia and the army. Nevertheless, they were not surrendered. They were men brave in defense of the motherland?

The Sierra had become a combat zone with the men that were fighting to release the Cuban nation. Where killed thousands in firing squads. Rodolfo Mazo Mazo could not tolerate the crimes committed against men who had no offense.

Rodolfo Mazo Mazo was a brave man who showed in all the years of struggle he concreted the value as a patriot in defense the Cuban people. Not, the slavery will ever arrive in our people by a system that not promises anything for the society. Rodolfo Mazo Mazo never allowed to be arrested by these militiamen and soldiers who made a fence to catch him dead or live. Rodolfo Mazo Mazo preferred to die before to surrender to the enemy.

How many truths can he said of these men who gave their lives for the country, because the people not accepted the horror of the massacres by men who had taken power by force of arms. Men who converted the executioners of their own people by subjecting it to the most horrible misery that mankind had ever seen. Rodolfo Mazo Mazo was a humble man and sacrifices his youth for the Fatherland enslaved.

Pedro: What led you to fight to defend the homeland that had fallen into the hands of the Communists from 1959?

Rodolfo: When I saw the Communists took over I realized that this system was not good for the Cuban people. I immediately made contact with some organizations and started fighting the regime that had not good intentions with the Cuban people. They would lose everything they had with this kind of government.

Pedro: What experiences have you had from that participated in the uprising in 1959 and 1960?

Rodolfo: I understand that the fight are not easy and in the battlefield plays the life by men or women living in peace and freedom to the rest of the world. Life in the mountains is not easy when you do not have the resources when you need them.

Pedro: What was the name of that organization when you threw the fight against the government that had taken power through armed struggle and violence?

Rodolfo: Not, that's not had name. We would take up arms and we rose in the mountains to overthrow the systems that were in power. That was just what we did when we take up arms to defend our country.

Pedro: What can you tell me when you began the struggle close of your home and its development? Especially when the fight began in the early years against the system that was in power

Rodolfo: The leader of the uprising was called Bernardo Corrales and that's when we began to fight fiercely against the enemy. They chased us with 20,000 soldiers and militiamen where we were fighting among the rocks and trees in the mountains. We were fighting against the crowd of militiamen and soldiers with all kinds of weapons. I came out unscathed from the uprising that killed many brave men in combat.

Pedro: What happened after you participated in the uprisings and movement which integrated you to continue the fight?

Rodolfo: The Movement that I participated was the Christian Democratic Movement (MDC) and Martiano Democratic Movement (MDM), which made the uprising in the mountains of the Province of Pinar Del Rio.

Pedro: What happened with the fight of the insurrection in the mountain of Pinar Del Rio and how many years was in prison on the Cuban communist system?

Rodolfo: On April 9, 1961, I was arrested and was in prison in Pinar del Rio, Isle of Pines, The Cabaña, Guanajay and other prisons. The political prisoners had had to pass difficult times for the situation that exist in the jails and prisons.

The Cubans prison is used to torture political prisoners wildly. The communist system is a system that applies all kinds of forces to destroy human beings, the torture, killings, punishment dungeons and food shortages and medicine. These are the atrocities that the communist system used across the years, because, Fidel Castro, Raul Castro, and Ramiro Valdes are motherfucker.

Pedro: Can you let me when you took to the Plan Morejon Farced Labor as it was that life, with all those soldiers with fire guns pointed at our head for 12 and 14 hours to make slave labor, as an experiment they did before, of the Forced Labor Camilo Cienfuegos, with all the cruelty used by communists?

Rodolfo: The Force Labor, Plan Morejon was the first who used to eliminate political prisoners. All was an experiment. They took a group of 217 political prisoners and ex-militaries took to the stone quarries of Nueva Gerona. In that place the government did an analysis of the behavior of political prisoners. Some of the prisoners as Ernesto de la Fe and Ramon Mestre were provided to guide the work we were doing in the stone quarries, to process the stones in the mills for grinding stones and turn them into gravel.

We were in the circulars and taken to punishment wards. When I finish the experiment, we returned to the circular back again. But we had to pay a heavy price because, of the 217 of the men that were in the Plan of Labor Force only 81 returned. The rest went to the Reeducation Plan.

The Morejon Plan began on October 18, 1963 with 217 political prisoners and ended on May 20, 1964, where 81 returned because the rest went to the Reeducation Plan.

So was the end of the communist barbarism. Among them Ernesto de la Fe better know as Gaya. He made the murals for the Communists. The other was Ramon Mestre also went to the Reeducation Plan with more 134. That's what happened with the tortures in the Plan Morejon.

Pedro: What was the deal with that was to Reeducation Plan?

Rodolfo: They had accepted all the privileges as meat, fruit, coffee, cigarettes and all kinds of food that the government gave them. But we do not accept any privileges. However, the 136 were for Reeducation Plan by accepting all. That is how I finish this tragedy after so much suffering in the stone quarries of Nueva Gerona.

Pedro: On June 29, 1964 we moved to Circular #4, and on July 6, 1964, in another massive transfer of the Circular #4 until #3, which began on Forced Labor Plan Camilo Cienfuegos on the 7th of July. There began the process cost us tens of dead and wounded. What was your problem when started a few days after the Plan Camilo Cienfuegos Forced Labor?

Rodolfo: I spent several days I did not go to work in block and when they found out I was not going to work. They carry me to the ditches of drains where I passed 4 days in this sewage water. Then I started in Block #11 in the Brigade #41. I did not know, if I returned alive to the circular.

Pedro: What happened to Benito Cruz Piñero that day you were in the block with him?

Rodolfo: the Pan Forced Labor Camilo Cienfuegos our life was uncertain because we not knew if they were going to kill all of us in this work brutal with the machine guns pointed to our head. That day Benito Cruz Piñero was doing his job normally and suddenly appears Cera with bayonet. Corporal Cera hurt with his bayonet to Benito Cruz. Cera was giving him several times with the bayonet.

Thus, the military was in the Forced Labor Camilo Cienfuegos on the Isle of Pines, where the men were murdered without fault.

Pedro: Do you remember some who were shot in the Block #11 and what happened?

Rodolfo: We were in Santa Fe when a soldier from conscription shot him by the back to Rosendo Rodriguez natural from Cienfuegos, Las Villas. When I saw that the military was shooting me throw the ground avoiding not hurting me. Rosendo was wounded by the back. The Sergeant came immediately to see what was the problem in the Block, and why was shooting. The soldier said that he was practicing with the political prisoners because he had not gone to the camp of firing. Rosendo was up to truck with a military for hospital, and we continue on slave labor. Those are the savages that the government used to perpetuate in the power.

Pedro: What did say the soldier when you got up the ground?

Rodolfo: Told me, never you escape from me. I do not hesitate a second. This soldier was the poison of communism which had in the blood.

Pedro: When finished this monstrosity of the Forced Labor Plan Camilo Cienfuegos. What can you tell me about the different prisons you had to go through all in its long years in captivity?

Rodolfo: I was transferred to the provincial prison of Pinar del Rio and Guanajay prison. Years later, I returned to the prison in Pinar del Rio, where I was freed from my 10 years in prison.

Pedro: What was your most difficulty and experience in prison through the years in captivity?

Rodolfo: In prison I had several experiences, starting with the Plan Camilo Cienfuegos Forced Labor in the Isle of Pines prison, where life was hanging by a threat. Other experiences are in jails and prisons, with the daily beatings, and punishment in the prison with the heat you it was horrible to live there. That I cannot forget.

Pedro: I recognize that your father knew many government officials Fulgencio Batista were Communists in Cuba. Who were these men?

Rodolfo: According to my father the leading Communist were Carlos Rafael Rodriguez, Blas Roca Calderio, Joaquin Ordoqui,

Jesus Menendez, Fidel Castro, Raul Castro, Ernesto Guevara de la Serna, Aracelio Iglesias, Lazaro Peña, Antonio Nuñez Jimenez, Raul Roa, Ricardo Alarcon, Ramiro Valdes, Sergio Del Valle and many more throughout the country.

Pedro: Those who have passed the whole process of the communist prisons know all the evil of the men who are in government massacring the population only because he disagreed with the dictatorial regime of men scoundrels, thieves and miserable. I understand all the sacrifice that Rodolfo Mazo Mazo did in the years of struggle to oust a group of criminals and terrorist murderers.

The country always appreciated all who have defended heroically giving their blood for it. Many martyrs have been killed in the firing squads in the country. For these reasons Rodolfo Mazo Mazo was a man of integrity who went to the battlefield to defend to the homeland. So are those who love the land where they were born. So was Rodolfo Mazo Mazo.

THE PROGRESSIVE PLAN

In 1971 and 1972 the organizations that were struggling for years to overthrow the communist government created a new plan called Progressive Plan. This plan had a different name, Reeducation Plan that was created in 1961 on the Isle of Pines when men were tired of fighting. They were cooperating with the ruled in volunteers work camps. That was exactly what they made defeated heads of organizations who surrendered to the communist government in 1971 and 1972.

These men left the fight betrayed thousands of martyrs that had been assassinated in the firing squad across the country. These men had come from the ranks of the Communist government when they started fighting to oust corrupt system men and murderers. However, they returned to the same place that they had left a few years, because they thought if they have capitulated and earning a salary of $190 pesos to the month and they could integrate them back to the positions when they held when they had deserted. This means that these men surrendered and went to work with his enemies or fellow travelers, men volunteers, tired, defeated and unable to continue the fight against communism.

These organizations created the Progressive Plan, which was a branch of Reeducation Plan. These men created much confusion in the political prison for having disintegrated in a 60 percent the Presidio Politico in cooperation with the communist authorities. Men who betrayed their ideals captivity abandoned their friends who were in jails and prisons closed when the communists started the murderer in prisons, huger strike, and punished in dungeon and living isolated for more than 12 years.

They did not care that these men died of disease; starvation dehydrated food shortage, or killed by a burst of machine guns from communist thugs. They left defeated, vanquished and humiliated by their surrender to the enemy. No, not I want to see things in black and white. That was the reality we live in absentia political prisoners, that died for their ideals and the sadness of seeing men that had had no strength to continue the fight.

I have had to live with all the suffering in jails and prisons, were men had no medicine to relieve a toothache, and see Carlos Calvo Sanabria pulling the teeth with a spring of his shoes because could not stand the pain and authority carried not him to the dentist to give him a medicine or to do a specimen removal. So are the bad guys that neither help the do nor help the good people. No, you cannot think that what I am saying is a fiction novel, this is the reality of what I have experienced in all my years between dungeons, dark cells, forced labor, solitary confined, the nakedness, the hunger strikes, tortures physical and psychological, the food shortage, lack of medicines and absolutely no access to the family for 12 years by the isolation that had. This is no fiction; this is reality I have had to live in long years of captivity in the jails and Prisons of Cuba.

Everyone has the right to life without having to suffer such cruelty by the hatred of men who only think of doing evil. No, I cannot think in my mind that men that represented to the organizations across the country had committed one of the biggest mistakes of their lives to join the ranks of their enemies. After they were imprisoned for many years and have not had the vision to predict before starting in the struggle to overthrow the communist system and only to destroy to the political prisoner. That was the cowardice and betrayal to the motherland of these men.

It is difficult to see the men demoralized in the last years of the struggle. The men who had the duty with to the country had surrendered to the enemy and who tortured while were in imprisonment. The betrayal is cowardly cruelty of man who leaves the fight without thinking of those who lost their lives fighting for the freedom. The cowards and their betrayal hurt in the soul. The man feels fear when he does things wrong and hides from the others. Because is a miserable and cowards. They live terrified of the veterans that scarified their lives for the country.

So are these scoundrels who prefer the contempt of others because they never knew the true of the brave that knew to defend his country with honor and shame. That's what's hurt to all these wretches who had gone to cooperate with the Communists from they came to the power in 1959.

The man who surrendered in the hardest moments in the Presidio Politico cannot lift his head against his companions and veterans who were abandoned when the Presidio Politico had that to be more united against the Marxist-Leninist executioners.

The leaders of the organizations had created the Progressive Plan in the prison of Guanajay. They became allies of communist criminals that had many thousands of men in the firing squads. Nevertheless, in the Guanajay prison, before, jail of women. The heads of organizations joined the Rehabilitation Plan to joining forces between Progressive Plan and Rehabilitation Plan.

These leaders negotiated with the Communist government to carry out the Progressive Plan in Guanajay prison, Province of Pinar del Rio, Cuba, and year later Havana Province. It was there that they began to cooperate with the regime and conditions imposed by them. That's how the Progressive Plan began and everything was fulfilled as they designed it.

There men were so evil that their irresponsibility caused the total isolation of political prisoners naked, with such ferocity that the communist government and their executioners left to starve political prisoners naked. I had to live when the communists were slaughtering those who were in prison in absentia in Puerto Boniato. They were doing so brutal accomplices of savagery against defenseless men in sealed cells with metal plates and without light because even that took away.

The betrayal of the majority of the leaders, according explained Roberto Torres with very strong language that could not be silent. No, do you not go to think that I am saying it is not real. No, the reality, have says with crudely, the claudicating they committed as men weak, defeated, tired and docile.

The capitulated leaders of these organizations were buried in the mud and could not get out of where they were. These men did not think of the rest of the political prisoners who died in the punishment cells of Puerto Boniato prison. Yes, they were years of suffering and torture against a group of men that not surrendered for more than a decade in prison, isolation and closed as animals in the cells of tortures the political prison were suffering.

The surrender of these organizations was total. They surrendered of the struggle and go to work Volunteering on farms with a salary of $190 pesos a month for their cooperation with the communist government. Government, which was involved in trafficking of cocaine, herein, Marijuana, terrorism and guerrilla subversion In Central America, South America and the Caribbean. They joined the ranks of his opponents by fear and cowardice. These men carry in their hearts the defeat, because they are fragile and deciles.

Thus, during the years of 1971 and 1972 political prisoners Naked in Puerto Boniato prison every day more, were cut off from the outside world. However, in the prison of Guanajay already begins to bear fruit Progressive Plan. Intellectuals and professionals, such as lawyers, doctors, engineering, economists, professionals, educationalists, journalists, writers, accountants and religious of all dominations, had taken advantage of the benefits it offered the regime in Progressive Plan. The intellectuals accepted the agreement with General Enio Leyva.

The Pact of the Progressive Plan had been embarrassing by most humiliating defeat in the history of Cuban for the political prisoners by those had betrayed the ideals of the martyrs executed at the firing squads and battlefields in the mountains of the Republic of Cuba.

The Progressive Plan Pact created and planned by intellectuals, professionals and businessmen was a national tragedy for Presidio Politico, because men were spiritless and they are instruments to the interests of the regimen. Nevertheless, they never had thought that betrayal sooner or later has its negative effect.

The Progressive Plan and Reeducation Plan had been blows strong for the political prisoner's naked and political prisoners with the Uniform Khaki Yellow on absentia, with heroism and bravery preferring death before surrender and betray their martyrs. Men were able to give examples of heroism, with honor, shame and dignity.

Treasons by the cowardice to face the cruel enemy and subjecting the people to slavery, misery, poverty, torture, Starvation, murder, terrorism and especially the destruction of the country. Because men are miserable bastards who do not built anything good that benefit the people, because they are corrupt, miserable and traitors to the Fatherland.

In 1972 the Presidio Politico had defined its position. Each group and each position was defined with the necessary strategy, as there were different positions in the prison. The positions were in rebellion. As the position Semi-naked, and the position dressed in the Uniform of Khaki Yellow. There was no other position in the Political Presidio. All the weight of Political Politico fell in these two positions since the beginning to the end, for 30 years in captivity with the last political prisoner Mario Chanez de Armas.

In 1973 the Progressive Plan was in full capacity with the volunteers working for the communist system. The Progressive Plan was created in the Guanajay prison in Havana Province, before Pinar Del Rio Province.

The surrendered leaders of the organizations ARP, M-3-11, MUR, AAA, CA, CID, M-20-05, MID, MIR, MRB, MDC, OA and others more described by Roberto Torres, Miguel Hernandez Miranda, Aldo Cabrera, Orlando Molina Contreras, Agustin Robaina and Rodolfo Mazo Mazo. These movements joined forced against the Presidio Politico Semi- naked and prisoners dressed in the Khaki Uniform Yellow on absentia. However, those who left for the Progressive Plan had been defended because they could not achieve the objective with the rest of political prisoners.

The Political Prisoners that were in the Rehabilitation for many years joined forces with the Progressive Plan. The rebel position had received the blow more devastating for political prisoners Semi-naked. But they had survived the treachery. The political prisoners Semi-naked had respect and patriotism with the thousands of martyrs that gave their lives on the firing squads.

The Progressive Plan and Rehabilitation Plan are the same with different names. The plans were created for men without faith, without hope, without ideals and without ideology. Anyone says otherwise is lying and does not fit the reality of facts.

These leaders of the organizations devoted to volunteer work won a salary of $190 pesos a month, with the condition that everyone have an exemplary conduct with a passport to leave to visit their families. Those Reeducated former political prisoners are becoming the executioners of their friends. Men had no returned of Progressive Plan or Rehabilitation Plan because were tired men, defeated, powerless, without honor, surrendered to the enemy, as Miguel Hernandez said.

In the Reeducation Plan were almost all former military from the government communist and the government unconstitutional of Cuba. In all these groups found Ramon Mestre, Ricardo Bofill pages, Dr. Rolando Cubales Secades, David Salvdor, Victor Mora, Dr. Abelardo Codinach, Ernesto de la Fe, and all the professional elite left for Reeducation Plan and Progressive Plan, with the Exception of Dr. Alberto Fiblas who had an excellent conduct. However, other doctors left for volunteer work plans as Dr. Lino Bernabe Fernandez, Dr. Pelayo Torres, Dr, Santiago Echemendia, Dr. Andres Cao Mendiguty, Dr. Jose Aguiar, Dr. Julio Abreu, Dr. Vladimiro Ramirez, Dr. Jose Rabasa, Dr. Valdes Dominguez, Dr. Jordan Fernandez, Dr. Velascos Sanchez, Dr. Darmau, Dr. Zaldivar, Dr. Carlos Portela, Dr. Manuel Romeu Fernandez, Dr. Bebo Borron and others but would make the list endless, with many thousands who joined these men, because they no longer had the strength to continue the fight and it capitulated.

The leaders of the organizations were weak and had surrendered mostly of the fight against communist. They preferred to agree with the regime of mutual agreement; to volunteer through their sentence were less severe, with good behavior and integrating all the communist system, according to what was agreed in the Covenant. All would be unconditionally released if all met the agreed requirements.

Actually the intellectual has no confidence in himself and becomes a conservative without concrete ideas and without any ideology regardless of any situation in the country.

The blow was strong for political prisoners Semi-naked do not gave up not an inch to the cowardice and treachery of the leaders of the most powerful organizations who had lost thousands of men executed in 1959 until 1970, when they agreed with the enemy without respect to many thousands of martyrs who had given their lives defending the people and institutions of the country. Men were killed in the firing of squads. The political prisoners of the Semi-naked have respected to the martyrs through the years. But, the men that were in the Rehabilitation Plan had not respected to these men that were killed in the firing squads, in the Forced Labor Plan in Isle of Pines and battlefields.

Most of the because of the organizations directed by the leaders in the volunteer work on farms with compensation of $190 pesos a month for all who were in the Progressive Plan and Reeducation Plan. The Progressive Plan was the same plan of Reeducation with different names. We know that the Communists have changed the name to all.

They made a Pact with the enemy in Guanajay jail while that naked Political Prisoners were isolated and were killed by communists, as well as hundreds of political prisoners dressed with the Khaki Uniform Yellow who were in jails and prisons in inhuman conditions. They did not care the death that committed by the criminals Marxist-Leninists. That was not important for them. Knowing that his friends were assassinated in jails and prisons closed.

The General Enio Leyva was satisfied with what he had achieved with those what have given up the struggle. The General had convinced intellectuals and professionals that were integrated the communist system unconditionally.

The handicapped organization leaders had surrendered or capitulated in masse in the most critical moments for the Presidio Politico Naked and dressed in Khaki Uniform Yellow.

Men carried 10 and 12 years imprisonment. The political prisoners in absentia had been betrayed by almost all organizations making up the block of rebellion of all organizations that began fighting in 1959 and 1960. Nevertheless, 12 years after had surrendered to their executioners with that despicable treachery characterizes meek and weak men.

They took the wrong path and will die with the pain of betrayal. Progressive Plan culminated on farms, construction and dairy to across the country, performing slave labor to humiliate more than to these cowards.

The communist government assigned minimum wage $190 pesos to the prisoners Rehabilitated. They have not respected to massively executed thousands around the country. These men had no strength to defend democracy, nor the people who underwent the barbarism of slavery. They were lent themselves to this shame. Yes, to change back to integrate the system communist, men docile, miserable and cowards.

They believed that the political prisoners who migrated years naked without communication in closed prisons would be free. They were wrong in their entirely and now live with much confusion ashamed of a most perverse way they acted.

The men had been surrendered to his enemies in exchange for his freedom. They never thought that the political prisoners in the prison Semi-naked could be released. That is what hurts them, they had to work eight years to ultimately have to live with the bitterness that they became slaves paid for their treachery and never will be able to tell their children that they were miserable cooperate with communist system. When, the barbarism system arrived that is in the power, the barbarism, crime and murder. So, they will have to die humiliated life being miserable and cowardly. They were unable to defend their ideals and patriotism.

However, the brave men betrayed were for their fellows. Their blood is shed in the battlefields, with heroism against communist criminals. Men who were able to oppose the shame of the betrayal of those without strength, their jaws trembled and cracked teeth.

The heads of the organizations tried to destroy a political prisoner Semi-naked and did it in part. However, they could not fully penetrate the prisoners in rebellion, they were men of honor. Intellectuals, professionals and leaders of organizations had been united to destroy The Presidio Politico naked and dressed in the uniform of Khaki Yellow In 1971 and 1972. The organization had had a triumph with thousands of political prisoners integrated into the ranks of the Progressive Plan. They could not to integrate the political prisoners Semi-naked or with the dressed in the uniform of khaki yellow on rebellion; they were men of honor and patriots.

They wanted to destroy the Presidio Politico, but they could not with all the coward and miserable. The man loves his country dies with ideals, patriotism and sacrifice for the Fatherland. The men brave never have betrayed his best friends in the battlefield and less to the have been killed in the firing squad. But, not so, with the scoundrels that be lent to all kinds of infamy. They will live embarrassed in front of Veterans, Heroes of the Fatherland.

This vile Covenant is unprecedented in the history of the Republic of Cuba. Men voluntarily surrendered or capitulated unconditionally. They carry on if the defeat will be without their entire existence of the mistake they made ashamed.

The heads of the organizations wanted to overthrow the communist government that they had put themselves in power. But for years later they capitulate unconditionally. The murderers Marxist=Leninists not respected human life. Nevertheless, the political prisoners Reeducated betrayed the martyrs and heroes that gave their lives fighting against the slavery and oppression by any rogue regime as it has been the system of the Castro government and the militaries docile.

That was the most dangerous treason committed by the leaders of Cuban Political Prisoners by the secrets of political prisoners. The leaders wearied of the organizations of political Prison. Men left demoralized and with a high level of guilt. By most despicable treachery that political prisoners in absentia have lived in the history of the Republic of Cuba. They had No interest with the population of 6.3 million people enslaved without mercy in the field of concentration and torture in the country.

THE CONCERN

Luis Leonardo Arroyo was born in Matanzas, Cuba in 1938. He studied Literature, Arts at Florida International University. He is a poet and writer. From a young Arroyo lived concerned about the fate of their homeland. In the 1957 entry in the Navy to defend the Cuban nation, the reason was threatened by communist guerrillas who attacked the Moncada Barracks assassinated sick soldiers who were hospitalized.

Luis Arroyo was arrested in 1960 and imprisoned for 27 years of the 45 he was penalized for to have initiated an armed uprising to overthrow the communist system that had taken power through terrorism and assassinations throughout the Republic of Cuba.

Luis L. Arroyo lived difficult moment in prison, almost on the verge of death when the four circulars were dynamited on April 18, 1961, with tens of tons of explosive. If the Invasion of Playa Giron triumphed, the Isle of Pines prison would disappear with all political prisoners. The risk was imminent and if was not would have immediately acted the Isle of Pines Prison disappear from the map with more than 5,000 political prisoners in its facilities.

Luis L. Arroyo with a group of technicians, managed to disable that monstrosity tons of dynamite and detonators connected to electrical cables. The intention of the communist system was to eliminate all political prisoners if the Invasion of Playa Giron has success in overthrowing the communist regime. Luis L. Arroyo is a humble man who knew to defend the homeland with heroism that had fallen into the clutches of Marxism-Leninism. Arroyo has devoted his life in defense of democracy, as a man of ideals and patriotism. He knew how to deal with all situations of political imprisonment and sacrifices of his fighting for freedom of Cuban people. The Cuban people had been enslaved and subjected to the cruelty of poverty and isolation from the outside world.

Luis L. Arroyo suffered the cruelty of Forced Labor Plan Camilo Cienfuegos on Isle of Pines for 33 months of torture and suffering where political prisoners were murdered in slave labor camps. The odyssey of Luis L. Arroyo did not end there. In 1967 he suffered the brutal nakedness imposed by the military forces weapons and bayonets. In 1968 he launched a hunger strike demanding improvements in feeding, family visits, medical care and better conditions in prison. The hunger strike call was successful of the Centennial for political prisoners who joined in the hunger strikes. The triumph of the points had demanded the government.

Luis L. Arroyo has been through critical moments. This man has suffered much in his life and had made great efforts in jails and prisons to keep the Presidio Politico united in the jails of Cuba. Luis L. Arroyo suffered several hungers strikes of 11, 20, 35 and 46 days without a cup of hot sugar water in the stomach. However, all do not. In 1970 Luis L. Arroyo was isolated in a cell of the Presidio Politico of Boniato, where he spent long years of captivity in totally in isolation punishment cells without access to their families, only faith in God and hope to go free with honor and shame.

Luis L. Arroyo has been a fighter for Human Rights throughout his life Luis L. Arroyo of humble origin, Intellectual, Poet and Writer who has overcome by their own efforts through the years. He is above all a great human being.

Luis L. Arroyo irreversibly lost partial vision in both eyes in prison as many political prisoners. But he never lost the faith of his release. He was free in 1987 after having spent 27 years in detention in almost all jails and prisons closed the country in subhuman conditions as a political prisoner in rebellious that he never bowed the enemy.

Luis L. Arroyo is a legend of Cuban Political Prisoners. The firmness, patriotism and honor as always do make the best sons.

Luis L. Arroyo has defended bravely the homeland of their ancestors. He has never rested in struggling for the liberty of the Cuban people.

Luis L. Arroyo lived most impressive historic moments of the surrender of the Brigade Playa Giron 2506. Was one of the devastating blows most of the fight against Marxism-Leninism, with the surrender on the battlefield by the lack of ammunition, the water, the food and the aid because they had been denied. The Brigade 2506 is surrendered, in less than 72 hours. Had been a mortal blow to the guerrillas fighting in the Escambray Mountains, where there were thousands of men under arms. The leaders of the underground organizations had fallen and the fight was decimated by the surrender of Brigade 2506.

The hope had vanished with the failure of the Bay of Pigs Invasion. The Cuban people had lost the opportunity of the overthrow of communism and all terrorist criminals led by Fidel Castro the thief, assassins and miserable. From that moment, the Cuban people were slaved.

Luis L. Arroyo never thought would live so many crucial moments in his life. Very sad moments when began of the labor forced plan in the Isle of Pines. The Forced Labor Plan in stone quarries of Nueva Gerona on 1963. The Forced Labor Plan Camilo Cienfuegos in 1964, where dozens of men were murdered patriots that not deserve such cruelty, Progressive Plan, the Nudity, the Huger strike, isolation in sealed cell and dungeons full of microbe without medical assistance, no light in the cell, no family visits and they died of starvation men.

All that had lived Luis L. Arroyo and political Prisoners in all his years of captivity due to savagery that characterize the communist.

27 years of torture in jails and prisons more fearful of the country where the executioners used the murderer against Cuba's political prisoners. However, the greatness of the man is in the soul and heart that were most strong than the evil of the communists. That is how the political prisoners in absentia defended the homeland which never forgot with patriotism and honor of each veteran in the struggle.

THE TRAGEDY

Evelio Cepero began the struggle in the 1960 when he saw the government had taken power. The government was not adequate for the Cuban nation. They began the struggle and prepared to oust the communist administration. Evelio Cepero and Chester Lacayo took the armed struggle to the overthrow the communist government.

We all know that the military Communists not respect the rule of law. These executioners of the Cuban people have subjected to slavery, hunger, misery, torture, terror, mass murder and genocide of the Cuban people. Evelio Cepero could not accept such massacres that being committed daily. That was the reason why the fight started with Evelio Cepero and Chester Lacayo to avoid cruelty, the slavery of the Cuban people and to remove from power the Castro government with all communists who were in government.

Chester Lacayo was arrested and Evelio Cepero was arrested months later. To all this we can say that the communist system created the terror through imprisonment, the torture, the firing squads across the country with weapons stockpiles that had brought secretly in the Soviet Union in the years 1959 and 1860.

The tragedy of the Cuban people began when Fulgencio Batista left the administration of the Republic of Cuba and handed to the communists who were in the Sierra Maestra, and Evelio Cepero disagreed with these guerrillas. He took the weapons with Chester Lacayo.

The failure of the 2506 Brigade made that the Communist regime will consolidate in the power and all the struggle of two years and a half was lost by defeat of the Invasion of Playa Giron that all it did was that all it did was to enslave the Cuban people.

Brigade 2506 was defeated by not having the resources necessary to continue fighting on the shores of the Zapata Swamp. They fought heroically without the resources needed to succeed, but they were defeated from the moment of disembark by to have no logistical support. They have that surrender in les of 72 hours, because they have not anybody support.

That was what happened, and the communist government was consolidated. In addition, the heads of the 2506 Brigade had too much confidence in the helping of a country that has never foregone to help the Cuban people free themselves from the disgrace of a bastard since 1898 when the colony of Spain was defeated.

So, it was like we lost the fight in 1960 and 1965, when outbreaks were decimated of the fighters Sierra of the Escambray. Evelio Cepero and I Know that 70 percent of the Cuban people are never agreed with the communist system. What happens is that 30 percent make more noise that the rest of the Cuban people.

With the defeat of the Brigade 2506 jails and prisons began to fill with thousands of political prisoners and dismantled all organizations in the country.

Our struggle has been of valiant men when the firing squad no ceased to assassinate to the men and women that were fighting the imprisoned, and many were shot as in the case of the Navy August 30, 1962. Were firing squads 472 men in one night? Evelio Cepero is convinced that the Cuban people have been a heroic people and has never bowed to live in that system horror and murder.

The fight was very difficult because we had not international aid and weapons we had to make face the communist regime that had crowed with Soviet weapons stockpiles and every country in the world. That's what hurts in the soul that our country has been slaved with the complicity of all capitalist countries of the world.

Castro, the thief of the Republic of Cuba, shortly before his death, his body bent and the erosion of time, becomes the laughingstock of humanity. He could not remember what he said with his dementia. Still, still visit the Presidents. Popes, Senators, and officials from other countries go to see how many days left to live, that will he remain in world, the man who has massacred its own people.

The war that started against communist tens thousands, assassinating to the men in the firing squads, hunger strikes, Forced Labor Camilo Cienfuegos, killed in jails and prisons, at sea and around 120,000 political prisoners in a population of 6,3 million inhabitant. That is love and patriotism as the men gave his life for the fatherland.

Evelio Cepero, for more than 50 years of enslavement of the Cuban people, not rested a day in the struggle for Cubans and to live in a free, no oppression, without enslave and without torture. The homeland is to live in it and not to be slaves of men who kill their people. Everyone has the right to life and no one can; kill a village for revenge and meanness. Freedom is the sunlight, the air, the rain, the night and day no can prohibit its beauty to exist.

Pedro: What can you tell me what happened in the Republic of Cuba when they took possession of the Marxist-Leninists?

Evelio: I can tell you that in the Cuban Revolution there era only dead of the Escambray of the heroics fighters, dead of Bay of Pigs. The boat of Cojimar, the Remorcador of March 13, the Aircraft of Brother to the Rescue, the Rule Boat, Bay of the Havana, firing Squads, Forced Labor Plan, Camilo Cienfuegos in Isle of Pines, the Hunger Strikes, Murders in Jails and Prisons, the Poverty, the Famine, Psychological and Physical Tortures, Ostracism of the Cuban people, Oppression, Persecution, Imprisonment and immorality since Castro took power in 1959. That is what is in Cuba for over half a century.

THE HUMILITY

Dagoberto Acosta Chirino was born in the town of Artemisa, Pinar del Rio, Cuba. In Artemisa he studied at private and public schools. From a young age was released to the battlefields against Marxist-Leninist regime that had taken power through armed struggle.

Years later he was arrested and detained for nearly two decades in jails and prisons in his country. Dagoberto suffered all kinds of torture in forced labor schemes in the Isle of Pines in 1964, for 33 months of brutal savagery. However, it did not end there. In 1967 he was subjected to nudity, without communication for 17 months. In 1968 and 1969 held two hunger strikes of 20 and 35 days where he was almost on the verge of death in prison of The Cabaña. In 1970 he was transferred to Puerto Boniato prison, where he remained until 1977 in total isolation, in punishment cells and dungeons totally without light, in sweatshops, where they were massacred several veterans of the struggle against the communist system.

Dagoberto was brutally tortured and punished for being in rebellious against the communist government of Fidel Castro the murderer, thief and terrorist and criminal. In that same year of 1977 he was transferred from the prison of Puerto Boniato to the Combined of Este in The Havana. Two years later he was released and traveled to the United Stated, where he lives actually.

Dagoberto lived difficult moments in the life for his integrity in the fight against the system that prevails in the Island of Cuba. This man, humble, devoted his youth to the freedom of his people who had fallen into slavery by a system of cruelty, all kind of terrorism to punish to the people with a criminal state and repression against the human life that may end with a bouquet of bullets in the chest. That is the reality that Dagoberto lived for many years in the jails and prisons of the Republic of Cuba by the cruelty of the communist Fidel Castro the thief, coward and his military communists.

Pedro: What you can tell me of your long years in jails and prisons of the Republic of Cuba and how you feel health?

Dagoberto: I am 75 years old, but I am young (Laughs). My physical condition is perfect and my sanity is normal, although I have been seriously ill.

Furthermore, prison and jails have left many traces in my life. Above all, I think, because I was very Rebellious in the years of captivity in the prison and the horrors of the cruelty in this world where we had so much suffering. The heart felt horrible pain in the difficult moments by our sacrifice against the slavery that uses a system cruel where is only waiting the protection of God.

We were victims of biological experiments in sealed cells of Puerto Boniato prison in the Eastern Province. All these experiences have had to endure the thousands of political prisoners in the jails and prisons of our country, through years of imprisonment and torture.

Fear is a cause and consequence of neurotic behavior and to some extent is also its definition, because it conditions and limits to the human beings. You cannot live with a conformist position alone viewer for over half a century.

I also want to say that peace is achieved through understanding and acceptance of the inevitable contradictions of life; pain and pleasure, success and failure, joy and sadness, birth and death. The problem can teach us to be humble and patient. However, we cannot change the world, but no need to change it to make it a place that unknown. The only thing in reality we have to do is concentrate on those little acts of kindness, things we can do every day.

People are attracted to people who demonstrate safety, they do not need made a good impression, to have reason all time, or take the glory. The majority of people feel affection for people who do not need to brag, speaking from the heart and not from the ego. So humanity die of sadness and grief without knowing what want.

Pedro: Dagoberto Acosta Chirino is a good and generous man, and never forgot the land of his birth. A veteran of many battles do not forgot of their ancestors because he is a man who never faltered with the patriotic ideal and not bowed to the enemy and had a vertical position until the last day it was releasing. He never abandoned his friends in jails and prisons, where human life goes slowly by the cruelty of a regime full of hatred and revenge without any kind of compassion for the human beings, because they are miserable bastards.

THE HISTORY

Felipe Del Rosario was born in Matanzas, Cuba 80 years ago. This man devoted his life to fighting for the homeland freedom that had fallen into the clutches of international communism. Felipe saw mobs with clubs in the hands assassinating to the men and women in the system prevailing in the island if Cuba for over half a country. Felipe and Eneida had three children: Sonia, Jesus, Rita and a grandson, Brandon, a family very religious and believing in God. So are Felipe, Eneida and their family.

Felipe suffered the rigors of the oppression of the regime communist. He was almost on the verge of death when the cell of the prison became a mass of fire with smock in the lungs and burns in the body. The fire devoured in minutes everything. Felipe Del Rosario lived difficult moments in his homeland and has never lost hope of seeing its country free of the disgraceful system that injures and kills. Felipe Del Rosario is a man of integrity who has given everything for the land that has never forgotten, as a man faithful to the cause of freedom of oppressed, such as is the people of Cuba.

Pedro: What can you tell me of the moments you have lived in the jails and prisons of the Republic of Cuba?

Felipe: As you can see, the pages of the history are full of hatred and bloodshed. However, amidst tragic circumstances are people doing extraordinary works of altruism and generosity. Why they are so bad and others are good?

Possible that some will become in cold blood murderers become extremely humanitarian? But sometimes emerges ferocious instincts in human behavior?

I would not he so pessimistic but the inclination of man's heart is from his youth, so even the children have an innate inclination to misbehave. It fact, we are all born with the tendency to do evil. In order to do well, we must make a great effort, and rowing against the current.

But human beings have the power of consciousness an innate sense of good and evil that affects most us for us to make all according to that is considered moral. So to those who lack moral formation can did good things. However, our inclination to do evil can cause us an internal conflict. But is there some other actor to include in our struggle between good and evil.

We have many good men. Also there are many bad men. But he who walks with people adopting incorrect behavior acquires his position. However, you should not go after the crowd for evil ends. Moreover, all is related to the honesty, straight and moral standards tend to imitate the good. However, the fact that we take care of the bad companies does not mean that evil will not go to influence us. As we are imperfect, the evil that inhabits the most, hidden from our life can proceed at any time. Besides, this not signify that you leave not home to expose the evil violence and revenge.

Given that all these factors influence our personality and behavior. We see to Fidel Castro and his commander's criminals to spread to the world with the evil. Who may have reason that they cannot be blamed for their misdeeds? But this reasoning is not valid. Everyone is responsible for their actions and thoughts.

All international action, whether good or bad is originated in the mind, if you think positive, will work well. If one allows that the selfish desires geminate in the mind. You may end up doing wrong. So, we can say that a person has the option to be as good or as bad as decides.

The saddest part is that men have forgotten God and the good things he has given us. Why man has this tendency to evil and chooses not the good? All human beings have the right to life and not to despair. That I do not understand because in my heart there is only love.

I can tell you that in my heart there is no hatred or bitterness towards my political opponents, despite all the hard times I spent in jails and prisons. My feelings are deeper that the wickedness of man. That's the most important thing in my life.

Pedro: What is faith and hope?

Felipe: Faith is the theological virtue by which we believe in God and believe all that he has said and revealed to us, and that Holy Church proposes for our belief, because he is truth itself. By faith "man freely commits his entire self to God." For this reason the believer seeks to know and do God's will. "The righteous shall live by faith."

The gift of faith remains in one who has not signed against it. But "faith apart from works is dead": when it is deprived of hope and love, faith does not fully unite the believer to Christ and does not make him a living member of his body.

The disciple of Christ must not only keep the faith and live on it, but also profess it, confidently bear witness to I, and spread it: "All however must be prepared to confess Christ before men and to follow him along the way of the Cross, amidst the persecutions which the Church never lacks." Service of and witness to the faith are necessary for salvation: "So everyone who acknowledges me before men, I also will acknowledge before my Father who is in heaven; but whoever denies me before men, I also will deny before my Father who is in heaven."

The theological virtues are the foundation of Christian moral activity; they animate it and give it its special character. They inform and give life to all the moral virtues. They are infused by God into the souls of the faithful to make them capable of acting as his children and of meriting eternal life. They are the pledge of the presence and action of the Holy Spirit in the faculties of the human being. There are three theological virtues: Faith, hope and charity.

Hope is the theological virtue by which we desire the kingdom of heaven and eternal life as our happiness, placing our trust in Christ's promises and relying not on our own strength, but on the help of the grace of the Holy Spirit.

The virtue of hope responds to the aspiration to happiness which God has placed in the heart of every man; it takes up the hope that inspire men's activities and purities them to order them to the Kingdom of heaven; it keeps man from discouragement, it sustains him during times of abandonment, it opens up his heart in expectation of eternal beatitude. Buoyed up by hope, he is preserved from selfishness and led to the happiness that flows from charity

Christian hope takes up and fulfills the hope of the chosen people, which has its origin and model in the hope of Abraham, who was blessed abundantly by the promises of God fulfilled in Isaac, and who was purified by the test of the sacrifice. "Hoping against hope, he believed, and thus became the father of many nations."

Christian hope unfolds from the beginning of Jesus' preaching in the proclamation of the beatitudes; they trace the path that leads through the trails that wait the disciples of Jesus. Hope is expressed and nourished in prayer, especially in the Our Father, the summary of everything that hope leads us to desire.

We can therefore hope is the glory of heaven promised by God to those who love him and do his will. In every circumstance, each one of us should hope, with the grace of God, to persevere "to the end" and to obtain the joy of heaven, as God's eternal reward for the good works accomplished with the grace of Christ. In hope, the Church prays for "all men to be saved."

Pedro: For me it was a great experience to have known this man for many years. He is good and without rancor towards those who tortured him for many years. With a heart without hatred or revenge, carries the pain in the soul and to see his people subjected to the slavery, the misery and famine. That is the greatness of the man.

THE CUBAN GENOCIDE

The genocide of the Cuban people has been heartbreaking in the history of the Republic of Cuba, where the men were sentenced to death, 30 and 20 years of prison, assassinated on the Isle of Pines in the Forced Labor, Camilo Cienfuegos. Gunned down in jails and prisons, at Sea and the firing squads by the military regime of Fidel Castro "Satan waits for you in the boiler of hell, assassin, thief and terrorist." Here is a partial list of men, women, elderly and children that where massacred by an atheist regime and despicable.

Abad, Luis
Abarca Alarcón, Ramón Alfonso
Abarca Castillo, Sergio Antonio
Abarca Leyva, Guillermo E.
Abarzua Zamorano, Carlos
Abdala Benítez, José Antonio
Abreu Pedroso, Eladio
Abreu Ruiz, Ángel
Abreu Villau, Enrique
Abreu, Antonio
Abreu, Bienvenido
Abreu, Marciano
Abreu, Mariano
Aburto Gallardo, Evaldo Segundo
Acevedo Becerra, Sebastián
Acevedo Cárdenas, José Manuel
Acevedo Cisterna, Eduardo Bernabét
Acevedo Espinoza, René
Acevedo Fariña, Germán
Acevedo Gutiérrez, Rubén Antonio
Acevedo Moreno, José Guillermo
Acevedo Pereira, Alfredo
Acevedo Rubio, Samuel Eduardo
Acosta Álvarez, Benjamín
Acosta Basulto, Manuel F.
Acosta Castro, Patricio Ricardo
Acosta Galan, Francisco
Acosta Villa Franca, Víctor
Acosta Villafranca, Víctor
Acosta, José Rodríguez
Acosta, Oriol
Acosta, Rubén
Acuña Ballestero, Reinaldo E.
Acuña Concha, Juan Antonio
Acuña Inostroza, Carlos M.
Acuña Reyes, René R.
Acuña Sepúlveda, Mario Daniel
Acuña Torres, Álvaro Javier

Achu Liendo, Rigoberto D. C.
Adasne Mora, José Abrahan
Adoy, Juan
Aduer Zulueta, Carlos Rodolfo
Aedo Aria, Luciano Humberto
Aedo Guerrero, Sergio
Aedo Herrera, Oscar Gastón
Aesa, Guillermo
Aguallo Olavarría, Héctor D.
Aguar Bello, Rafael Eduardo
Agud Pérez, Faruc Jimmy
Agüero Paredes, Rolando
Agüero, Marcelo
Agüero, René
Aguiar, José de la C.
Águila Galano, Francisco
Águila Pérez, Pedro
Águila, Francisco
Aguilar Carvajal, Alicia Marcela
Aguilar Cubillos, Jorge Ricardo
Aguilar Garrido, Jacobo Daniel
Aguilar Núñez, Sergio Emilio
Aguilera Bustos, Carlos Segundo
Aguilera Contreras, Ramón Luis
Aguilera Gil, Onelio
Aguilera Olivares, René G.
Aguilera Pereira, Uberlindo De R.
Aguilera Salas, Hernando
Aguilera Vázquez, Víctor M.
Aguilera, Juan
Aguilera, Luis Fernando
Aguilera, Roberto
Aguiles, René
Aguirre Ballesteros, Juan Antonio
Aguirre Moya, Hernán
Aguirre Pruneda, Reinaldo A.
Aguirre Tobar, Paulino A.
Aguirre Vidaurreta, Francisco
Aguirre, Domitila Mercedes
Aguirre, Tomás
Agustín Gutiérrez, José
Aillañir Huenchual, Carlos
Airado Pérez, Cristóbal
Álamo Contreras, Jorge Eduardo

Alaníz Álvarez, Luis Eduardo
Alarcón Alarcón, Jaime
Alarcón, Higo
Alarcón, Miranda
Alayón, Pelayo
Alba García, Orlando
Alba Moya, Ramón
Albear Ortega, José Aladino
Albear, Javier Segundo
Alberto Méndez, Juan
Albino Pereira, Fernando
Albizar, Eugenio
Albornoz Acuña, Miguel Del C.
Albornoz González, Alberto
Albornoz González, Alejandro
Albornoz González, Felidor E.
Albornoz González, José Guillermo
Albornoz Matus, Sergio Williams
Albornoz Muquillaza, Claudia M.
Albuerne Villanueva, Aurelio
Alcaino Campos, Jorge Segundo
Alcalá, Ramón
Alcalde Puig, Rosa
Alcapia Cienfuegos, Sergio A.
Alcayaga Aldunate, Augusto
Alcayaga Varela, Carlos Enrique
Alcázar Águila, Jaime Alejandro
Aldoney Vargas, Jaime
Alegría Arriagada, Sergio Segundo
Alegría Higuera, José Sergio
Alegría Mundaca, Juan Alberto
Alemán Guardarrama, Pedro
Alemán Guardarrama, Rafael
Alemán, Antonio
Alemán, Carlos
Alemán, Roberto
Alfaro Castro, Hugo Enrique
Alfaro Retamal, Waldo Cesar
Alfonso Cruz, Roberto
Alfonso González, Daniel
Alfonso Hidalgo, Carlos
Alfonso Muñoz, Pedro Marco
Alfonso Sánchez, José A.
Alfonso, Celia

Alfonso, Celio
Alfonso, Estanislao
Alfonso, José Luis
Alfonso, Mario
Alfonso, Roberto
Alfonso, Sergio
Alfonso, Sergio Espina
Almanza Romero, Pilar
Almeida Hinojosa, Julio M.
Almeida Martínez, Delio
Almeida Socarras, Ramiro
Almeida, Alfaro
Almeida, Heriberto
Almeira, Luis F.
Almeira, Valle
Almendras Almendras, Nelson C.
Almirot, José
Almonacid Arellano, Luis Alfredo
Alonso Alomá, Agustín
Alonso Lureiro, Ernesto
Alonso Suárez, José Antonio
Alonso, Antonio
Alonso, Dany
Alonso, Rafael
Alonso, Roberto
Aloy Rivero, Juan
Alsina Hurrios, Juan
Alsina Hurtos, Joan
Altamirano Monje, Elvin Hipólito
Altamirano Navarro, José Otto
Alteguez Mualen, Luis Antonio
Alvarado Anaya, Mario
Alvarado Ortiz, Carlos Segundo
Alvarado Vargas, Sergio Osvaldo
Álvarez Aballí, Juan Carlos
Álvarez Álvarez, P. de la Caridad
Álvarez Amador, Jesús
Álvarez Amador, José
Álvarez Barría, José Orlando
Álvarez Bernal, Jorge
Álvarez Bocanegra, Amado
Álvarez Cañas, Guillermo Amador
Álvarez Castillo, Castillo
Álvarez Castillo, Fernando

Álvarez Castro, Ángel
Álvarez Castro, Pedro Ángel
Álvarez Concepción, Máximo
Álvarez Cruz, Bernal
Álvarez de la Rosa, Carlos
Álvarez Díaz, Fernando
Álvarez Díaz, Francisco
Álvarez Díaz, José
Álvarez Fernández, Arturo
Álvarez Fonseca, Orlando
Álvarez González, Jorge
Álvarez Guerra, Ángel C.
Álvarez Guerra, Lissette
Álvarez Hernández, Arturo
Álvarez Izaguirre, Gerardo
Álvarez Kenan, Arnaldo
Álvarez Leyva, Ángel
Álvarez López, Lister
Álvarez López, Patricio Amador
Álvarez Machín, Eduardo
Álvarez Molina, Eddy
Álvarez Molina, Eduardo
Álvarez Morales, Reynaldo
Álvarez Olivares, Den Río Max.
Álvarez Pizarro, Gumersindo
Álvarez Raman, Rafael
Álvarez Ramón, Rafael
Álvarez Ríos, Luis
Álvarez Rodríguez, Alfredo
Álvarez Rodríguez, Luis
Álvarez Roque, Andrés
Álvarez Santibáñez, Federico R.
Álvarez Toro, María Victoria
Álvarez, Alejandro
Álvarez, Antonio
Álvarez, Blacaman
Álvarez, Daudeano
Álvarez, Digno
Álvarez, Fernando
Álvarez, Gerardo
Álvarez, Guillermo
Álvarez, Jesús
Álvarez, Jorge Casiano
Álvarez, José Antonio

Álvarez, Leofilo
Álvarez, Léster
Álvarez, Luis Raúl
Álvarez, Mario A.
Álvarez, Rafael Ángel
Álvarez, Ramón
Álvarez, Sergio
Álvaro, Humberto
Álvaro, José L.
Alvelo Sosa, Jesús
Alvízar, Eugenio
Alzamora González, Luis Porfirio
Allende Fuenzalida, Simón Cirineo
Allende Gossens, Salvador
Amador Cruzada, Radamés
Amador, Oscar
Amarán, Pedro
Amaury, José
Amechazurra Castro, Bebo
Amigó Carrillo, Mario Alberto
Amores, Gil Alberto
Amores, Roberto
Ampuero Ángel, Alberto Antonio
Ampuero Gómez, Juan Carlos
Anasiu Lascham, Pablo
Anaya Carrasco, Yamira
Anaya González, Hugo
Anaya González, José Eduardo
Anaya Palomino, Jaime
Anaya Rojas, Jorge Enrique
Anaya, Armando
Anaya, Jaime
Anaya, José Agustín
Anaya, Lázaro
Anaya, Secundino
Andariaga, Tomás
Andrade Andrade, María Lidia
Andrade, Armando Arínez
Andrades Balcazar, Luis H.
Andras Rimler, Tibor
Andreus Contreras, Juan
Andurandegue Sáez, Pedro Julio
Anfrens Fuentes, Roberto Enrique
Ángel Marilican, José René

Angueira Suárez, Álvaro
Angulo Matamala, Rolando G.
Anito Machacan, Luis Felidor
Antilaf Epulef, Miguel Ángel
Antiman Namuelulin, Rubén A.
Antonio Opazo, Pedro Segundo
Apablaza Henríquez, Clorinda
Aqueveque Atileo, Iván Marcelino
Aqueveque Iván, Marcelino
Aquit Manrique, Diosdado
Arado Ortiz, Mario Orlando
Aragón Aragón, Clemente
Aragón, Fidel
Aragonés, Reymundo
Arana Saldaña, Percy Max
Aranda Bruna, Hugo Hernán
Aranda Castillo, Eugenio
Aranda Díaz, José Domingo
Arandas Contreras, Daniel Bravo
Araneda Contreras, Vladimir A.
Araneda Reyes, Luis Alberto
Aránguiz González, Jorge Antonio
Aravena Álvarez, Luis Alberto
Aravena Mardones, Jorge Claudio
Aravena Mejías, Juan Fernando
Araya Araya, Pascual Antonio
Araya Araya, Pedro Abel
Araya Figueroa, Freddy Alex
Araya Fuentes, Carlos Segundo
Araya Fuentes, Oscar Emelio
Araya Garrido, Héctor Eugenio
Araya Mandujano, Jorge Manuel
Arcanio Quintana, Segundo
Arce Alarcón, Ramón Alfonso
Arce González, Enrique Hernán
Arce Peters, Patricia Angélica
Arce Tolosa, Teófilo Segundo
Arcía, Israel
Arcia, Raúl
Arcia, René
Arciaclara, Raudel
Arconsil, Estanislao
Arcos Jerez, Rafael
Ardanaga, Tomás

Arellano Ochoa, Oscar Leonardo
Arellano Pinochet, Héctor Benicio
Arellano Rojas, José Antonio
Arellanos Gómez, Juan de la Cruz
Arellanos Muñoz, Jorge Sebastián
Arenas Bejas, Mauricio Fabio
Arencibia Arancibia, Manuel Jesús
Arencibia Busto, Ricardo
Arencibia Cantillana, Carlos E.
Arencibia Castillo, Miguel Hernán
Arencibia Odio, Israel
Arencibia, Anacleto
Arencibia, José
Arencibia, Orlando
Arévalo Sosa, Jesús
Arfonso, Estanislao
Argote Duany, Ernesto
Argoto, Manuel
Arguelles Toro, Mario
Argüelles, Andrés
Argüelles, Félix
Argüelles, Lorenzo
Argüello, Luis
Arguín, Roberto
Arias Callejos, Armando
Arias Gómez, Aracelia
Arias Matamala, Isidro
Arias Matamala, Isidro Segundo
Arias Medina, Armando
Arias Navarrete, Hugolino H.
Arias Pino, Luis Fidel
Arias Quesada, Juan Domingo
Arias Ramírez, Luis Armando
Arias Vegas, Alberto V.
Arias, Armando
Arias, Armando
Arias, Esteban
Aris Polo, Mario
Arismende Medina, Oscar
Arismendi Pérez, Adolfo Omar
Armaguer, Tomás
Armas Ayala, Sergio
Armas, Miguel de
Armengol, Arístides

Armentero Aruca, Sergio
Armentero, Catalino
Armentero, Félix
Armijó Castillo, Juan Carlos
Arocha, Raúl
Aroes de la Chan, Alberto
Aros Pardo, Alfonso Luis
Arpuro, Lázaro
Arqueros Silva, Mario del Carmen
Arratía Reyes, Leonardo Abraham
Arrechavala, Miguel
Arredondo Báez, Enrique Dante
Arredondo González, Juan G.
Arredondo Sánchez, Hugo Néstor
Arriagada Cortés, José Manuel
Arriagada Jara, José Santos
Arriagada Saldias, Guillermo
Arriagada Zúñiga, José Gabriel
Arrieta, Roberto
Arros Yeñez, Oscar Segundo
Arroyo Maldonado, José
Arroz Calderón, Gilberto
Arsugaray Santana, Sergio
Arsugaray, Sergio
Arteaga, José María
Artiaga Manso, Gonzalo
Artiaga, María
Artilles Olivera, Felipe
Astudillo Celedón, José Luis
Astudillo González, José Eduardo
Astudillo Monsalve, Carlos H.
Aswee, Luis
Aumada Guerrero, Raúl
Auzcar Mener, José
Avendano Busques, Francisco
Ávila Cardoso, Reynaldo
Ávila Delgado, Antonio Gerardo
Ávila Garay, Juan Francisco
Ávila Maldonado, Mario Alberto
Ávila Márquez, Roberto Segundo
Ávila Pizarro, Jorge
Ávila Ramírez, Adolfo Rigoberto
Ávila Rocco, Donato Segundo
Ávila Sánchez, Luis

Ávila, Emilio Carlos
Ávila, Nápoles
Ávila, Ruperto
Avilé, Manuel
Avilés Miranda, José Aristeo
Ayala Hernández, Magda Evelyn
Ayala, Antonio
Ayanao Montoya, Moisés
Azea Muñoz, Juan Nemías
Azema Muñoz, Juan Nemías
Babusen, Roberto
Bacallao Rodríguez, José
Bacallao Zubieta, Juan
Bacallao, Luis
Bacciarini Zorrilla, Raúl Enrique
Báez, Juventino
Baeza Contreras, Luis Humberto
Baeza Opazo, Héctor Alejandro
Bahamonte Rogel, Linfor del C.
Baigori Hernández, Carlos Raúl
Baire Linares, Enrique
Balboa Cisternas, Gladys del T.
Balboa López, Ángel Luis
Balboa Troncoso, Omar Enrique
Balmazeda, Raúl
Balzal, Candelario
Barahona Palma, Roberto Ernesto
Barahona Reyes, Meer
Barboa Fernández, Carlos
Barca Lano, Luis Virgilio
Barcena, Alejandro P.
Barios Varas, Luis Hilario
Barios, Carmeles
Barios, Chucho
Baró Gutiérrez, Abel E.
Baró Merodio, Leonardo
Barra Duarte, Juan Pablo
Barra García, Luis Alberto
Barra Martínez, Ricardo Antonio
Barra Umaña, Luis Arturo
Barrabal, Renaldo
Barrabí, Berbaedo
Barrales González, Víctor Manuel
Barrales Rivera, Hernán Rodolfo

Barrantes Alcayata, Marcos E.
Barraza Anabalon, Juan Pablo
Barraza Enríquez, Eduardo O.
Barraza Enríquez, Vicente O.
Barraza Guerra, José Tulio
Barraza Torres, Luis Leopoldo
Barreiro, Manuel
Barrel Lemus, Roberto A.
Barrera Riquelme, Luis Alberto
Barreras, Antonio
Barreras, Pedro
Barrero Fernández, José
Barrero Fernández, José
Barrero Silva, Antonio
Barreto Silva, Antonio
Barreto, Jaime
Barreto, René
Barreto, Rogelio Sopo
Barría Barría, José Antonio
Barría Ordóñez, Pedro Purísimo
Barrientos Aedo, Juan Esteban
Barrientos Añazco, Hugo Orlando
Barrientos Matamala, Raúl Jaime
Barrientos Warner, José René
Barriga Soto, José Orlando
Barrios Andrade, Marcelo Esteban
Barrios Podré, José
Barrios Ramírez, Frank
Barrios Ramírez, Severino
Barrios Valencia, Alejandra
Barrios, Jorge
Barros Cartagena, Antonio M.
Barros López, Felipe
Barroso, Octavio
Bascuñan Mourgues, Dewet C.
Basoa Alarcón, René Rodrigo
Bastias Bustos, Juan Napomucero
Bastias Martínez, Jaime Max
Bastidas Zegers, Carlos Omar
Basulto, René
Batista Abelardo, Antonio
Batista, Ramón
Bautinal Bell, Juan
Beatón Martínez, Manuel

Becerra, Ramón
Becker Alfaro, Víctor Hugo
Beiza Beiza, Amalindo D. Carmen
Beltrán Carimen, Luis Eduardo
Beltrán de la Rosa, Ernesto
Beltrán Lizama, José Tomás
Beltrán Mendoza, Pablo
Beltrán Sandoval, Ramón B.
Beltrán, Héctor Eduardo
Bell Tamayo, Francisco
Belles López, Alberto Rodrigo
Bello Bello, Waldo Antonio
Bello Fajardo, Efrén
Bello Suárez, Raimundo
Bello, Juan
Benaiges Albert, Luis Marcelo
Benítez Herrera, Leopoldo
Benítez Leal, Modesto
Benítez Ortega, Víctor Segundo
Benítez Sosa, Roberto
Benítez, Blanco
Benítez, Felipe
Berenguer, Manuel Roig
Berger Guralnik, Carlos
Bermedo Becerra, Ángel Román
Bermúdez Abreu, Jorge
Bermúdez Ballón, Máximo Adolfo
Bermúdez Gaete, Juan Rafael
Bermúdez Torriente, Juan
Bermúdez, Luciano
Bermúdez, Pedro
Bermúdez, Ramón
Bernal Aguirre, Omar del Carmen
Bernal Yanes, Fredy
Besú, Antonio
Betancourt Yevenes, Juan Carlos
Betancourt, Facundo
Betancourt, José
Betancourt, Maurilio
Betancourt, René A.
Betanzos Ortega, Emilio
Bicet Polo, Ángel
Blanco, Cuco
Blanco, Fernando

Blanco, Ignacio
Blanco, Juan
Blanco, Oscar
Blanco, Sergio
Boitel Abraham, Pedro Luis
Boitel, Juan José
Bolaños, José S.
Bolaños, Orlando
Boncompte Andrew, Juan José
Bonet, Nelson
Borbón Rivero, Ruperto
Bordas Paz, José Francisco
Borges Rojas, Oscar
Borges, Ismael
Boroiza Carrasco, Juan Segundo
Borrell, Pedro
Braijel Vestal, Hermenegildo
Braniff Rojas, Grover V. Segundo
Bravo Aguilera, René Eduardo
Bravo Aguilera, Sergio Jaime
Bravo Álvarez, Fidel Alfonso
Bravo Fuentes, Hugo Patricio
Bravo González, Pedro Humberto
Bravo Montalvo, José
Bravo Vega, Alejandro Ramiro
Bravo Zúñiga, Carlos Raúl
Bravo, Álvaro
Bravo, Tomás
Brewe Torres, Julio Enrique
Briceño Briceño, Manuel
Brito Álvarez, Juan de Dios
Brito Noa, Celestino Ángel
Brizuela Pontigo, Ernesto Carlos
Brizuela, Raúl
Bruna Bruna, Juan Segundo
Brunet Lugones, Rafael
Brunet, Carlos
Brunet, Waltirio
Bugallo Celuzi, Oscar Héctor
Burgos Mautz, Sergio Arnoldo
Burgos Muñoz, Manuel Alberto
Burgos Sepúlveda, Aníbal
Bush Morales, Luis
Busket Aguilar, Antonio

Bustamante Llancamil, María E.
Bustamante Mancilla, Carlos A.
Bustos Bustos, Mario Francisco
Bustos Canales, Carlos Alejandro
Bustos Marchant, Juan Ramón
Bustos Morales, Benjamín
Caballero González, Julio
Caballero Ulloa, María Margarita
Caballero, Bernardo
Caballero, Florencio
Caballero, José
Caballero, Renato
Caballeros Chávez, José A.
Cabaña Conde, Ramón
Cabedo Aguilera, Jorge Alejandro
Cabello Bravo, Winston Dwight
Cabello Cabello, Tomás Orlando
Cabezas Bueno, José Ángel
Cabezas Castro, Juan Carlos
Cabezas Gacitúa, Julio Cesar
Cabrera Aburzúa, Haroldo Ruperto
Cabrera Balariz, Elizabeth del C.
Cabrera Fernández, Miguel
Cabrera Heredia, Eulalio
Cabrera Hernández, Gerbacio
Cabrera Hinojosa, Ester Angélica
Cabrera Medina, Euladio
Cabrera Navarro, Aldo
Cabrera Navarro, Alejandro
Cabrera Neira, Bernabé
Cabrera Oliva, Josué Manuel
Cabrera Ortiz, Transito del Carmen
Cabrera Pastrana, Jesús
Cabrera Pérez, Alberto
Cabrera Rivero, Francisco
Cabrera Sosa, Rolando
Cabrera Sousa, Rolando
Cabrera Steri, Dori
Cabrera, Abilio
Cabrera, Elizardo Cristóbal
Cabrera, Irenio
Cabrera, Jesús
Cabrera, Mariana
Cabrera, Muno

Cabrera, Sandalio
Cabrera, Silvio
Cabrera, Ulises
Cáceres Gatica, Jorge Rolando
Cáceres Morales, Jaime Andrés
Cáceres Muñoz, Manuel David
Cáceres Pavez, Guillermo de J.
Cáceres Peña, Lincoyan Nery
Cáceres Peredo, Daniel
Cáceres Santibáñez, Roberto H.
Caciano Álvarez, Jorge
Cachimba, Miguel
Cadet Vázquez, José Modesto
Calá de la Rosa, Leonel
Calá Reitor, Cesar
Calank Corola, Abel
Calderín, Armando
Calderón Aureliano, Emelio
Calderón Martínez, Armando
Calderón Nilo, Francisco Javier
Calderón Piñeda, Juan Manuel
Calderón Saldaña, Santos Pascual
Calderón, Eduardo
Calderón, Erasmo Ricardo
Calderón, Juan
Caldes Contreras, Jaime Humberto
Caldiño Insua, Ramón
Calfuquir Enríquez, Patricio
Calviño Insua, Ramón
calvo Martínez, Carlos Manuel
Calzadilla Pérez, Osvaldo
Calzadilla Romero, Irán del Trasito
Camacho Guerra, Norberto
Camacho, Casildo
Camacho, Gaudencio
Camacho, Luis
Camacho, Miguel
Camacho, Norberto
Camejo Herrera, Roberto
Camejo Reyes, Diosdado
Campa Aldeacoa, Mario
Campos Aldeacoa, Mario
Campos Carrillo, Felipe Porfirio
Campos Fardilla, Jorge Sergio

Campos Linares, José Martí
Campos López, Rubén Antonio
Campos Martínez, Carlos
Campos Pinilla, Yolanda H.
Campos Placeres, José Antoni
Campos Regino, Daniel
Campos Rivero, José
Campos Rojas, Elsa de las M.
Campos, Benito
Campos, Carlos
Camu Veloso, Arnoldo
Canales Venegas, Benjamín A.
Canales Venegas, Isaías Rodolfo
Canales Vivanco, Luis Alberto
Candía Acevedo, Mario Ángel
Candía Núñez, Hugo del Rosario
Candia Reyes, Segundo Enrique
Candia Salinas, Sergio Orlando
Candía Vázquez, Carlos Germán
Canedo Rojas, Mario Armando
Canelo Naureira, Luis Enrique
Canelo, Jorge Humberto
Canet, Miguel
Cano Vidal, María del Carmen
Cansino Alcaino, Eduardo G.
Cantera, Pedro
Cantero, Pedro
Cantero, Rolando
Cantil, María
Cantú Salazar, Manuel Beltrán
Cantuarias Grandon, Gustavo
Canvacho Roa, Oscar Segundo
Cañas Acevedo, Juan Ramiro
Cañizares, Julián
Capó, Héctor
Capó, María
Capos Gatica, Juan Fernando
Capote Fíallo, José Manuel
Capote Landín, Domingo
Capote Medina, Andrés
Capote, José
Caraballo Betancourt, Mario
Caraballo Pacheco, José Luis
Carabeo, Orestes

Carballo, Enrique
Carbonell, Rogelio
Cárcamo Cárcamo, Román Oscar
Cárcamo Carrasco, Germán Simón
Cárcamo Garay, José Mario
Cárcamo Navarro, Dagoberto S.
Cárcamo Rodríguez, Julio A.
Cárcamo Rojas, Saúl Sebastián
Carcamo Saldaña, Mario Arnaldo
Carcamo, Juan Bautista
Carda, Joaquín
Cardaron Cortés, Luis Ernesto
Cárdenas Ariel, Alberto Iván
Cárdenas Arriagada, Valentín
Cárdenas Díaz, Andrés Alfonso
Cárdenas Gómez, Edgard Eugenio
Cárdenas Montes, Luis
Cárdenas Paredes, Ramón
Cárdenas Pérez, Juan Carlos
Cárdenas Villegas, Marcelino
Cárdenas, Eduardo
Cárdenas, Ermeregildo
Cardo Reyes, Daniel
Cardo, Daniel
Cardo, Manuel
Cardona Valdez, Rosendo
Cardoso, Pedro
Carero, Aurelio E.
Caridad González, Vicente
Caridad Rodríguez, Luis
Caridad Rodríguez, María
Carilaf Díaz, Gregoria
Carmenarte, Ramón
Carmona Acevedo, Augusto H.
Carmona Concha, Ángel Patricio
Carmona Concha, Camilo Cariel
Carmona Parada, Ángel Patricio
Carmona Pérez, Gabriel
Carmona, Bernardo
Carnona, Roberto
Caro Bastias, Luis Humberto
Caro Benítez, Ricardo Alejandro
Caro Pérez, Ángel
Caro, Eladio

Carpanchai Choque, Jerónimo J.
Carracedo Ulloa, José
Carralero Anaya, Antonio
Carralero, Elpidio
Carrales, Bernardo
Carranza, Juan
Carrasco Barrios, Ricardo Eduardo
Carrasco Bascuñan, Nelson R.
Carrasco Cáceres, Carlos Aurelio
Carrasco Gatica, Alejandro Luis
Carrasco Maldonado, René C.
Carrasco Peña, Blanca Marina
Carrasco Pereira, Fernando A.
Carrasco Rivero, Jorge
Carrasco Tapia, José H.
Carrasco Toloza, Rubustiano
Carrasco Torres, José Manuel
Carrasco Valdivia, Mauricio
Carrasco Vázquez, José Herman
Carreño Aguilera, Iban Sergio
Carreño Calderón, José Belisario
Carreño Zúñiga, Juan Enrique
Carreño Zúñiga, Víctor Hugo
Carreón, Alfredo
Carreras Zayas, Jesús
Carrero Chenqueo, Ramón
Carrero, Joaquín
Carrero, Victorio
Carrillo Almonacid, Juan de Dios
Carrillo Tornería, Isidoro del C.
Carrillo, Yean
Carrión, Alfonso
Carroza Carroza, José Luis del C.
Cartaya, Orestes
Carvajal González, Agapito
Carvajal González, Fernando
Carvajal, Listtre Quiroga
Carvallo Lira, Enrique Armando
Carzadilla, Urbano
Casamayor Montane, Arcadio
Casanova Pino, Mario Eduardo
Casero Pérez, Rolando
Casielles Amigó, Julio
Casillas Lumpuí, Arcadio

Casola Bernal, Augusto
Casola Sandanas, Armando
Castañeda, Cristóbal
Castañeda, Wilfredo
Castaño Quevedo, José
Castaño, Quevedo
Castellanos Castro, Lázaro
Castellanos Fernández, Antonio
Castellanos, Jesús
Castellanos, Pura
Castellanos, Reinaldo
Castellón, Antonio
Castellón, Pedro
Castilla Lemus, Heliodoro
Castilla Lumpuí, Joaquín
Castillo Ahumada, Luis Antonio
Castillo Ahumada, Mario Antonio
Castillo Ahumada, Salvador Fidel
Castillo Alegría, Moisés del C.
Castillo Alegría, Víctor Moisés
Castillo Andrade, Maguindo A.
Castillo Arcaya, Roberto
Castillo Baldivia, Leo
Castillo Barrueto, Víctor Manuel
Castillo Calgagni, Hernán Horacio
Castillo Castillo, Gabriel Antenor
Castillo Castillo, Román Armando
Castillo del Pozo, José
Castillo Fornaris, José Luis
Castillo Gaete, Roberto José
Castillo Gaete, Rogelio José
Castillo Hormazábal, Andrés J.
Castillo Lemus, Eleodoro
Castillo Martínez, José Manuel
Castillo Muñoz, María Loreto
Castillo Narrientos, René Enrique
Castillo Ortega, Carlos
Castillo Oyarce, Ricardo Sergio
Castillo Ramírez, Pedro
Castillo Soto, Manuel Segundo
Castillo Valdivia, Francisco
Castillo, Abel
Castillo, Ángel Luis
Castillo, Antidio

Castillo, Carlos
Castillo, Gerardo
Castillo, José Antonio
Castillo, Luis
Castillo, Martín
Castillo, Ramón
Castillo, Sergio
Castillo, Ventura
Castro Arce, Armando
Castro Caldera, Raúl Humberto
Castro Castro, Samuel Roberto
Castro Contreras, Armando
Castro Heredia, Armando
Castro Hurtado, Gustavo H.
Castro López, Carlos Alberto
Castro Lora, Víctor
Castro Ojeda, Gilberto
Castro Rojas, Germán Gustavo
Castro Saavedra, Sergio Manuel
Castro Sáez, Héctor Guillermo
Castro Seguel, Alex Robinson
Castro Vidal, Luis Emilio
Castro, Armando
Castro, Bebo
Castro, Emelio
Castro, Emilio
Castro, Gilberto
Castro, Guillermo
Catalá, Juan José
Catalán Arriaza, Olivia Hijo D.
Catalán Lizana, Luis Eloy
Catalán Ojeda, Pedro Luis
Catalón Ferrero, Miguel Ángel
Cattani Ortega, Francisco
Cavada Soto, José Ismael
Cayo Cayo, Bernardino
Cayuan Caniuqueo, Mauricio S.
Cayul Tranamil, Segundo
Cayunao Villalobos, José Enrique
Cazadilla Vivanco, Gregorio
Cea Iturrieta, Mauricio Carmelo
Ceballo, Antonio
Cebarrio López, Felipe
Cedeño, Néstor

Cedeño, Sabino
Ceguera Conesa, Aquilino
Celedon Lavín, León Eduardo
Cepeda Venegas, Jorge Antonio
Cepero Alfonso, Ismael
Cepero García, Felipe
Cera Pineda, Nelson
Cerda Aburto, Jorge Enrique
Cerda Albarracín, Jorge
Cerda Ángel, Eduardo Elías
Cerda Lucero, Juan Bautista
Cerda Zúñiga, Pedro Antonio
Ceresada, Nodal
Ceria Alfad, José Miguel
Cerón Barros, Juan Arturo
Cerrera Almendares, Eduardo
Cervantes, Juan Gualberto
Céspedes Céspedes, Rodrigo A.
Céspedes Riquelme, Mario Hernán
Charlote Espileta, Olegario
Cienfuegos Cavieres, María V.
Cifuentes Daroch, Pedro Antonio
Cisterna Bocaz, Miguel Ángel
Ciudad Vázquez, Teresa Eugenio
Claucedo González, Demetrio
Clausell García, Ángel M.
Clauset Gato, Raúl
Clauset, José
Clement Hecnenlietner, Vicente P.
Cobo Ahumada, Jorge Raúl
Codines, Jerónimo
Cofre Catril, Juana Del Carmen
Cofre Quezada, Juan Gilberto
Coidan Leyva, Spiro Adrián
Colas, Roberto
Colihuinca Rajlat, Juan Antonio
Coloma Acuña, Manuel Jesús
Collazo Valdez, Rosendo
Collio Collio, Luis Alberto
Comopira, Pedro
Companioni Díaz, Manuel
Conchas Callejas, Raúl Dalton
Conde Green, Miguel
Conde, Marcos

Conesa Iglesia, Norberto
Cono Gaspar, Pedro
Constanzo Vera, José Alfonso
Consuegra Hernández, Ubaldo
Consuegra, Joaquín
Contreras Cáceres, Audito Neptalí
Contreras Carrasco, Ezequiel S.
Contreras Escamilla, Luis H.
Contreras Fuentes, Hernán D.
Contreras Garay, Ángel
Contreras Godoy, Jorge Ángel
Contreras González, Antonio
Contreras González, Jorge Edilicio
Contreras González, Juan Orlando
Contreras Juan, Andrew
Contreras Mazo, Braulio
Contreras Menares, Manuel Andrés
Contreras Oviedo, Luis Alberto
Contreras Plotsqui, Ezequiel Z.
Contreras Raviche, Eloy F.
Contreras Santander, Agustín
Contreras Sinpertigue, Jorge René
Contreras, Carlos
Contreras, Jorge
Corbalán Castillo, Luis Alberto
Cordero Díaz, Cándido
Cordero Izquierdo, Reinaldo
Cordero Spin, Miguel
Cordero, Fulogio
Cordero, Ramón
Cordobez Hernández, Rubén
Córdova Croxato, José Rufino
Córdova Yáñez, Juan Miguel
Coria Calderón, Juan Jorge
Corlad Sarpi, Carlo Emilio
Cornejo Carvajal, Jorge A.
Coro, Alberto
Corrales, Bernardo
Correa Arce, Ruiter Enrique
Correa Ortiz, Germán
Correa Ortiz, Hernán
Correa Rodríguez, Nicomedes S.
Correa Vergara, Luis Alberto
Correa, Ramón

Corredera Reyes, Mercedes del P.
Corredera, Carlos
Correoso, Aníbal
Cortaza Hernández, Manuel R.
Cortés Álvarez, Hipólito Pedro
Cortés Álvarez, Pedro Hipólito
Cortés Anaya, Rubén Del C.
Cortés Castro, Bernardo Del T.
Cortés Contreras, Abelardo de la C.
Cortés Cortés, Oscar Armando
Cortés Díaz, José Rosamel
Cortés Díaz, Justo Benedicto
Cortés Jelves, Pedro Blas
Cortés Luna, Gabriel Marcelo
Cortés Luna, Marcelo Gabriel
Cortés Morales, María Donato
Cortés Navarro, Andrés Nicanor
Cortés Pino, Fabián Onofre
Cortés Pino, Luis Enrique
Cortés Rodríguez, Germán de J.
Cortés Velázquez, Hernán A.
Cortés, Armando Oscar
Cortínez Olguín, Omar Julio
Cortz Maldonado, Benito E.
Corvalán Cerda, Agustín Sergio
Cosafreda Rodríguez, Joaquín
Cosejo, Lázaro
Cosío, Natalio
Coso Pérez, René
Cossío Pérez, Moisés del C.
Costa Cairo, Gilberto
Cotal Álvarez, Luis Raúl
Coto Gómez, Filiberto
Coto Sánchez, Juan
Coto, Gilberto
Covarubias, Robert
Crespo Regino, Daniel
Crespo Regino, Danny
Crespo, Luis Lara
Crisol Segura, José
Crusarmiento, Ramón
Cruz Abrey, Enrique
Cruz Alfonso, Roberto

Cruz Álvarez, Bernal
Cruz Caro, Alberto
Cruz Mederos, Juan Luis
Cruz Morales, Francisco
Cruz Oropesa, Efraín
Cruz Ortiz, Manuel Félix
Cruz Pérez, Emelio
Cruz Santiago, Gregorio
Cruz Sarmiento, Ramón
Cruz Zavala, Alfonso Carlos
Cruz, Carlos Manuel
Cruz, Domingo
Cruz, Félix
Cruz, Manuel
Cruz, Pedro
Cruz, René
Cruz, Roberto Alfonso
Cruz, Sergio
Cruzarmiento, Ramón
Cuadra Espinoza, Guillermo J.
Cuadras Hernández, Carmelo
Cubelas Rodríguez, Antonio
Cubillos Portilla, Eduardo
Cuellar, Jesús
Cuellar, Julián Cela
Cuellas Arbornoz, Florencio E.
Cuellas Concepción, Rolando
Cuellas Jiménez, Jesús
Cuello Álvarez, Guillermo N.
Cuervo Fernández, Gustavo
Cuervo, Vicente
Cueto Sánchez, Juan
Cuevas Alfonso, Jaime
Cuevas Díaz, Benicio Bruno
Cuevas Díaz, Benito Bruno
Cuevas Herrera, Adalberto
Cuevas Moya, Alberto Carlos
Cuevas Parra, Bernardo Querubín
Cuevas Soto, Adalberto
Cuevas, José
Cuevas, Manuel
Cuevas, Vicente
Cuñada, Miguel
Curamil Castillo, Francisco S.

Curaqueo Alarcón, David D.
Curbelo del Sol, Carlos
Curbelo, Carlos
Curbelo, Rubén
Cusco Viera, José
Cuthberthi, Sofía Ester
Chacón Flores, Antonio
Chacón Orellana, Pedro Raúl
Chacón Villanueva, Sergio Gastón
Chamiso, Leonardo
Chamizo Almora, Andrés
Chamorro Leyva, Guadalupe
Chamorro Monardes, Hernán E.
Chamorro Salinas, Carlos Octavio
Chamorro Torres, Manuel A.
Chan, Luis
Chandía Miranda, Luis Fernando
Chandía San Martín, José del C.
Chanez Cjanez, Nicolás
Chanquet, Jorge Roberto
Chanter, Eduardo
Chao Flores, Antonio
Charlot Espileta, Olegario
Charme Barros, Eduardo
Chávez Oyarzún, Cosme Ricardo
Chávez Pichipil, Hilda del Carmen
Chávez Reyes, Carlos
Chávez Riovas, Juan Antonio
Chávez Rivas, Juan Antonio
Chávez, Augusto
Chávez, Joseíto
Chávez, Mario
Chaviano Martínez, Rafael
Chaviano Reyes, Armando
Chemat, Rafael
Chon Marcos, José
Dachelet Martínez, Alberto A.
Dago Lamas, Apolinar
Danubeitia, Francisco Manuel
David Vecerra, Julio Fernando
Dávila Rodríguez, José Héctor
de Dios, Calixto J. de Dios
de la Barra de la Barra, Sergio
de la Barra Villarroel, Alejandro

de la Barra, Osvaldo Sergio
de la Fuente Castillo, Claudio P.
de la Guardia Guardia, Antonio
de la O, Arístides
de la Rosa Beltrán, Evelio
de la Rosa Bonilla, Andrés
de la Rosa, Arturo
de la Vega Rivera, José
de la Vega Rivera, Mario F.
de los Mozos Corvalán, Irma M.
de Souza Khol, Nelson
debac Herrera, Blanca Maria
del Bravo, Ricardo
del Canto Rodríguez, José E.
del Firro Santibáñez, Amador
del Pero Bustos, José Antonio
del Transito Santander, Ignacio
del Valle Galindo, Fernando
del Valle, Alfredo
Delgado López, Roberto
Delgado Marino, Oscar Jesús
Delgado Pérez, Carlos
Delgado Reyes, Gerardo
Delgado Sosa, Genaro
Delgado Tapia, Alicia Ana
Delgado Vallejos, Bertilio
Delgado, Ángel
Delgado, Daniel
Delgado, Eliecer
Delgado, Israel
Delgado, Jesús
Delgado, José
Delgado, Roberto
Despaigne Moré, Enrique
Devia Devia, José Rosa
Díaz Agüero, Beatriz Selena
Díaz Barrios, Carlos Hernán
Díaz Barrios, Hernán Carlos
Díaz Castro, Miguel Mario
Díaz Cliff, Juan Antonio
Díaz Contreras, Elizabeth
Díaz Fierro, Juan Carlos
Díaz González, Mario
Díaz González, Ramón

Díaz Inostroza, José Manuel
Díaz Jiménez, Arturo Fernando
Díaz León, Miguel Antonio
Díaz Liyo, Humberto Guillermo
Díaz López, Enrique Jorge
Díaz López, Jorge Enrique
Díaz López, Juan Jonás
Díaz Madruga, Claro Ernesto
Díaz Madruga, Ernesto
Díaz Maldonado, Laura Yolanda
Díaz Manríquez, Luis Alberto
Díaz Müller, Alfredo Fernando
Díaz Muñiz, Rafael
Díaz Muñoz, Luis
Díaz Nilo, Luis Santiago
Díaz Reyes, Luis
Díaz Rodríguez, Ezequiel
Díaz Romero, José Luis
Díaz Salinas, Luis Guillermo
Díaz Soto, Eduardo Antonio
Díaz Walter, Placido
Díaz, Antonio
Díaz, Arturo Enrique
Díaz, Claro
Díaz, Enrique
Díaz, Evelio
Díaz, Rey
Dinamarca Vidal, Nelson A.
Domke San Martín, Manuel F.
Donaire Rodríguez, Rolando A.
Donato Sanrivera, Clementina H.
Doniz, Fernando
Donoso Ávila, Carlos Emilio
Donoso Cortés, Manuel Gilberto
Donoso Dañovettia, Manuel F.
Dorner Caimapu, Mario Enrique
Dotemendez, Adriana D. la M.
Duarte Reyes, Ramón Leopoldo
Dueñas Gandín, Juan
Dufrenárvaes, Ingrid Jannette
Duque Duque, Carlos Enrique
Durán Castillo, Gonzalo Nelson
Durán Durán, Carlos Noé
Duran Toledo, Mario Ramón

Duran Torres, Omar Oscar
Duran Zúñiga, Neptalí Rubén
Duran, Diego
Echevarría Chacón, Gonzalo
Elden Pehuén, Mercedes L.
Elgeta, Gastón Manuel
Ellis Venegas, Patricio Orlando
Enriques Espinosa, Miguel H.
Escanilla Escobar, Claudio Jesús
Escobar Astudillo, Fernando V.
Escobar Camuz, Juan Joaquín
Escobar Chavarria, Ramón Luis
Escobar Escobar, Humberto
Escobar Ferrada, Ángel Manuel
Escobar Lagos, Lorena Del Pilar
Escobar Miranda, Guillermo M.
Escobar Mondaca, Edelmira E.
Escobar Zúñiga, Nemesio
Escobedo Cáliz, Alfredo Carlos
Eseiffert Dossow, Norberto
Esparza Osorio, Tomás Segundo
Espejo Flores, Gabriel Nelson
Espejo Gabriel, José
Espejo, José Gabriel
Espina Alfonso, Sergio
Espinosa Ojeda, Joaquín Segundo
Espinosa Santic, José Enrique
Espinosa Valenzuela, José Santos
Espinoza Farías, Jorge Patricio
Espinoza Farías, Patricio Jorge
Espinoza Figueroa, Juan Carlos
Espinoza la Torres, Rosa Emilia
Espinoza Medel, Florentino
Espinoza Muñoz, Juan Carlos
Espinoza Olmedo, Marcos A.
Espinoza Parra, Elías Juan
Espinoza Santis, Enrique José
Espinoza Troncoso, Guido Arturo
Espinoza Valenzuela, Ángel D.
Espinoza Valenzuela, Juan S.
Espinoza Villalobos, Berlindo L.
Espinoza Villalobos, Luis U.
Esteban, Ogan
Estol, Miguel Emilio

Estrada Bustos, Daniel Germán
Fajardo Arancibia, Rafael A.
Fajardo Hidalgo, Sergio Alberto
Fajardo Muñoz, José Manuel
Falcón, Francisco
Faneque, Manuel
Faramiñan Fernández, Guido
Farfán Verdugo, José Agustín
Farías Naranjo, José Carlos
Farías Padilla, José Miguel
Farías Pastene, Ibero
Farías Quiroz, Elena de Tránsito
Farías Urzua, Oscar Armando
Fariña Concha, Valentina Tatiana
Faudez Latore, Julio del Carmen
Faudez Muñoz, Fernando Omar
Faudez Ortiz, Carlos Enrique
Faudez Ortiz, Santiago Omar
Fe Alfonso, Erasmo A. Vicente
Fe Alfonso, Vicente
Felipe Hernández, Luis
Felipe Paludon, Fulgencio
Félix, Cornelio
Fenan Rivero, Myladys
Fernández Burgos, Pedro Antonio
Fernández Cabrera, Miguel
Fernández Casanova, Luis
Fernández Cobo, Roberto
Fernández Coloma, Victoriano S.
Fernández Cuevas, Dagoberto J.
Fernández Cuevas, Miguel Alberto
Fernández Díaz, Jorge
Fernández Fernández, Emilio
Fernández Fernández, José
Fernández Fernández, Ramón
Fernández Hill, Esteban
Fernández Lagos, José Miguel
Fernández López, Gilberto
Fernández Martínez, José
Fernández Núñez, Manuel S.
Fernández Pérez, Carlos
Fernández Ponce, Rolando
Fernández Ramos, Pantaleón
Fernández Rebolledo, Manuel M.

Fernández Rico, Mario
Fernández Rivera, Jorge Antonio
Fernández Rodríguez, Cindy
Fernández Ross, Ramón
Fernández Suero, Cecilio
Fernández Toledo, Roberto
Fernández Trujillo, Humberto
Fernández Varela, Rafael
Fernández, Aurelio
Fernández, Nidio
Fernández, René
Fernández, Walter
Ferrada Piña, Luis Humberto
Ferrara Sandoval, Luis Arnoldo
Ferreira Romos, Daniel
Ferreira Vásquez, José María
Ferrer Silva, David
Ferrias, Armenio
Fierro Fierro, Armando José
Fierro Pérez, Bautista Juan
Fierro Santibáñez, Roberto A.
Figueras Ubach, Félix Francisco
Figueredo, Blas Rosa
Figueredo, Héctor
Figueroa Bustos, José de la Cruz
Figueroa, Domingo
Figueroa, Hernán Cea
Flores Acevedo, Fernando Sotanor
Flores Antivilo, Segundo Norton
Flores Caroca, Floridor de Jesús
Flores Duran, Gabriel Sergio
Flores Echeverría, Arnaldo
Flores Mardones, Nicolás Iván
Flores Martínez, Justo Segundo
Flores Pérez, Arcadia Patricia
Flores Poblete, Gabriel Enrique
Flores Sepúlveda, Carlos F.
Flores Zapata, Jorge Nelson
Flores, Francisco Guillermo
Folmer Klnner, José Luis
Foltzick Casanova, Balmorir V.
Fonseca Castro, Antonio Eduardo
Fonseca, Mario
Fontela Ruiz, Desiderio

Fonton, Rafael
Fortunato Morejón, Luis
Fragela, Roberto
Francecena Valdés, Silvio
Franco Mira, José
Frankovich Pérez, María D. de la C.
Fredes Fernández, Reinaldo
Freire Caamaño, Eliecer S.
Freire Camaro, Sigisfredo Eliecer
Fres Gallardo, Elías Gonzalo
Fres Gallardo, Gonzalo Elías
Fritz Monsalvez, Eulogio del C.
Frometa, Valentín
Frontela, Manuel
Fuentealba Herrera, Carlos R.
Fuentes Cáceres, Abelardo Daniel
Fuentes Concha, Nadia Del C.
Fuentes Cortés, Rubén
Fuentes Fernández, Oscar Vicente
Fuentes Fuentes, Luis Humberto
Fuentes Garín, Eugenio del C.
Fuentes Lagos, Antonio Jorge
Fuentes Lucero, José Jesús
Fuentes Ovando, Rosa Patricia
Fuentes Ravanal, Guillermo Juan
Fuentes Segovia, José Armando
Fuentes Sepúlveda, Andrés A.
Fuentes Sepúlveda, Pedro Aladín
Fuentes Silva, Sergio
Fuentes Soriano, Luis Alberto
Fuentes Toledo, Franco Jorge
Fuentes Zamorano, Juan Alberto
Fuentes, Rogelio Antonio
Fuenzalida Enrique, Víctor
Fuenzalida Fernández, Rodolfo J.
Fuenzalida Fuenzalida, Víctor E.
Fuenzalida Madrid, José Orlando
Fuenzalida Moreles, Antonio F.
Fuenzalida, Enrique Víctor
Fundora Fernández, Jorge
Fundora Sánchez, Ramón
Fundora, Jorge
Fundora, Ramón

Gabiella, Ángel
Gabitua Martínez, Ricardo Juan
Gacitua Martínez, Juan Richard
Gaete Celis, Luis
Gaete Espinoza, Jorge Leonel
Gahona Ochoa, Luis Alberto
Gahona Orellana, Washington M.
Gajardo Nuche, Cesar
Galán Zaldívar, Máximo
Galarce León, Luis Humberto
Galaz Salas, Domingo Octavio
Galaz Vera, Carlos Alberto
Galdames Rojas, Orlando
Gálvez Fuentes, Kuis Aurelio
Gálvez Guzmán, Eduardo F.
Gálvez Hersley, Ricardo
Gálvez Norambuena, Víctor Omar
Gálvez, Fernando Grandon
Gálvez, Raúl Fernando
Gallardo Chávez, Arturo Oscar
Gallardo Chávez, Ester C.
Gallardo Chávez, Oscar A.
Gallardo Moreno, Catalina Ester
Gallardo Moreno, Roberto
Gallardo Muñoz, José Manuel
Gallardo Núñez, Juan Jorge
Gallardo Pacheco, Alberto R.
Gallardo Vegas, Humberto E.
Gallardo Villagrán, Mario A.
Gallardo Zapata, Ernesto
Gallegos Saball, Benedicto A.
Gallegos Santis, Carlos Oscar
Galleguillos Sepúlveda, Rafael E.
Gallo Cruz, Modesto
Gamboa Farías, Alfonso Antonio
Gamboa Pizarro, Luis Alfredo
Gambor Alarcón, Luis S.
Gámez Sáez, Joaquín Alfonso
Gamonal Suárez, José Adolfo
Ganga Torres, Luis Andrés
Gao Alarcón, Mario Armando
Garate Torres, Segundo Nicolás
Garay Tobar, Lina Dora
Garay, Ángel Esteban

Garcel, Pedro
García Álvarez, Andrés
García Arencibia, Diosdado
García Barrios, José Boertido
García Cancino, Narciso Segundo
García Cuevas, Enrique
García Díaz, Carlos
García Garay, Antonio Jesús
García García, Héctor Victoriano
García González, Manuel Antonio
García Guerra, Ismael
García Gués, Hernando
García Gutiérrez, Tabitha Carolina
García López, Eladio
García Morales, Santiago S.
García Posada, Ricardo Hugo
García Turino, Marco Tulio
García Valdés, Armando
García, Ángelo
García, Carlos
García, Eduardo
García, Elio
García, Zacarías
García-Menocal Fowler, Raúl
Garfias Gatica, Dagoberto E.
Garona Ochoa, Alberto Luis
Garreton Romero, Víctor A.
Garrido Espinoza, Fermín E.
Garrido Fernández, René Hernán
Garrido Letelier, Atilio Dante
Garrido Muñoz, Daniel Jacinto
Garrido Ocarez, Carlos H.
Garrido Queulo, Christian L.
Garridos Barrios, Sergio Enrique
Garte Ávila, Miguel Segundo
Garzan Morillo, Benjamín
Gatita Coronado, Víctor Joel
Gatita Vázquez, Manuel Jesús
Gayoso González, David Oliberto
Gfell Henríquez, Francisco A.
Gil Carril, Osvaldo
Godoy Bello, Gerardo
Godoy Echegoyen, Carlos Gabriel
Godoy Hernández, Jorge Enrique

Godoy Mancilla, Darío Armando
Godoy Sandoval, Luis Alberto
Godoy, Jorge Abel
Godoy, Nelson Astolfo
Gojanovic Arias, Drago Vinko
Gómez Aguirre, Ana Teresa
Gómez Andrade, Susana del R.
Gómez Arriagada, Sergio Arturo
Gómez Cedeño, Leonor
Gómez Concha, José Domingo
Gómez Espinoza, Nelson F.
Gómez Frías, Oscar Armando
Gómez Gutiérrez, Pedro Eleazar
Gómez Hidalgo, Lina de las M.
Gómez Iturra, Juan C. Humerto
Gómez Iturra, Juan Carlos R.
Gómez Monsalve, Víctor S.
Gómez Retamales, Jorge G.
Gómez Velásquez, José René
Gómez, Esteban
Gómez, Máximo
Gongotoma Vallejo, Alberto
González Albornoz, Mario A.
González Álvarez, Gerardo
González Allende, Manuel José
González Angulo, Enrique
González Avalos, Jorge Iván
González Barroso, José
González Beliran, José Luis
González Bello, Macdiel
González Benítes, Ladislao
González Bravo, Miguel Ángel
González Cárnica, Ángel A.
González Delgado, Juan Walter
González Farías, Robinson
González Francisco, Pedro
González Fredes, Fernando D.
González Fundora, Ramón
González Garriga, Ángel B.
González González, Gerardo
González González, José Manuel
González González, Moisés P.
González González, Patricio L.
González González, Ramón

González Inzunza, Juan Carlos
González Jara, Rodolfo Raúl
González Lines, Andrés
González Lizama, Roberto Omero
González Lorca, Néstor A. Iván
González Mardones, Danilo Jesús
González Maureira, Servando A.
González Miranda, Sara Rosa
González Moena, Ana Jeannette
González Mondaca, Luis Osvaldo
González Mondaca, Patricio
González Morales, Francisco J.
González Morales, Francisco R.
González Nicolau, Hernán Sergio
González Norambuena, Mauricio
González Ortega, Ramón D.
González Pandiera, Gregorio
González Pedro, Humberto
González Pedroso, Filiberto
González Pérez, Rosendo
González Quevedo, Adelina
González Ramos, Néstor
González Rojas, Antonio Segundo
González Roqueta, Julia
González Saavedra, Alamiro S.
González Salgado, Cesar Rubén
González Sanhueza, Segundo
González Sepúlveda, José G.
González Tognarelli, Fernando
González Vargas, Manuel Zacarías
González Velderia, Pedro De N.
González Venega, David Héctor
González Yánez, Héctor Enrique
González, Benereo
González, Casin
González, Enrique
González, José
González, Juan R.
González, Luis
González, Porfirio
González, Roberto
González, Salvador
González, Teófilo
Gonzalo, Felo

Granado, Rufo
Guajardo Betancourt, Celso A.
Guajardo Palma, Osar C.
Guañio, José
Guarda Olivares, Julio Arturo
Guarda Sáez, Juan Eduardo
Guardia Oliveres, Raúl Del C.
Guerra Bello, Anastasio
Guerra Capote, Raquel
Guerra Domínguez, Luis
Guerra Fernández, Mario José
Guerra Herrera, Roberto
Guerra, Julio
Guerra, Miguel
Guerra, Tomás
Guerrero Ceballos, Manuel L.
Guerrero Guerrero, Pascual A.
Guerrero Guzmán, Miguel Ángel
Guerrero Hostales, Carlos
Guerrero Vaganay, Enrique
Guevara Mardones, Fernando E.
Guillen, Porfirio
Guiral, Enrique
Gulauma, Roberto
Gusmay, Rolando
Gutiérrez Aravena, Domingo R.
Gutiérrez Ascencio, José Fernando
Gutiérrez Benavides, Carlos
Gutiérrez García, Juan
Gutiérrez Garrido, Felipe Antonio
Gutiérrez Gómez, Marcelo del C.
Gutiérrez Gutiérrez, Juan Antonio
Gutiérrez Gutiérrez, María Cristina .
Gutiérrez Núñez, Enrique Jorge
Gutiérrez Rodríguez, Jack E.
Gutiérrez San, Jorge
Gutiérrez San, Martín Jorge
Gutiérrez Soto, Carmen
Gutiérrez Valdés, Antonio
Gutiérrez Valdés, Pedro
Gutiérrez, Estervino
Guzmán Altamirano, Carlos A.
Guzmán Cuevas, Oscar Jesús
Guzmán Fuentes, Marcelo Omar

Guzmán Muñoz, Francisco Ramos
Guzmán Muñoz, Guillermina Inés
Guzmán Santacruz, Roberto
Guzmán Soto, Luis Enrique
Guzmán Urrutia, Jorge Patricio
Hacue Arellano, Juan Santos
Hamame Sanur, David
Hamer Barros, Luis Eduardo
Hanet, José
Harasic Mervil, Jorge Quinto
Hardiman, Manuel
Hechebarría Montai, Pedro
Hechebarría, Luis
Hechebarría, Miguel
Hechenleitner, Vicente Clement
Hechevarría Montei, Pedro
Hechevarría, Fernando
Henríquez Aguilar, Sandra Janet
Henríquez Aravena, Hernán Arturo
Henríquez Araya, Juan Waldemar
Henríquez Burgos, Heriberto
Henríquez Calderón, Héctor Hugo
Henríquez Gallegos, Wilson D.
Henríquez Henríquez, Juan Jesús
Henríquez Magla, Evelyne
Heredia, Ramón
Heria Bravo, Rafael
Heria Bravo, Rafael Félix
Hermosilla Muñoz, Luis Hilario
Hernán Hernández, Gustavo
Hernán, Manuel
Hernández Alarcón, Juan Carlos
Hernández Albornoz, Miguel A.
Hernández Alemán, Justo
Hernández Almendares, Rafael
Hernández Anaya, Pedro G.
Hernández Andrade, José G.
Hernández Andrade, Roberto D.
Hernández Arencibia, Navildo
Hernández Borges, Manuel
Hernández Briondo, Víctor
Hernández Caneiva, Víctor
Hernández Cansío, Natalio
Hernández Carranza, Rafael

Hernández Castillo, Sergio
Hernández Cosío, Miguel
Hernández Cruz, Julián
Hernández Chacón, Alexis
Hernández Elgueta, Guillermo H.
Hernández Esteves, Rigoberto
Hernández Fernández, Eusebio
Hernández Garcés, Héctor E.
Hernández García, Luis
Hernández García, Pedro René
Hernández González, Armando
Hernández González, José
Hernández Guajardo, Juan F.
Hernández Hernández, Roberto
Hernández Hill, Hernando
Hernández Iglesias, Manuel
Hernández Martínez, Eredio
Hernández Martínez, Eredio
Hernández Martínez, Felipe
Hernández Martínez, René
Hernández Más, Jacinto
Hernández Medina, Argelio
Hernández Mondaca, Juan Luis
Hernández Montes, Félix
Hernández Morales, Evelio
Hernández Morales, José
Hernández Moreno, Gilberto
Hernández Neira, Luis Alberto
Hernández Peña, Carlos
Hernández Pérez, Fidel
Hernández Pupú, Erenio
Hernández Rodríguez, Evelio
Hernández Suárez, Amado
Hernández Suárez, Armando
Hernández Valdés, Dámaso
Hernández, Abdulio
Hernández, Adalberto
Hernández, Agapito
Hernández, Agustín
Hernández, Alemán
Hernández, Alfredo
Hernández, Antonio
Hernández, Arsenio
Hernández, Benito

Hernández, Cansío
Hernández, Enrique
Hernández, Erineo
Hernández, Francisco
Hernández, Gregorio
Hernández, Hipólito
Hernández, Horacio
Hernández, Humberto
Hernández, Jesús
Hernández, Joaquín
Hernández, José
Hernández, Juan A.
Hernández, Juan Antonio
Hernández, Julio
Hernández, Leobaldo
Hernández, Leonardo
Hernández, Leopoldo
Hernández, Luis
Hernández, Mario Bernardo
Hernández, Micael
Hernández, Napoleón
Hernández, Natalio
Hernández, Natalio
Hernández, Ramón
Hernández, Rey
Hernández, Rivera
Hernández, Roberto
Hernández, Valentín
Herrera Caballero, Fernando
Herrera Cabello, Alfredo
Herrera Clavera, Juan Antonio
Herrera Delgado, Cecilio
Herrera Duque, Eleodora
Herrera González, Luis Ricardo
Herrera Ledesma, Eleodoro
Herrera Manríquez, Guillermo H.
Herrera Rivero, Nelson Adrián
Herrera Rivero, Salustio
Herrera Urrutia, Juan Leopoldo
Herrera Villegas, José Manuel
Herrera, Antonio
Herrera, Benito
Herrera, Facundo
Herrera, Juan L.

Herrera, Leopoldo
Herrera, Leticia
Herrera, Salvador
Hidalgo Blanco, Ramón
Hidalgo Contreras, Juan Ruperto
Hidalgo González, Juan Manuel
Hidalgo Retamal, Carlos Miguel
Hidalgo Rivas, Manuel Segundo
Hidalgo Valdés, Juan
Hidalgo, Israel
Higueras Zúñiga, Isaías
Hill Corrales, Fernando
Hinojosa Céspedes, Vicente A.
Honores Aguirre, Hernán Del C.
Horman Lazar, Charles Edmund
Hormazabal Pino, Nelson Luis
Hormazabal Romero, Salvador A.
Huazqui Barria, Roberto Eder
Huenucci Antil, Mauricio
Huenul López, Lincoyan Carlos
Huerta Acevedo, Gregorio Del T.
Huerta Beiza, Víctor Hugo
Humeres Verdugo, Camilo E.
Hurtado Martínez, Manuel H.
Ibáñez García, Manuel Jesús
Ibarra Echeverría, Carlos L.
Ibarra Espinoza, Carlos A.
Ibarra Fuentes, Guillermo
Ibarra Pino, Manuel
Ibarra Saavedra, Julio M.
Iglesia Pons, Isaías
Igor Spormann, Gustavo B.
Illa, Victoriano
Inarejo Araya, Marcos Segundo
Inarejo Igor, Luciano José
Infante Hidalgo, Braulio
Infante Idal, José Gabriel
Infante Suárez, Bienvenido
Inostroza Flores, Guillermo
Inostroza Lamas, Caupolicán
Inostroza Lamas, Caupolican H.
Inostroza Mallea, Juan Luis
Inostroza Ñanco, José Víctor
Inostroza Orellana, Luis Alberto

Insua Cossío, Juan Guillermo
Insua González, Jesús
Irene Sotolongo, Juan
Iribarren González, Fernando E.
Irrutia González, Ermin Néstor
Isabel Torrado, María
Issac Mendieta, Roberto
Iturra Gómez, Carlos Humberto
Iturra González, Erwin Néstor
Iturras Contreras, Carlos F.
Iturriaga Rodríguez, Leovigildo
Iván, Gerardo Lema
Izquierdo García, Alberto
Izquierdo Portuondo, Enrique
Izquierdo, René
Izquierdo, Tomás
James, Alberto
Jara Álvarez, Aquiles Juan
Jara Aravena, José Eduardo
Jara Córdoba, Julio Antonio
Jara Cortés, Carlos Eduardo
Jara Espinoza, Ramón Osvaldo
Jara Herrera, José Juan Carlos
Jara Herrera, Juan Carlos
Jara Jara, Mario
Jara Latorre, José Orlando
Jara López, Bernardo Ramón
Jara Martínez, Víctor Lidio
Jara Ríos, Eliseo Segundo
Jara Santibáñez, Manuel Elías
Jara Valenzuela, Heremías Noé
Jaramillo Figueroa, Osvaldo
Jarlan Purcel, Benjamín Alfredo
Jeldres De la Cuadra, Claudio E.
Jeldres Jeldres, Juan Antonio
Jelírez Beltrán, Enrique Mario
Jelves Morales, Dide Jinning
Jerez Padilla, Raúl A. de la Cruz
Jiberga, Salustiano
Jiménez Alfaro, Tucapel Francisco
Jiménez Álvarez, Manuel
Jiménez Díaz, Guillermo
Jiménez García, Juan Miguel
Jiménez Jiménez, Jaime

Jiménez Lucero, Bernardo S.
Jiménez Machuca, Armando E.
Jiménez Morales, Amelio
Jiménez Muñoz, José Alejandro
Jiménez Vidal, Juan Francisco
Jiménez, Arnaldo
Jiménez, Edmundo
Jiménez, Macho
Jiménez, Ricardo
Jiménez, Rosario
Jofre, Silverio
John Olivera, Alberto
Jordán Domic, Jorge Mario
Jordán, Pedro
Jorge Salazar, Jorge Rolando
Jorin Vega, Osmin
Jorquera Jorquera, Luis Alberto
Jorquera Leyton, Gonzalo Mario
Juica Cortés, Erick Patricio
Junco Soler, Sotero
Junco, Jesús
Junco, Silvino
Junco, Tomás
Jurado Rosales, Raúl
Karelovic Kirigin, Danilo Simón
Keyok Fredes, Arturo
Kin Yum, Jorge
King Young, Jorge
Krauss Iturra, Víctor Fernando
Krul, Teodoro Konoba
Kunze Duran, Tito Guillermo
La Rosa, Francisco
La Villa, Andrés
Labbe Peñaloza, Luis Eugenio
Labna Jiménez, Héctor Marcelo
Labra Saure, Pedro Claudio
Labrada Martínez, Heriberto
Labrada Martínez, Jorge
Lacorte, Miguel Ángel
Lagos Bravo, Luis Humberto
Lagos Escobar, Guido Onofre
Lagos Marín, Nelson Ernesto
Lagos Reyes, Ricardo Raúl
Lagos Salnas, Carlos Eduardo

Lagos Silva, Luis Alberto
Lamana Abarzúa, Jorge Andrés
Lamich Vidal, Jorge Rubén
Lanza Flores, Margarito
Lanza Ortega, Ramón
Lara Ruiz, Francisco Urcisinio
Lara Valdés, Cristian Alfonso
Lara, Artemio
Larena Inostroza, José Miguel
Larenas Molina, Carmen Gloria
Larrabide López, Raúl Leopoldo
Larrea, Manuel
Lascano Campos, José Renato
Lastra Ayala, Lastania Del C.
Latorre Rodríguez, Elizabeth
Latorre, José Modesto
Latorre, Modesto José
Laubra Brevis, Juan De Dios
Laurel Almonacid, José Alberto
Lausic Glasinovic, Cedomil L.
Lavanderos Lataste, Mario L. Iván
Lavani, Euladio
Lavín Loyola, Claudio Arturo
Laza Miranda, José Luis
Lazo Arriagada, Luis Alonso
Lazo Pastrana, Alberto
Lazo Quinteros, Raúl Del Carmen
Lazo, Jesús
Leal Díaz, Miguel Ángel
Leal Frías, David Alejandro
Leal Pereira, Arsenio Orlando
Leal Riveros, Víctor Ricardo
Leal Sanhueza, Heriberto Del C.
Lebrigio Flores, Jorge
Lefian Rodríguez, Hernán A.
Lefiqueo Antilef, Dagoberto
Leiva Adasme, Eduardo
Leiva Jiménez, Oscar Armando
Leiva Molina, Sergio Gustavo
Leiva Muñoz, Manuel Antonio
Leiva Narváez, Ramón Nonato
Lejdermann Konoyoika, Bernardo
Lema Rodríguez, Juan Patricio
Lemus Muñoz, Exequiel Alejandro

Lendo Vega, José Gregorio
León Fuentes, Patricio Wenceslao
León Jiménez, Bernardo
León Jiménez, José
León Jr., Genaro
León Morales, Carlos René
León Pausen, Javier De Jesús
León Ramírez, Eulogio
León Rodríguez, Jorge
León Rondón, Arbelio
León Sr., Genaro
León Venegas, Pedro
León, Armando
León, Genaro
León, Isace
León, José
León, Luis
Leónidas Contreras, Elizabeth
Leónidas, Isabel Díaz
Lepe Moraga, Héctor Manuel
Lepin Antilaf, Segundo
Letelier Del Solar, Orlando
Letelier Parra, Juan José
Leutun Miranda, Francisco S.
Levimilla Juan, Eleuterio
Levio Llaupe, Andrés
Levocoy Emelcoy, José Alfredo
Leyva, Eutiminio
Leyva, Justo
Lezcano Blanco, Avelino
Lezcano Blanco, Evelio
Lillo Alarcón, Luis Humberto
Lima Valenzuela, Ciro
Lima, Alejandro
Linares Cerrano, Francisco
Linares Drake, Ángel
Linares Galarce, Francisco S.
Linares Rodríguez, Sixto
Lincopan Culfulaf, Francisco J.
Lira Bravo, Segundo del Carmen
Lira Morales, Juan Manuel
Lira Yáñez, Jorge Nicolás
Lizama Irrazábal, Francisco J.
Lizama Trafilaf, René Alejandro

Lizama, Manuel
Lizarde, Reinaldo
Lizardi Flores, Humberto
Lizardi Lizardi, Luis Alberto
Lobos Cañas, Luis Alberto
Lobos Utribinas, Oscar Antonio
Logos Rodríguez, Antonio A.
Loó Prado, Arturo Julio
López Chamizo, Andrés
López Chávez, Roberto
López Elgueda, Ricardo Octavio
López Estay, Cristina del Carmen
López Leyton, Rafael De la Cruz
López López, Manuel Antonio
López Olmedo, Víctor Enrique
López Palma, Sergio Antonio
López Torres, Juan Segundo
López Zúñiga, Francisco H.
López, Luis
Lorenzo, Lorenzo Suárez
Luaces Ortega, Ramón
Lucero Aldana, Oscar Roberto
Lucero Muñoz, René Eusebio
Luna Gabriel, Marcelo
Luque Schurman, José
Luzardo, Ismael
Llancaqueo Millin, Segundo E.
Llanera Andrade, José A
Llanes, Amados
Llanes, Eusebio
Llanio, José Ricardo
Llanos Guzmán, Héctor Horacio
Llaquien, Víctor
Llerena Calderín, Antonio
Lleucun Lleucun, Juan
Macaya Barrales, Alfonso S.
Maceda Toledo, Hilario
Maceo Maryí, Pedro A.
Machado, Carlos
Machado, Carlos
Machín García, Erasmo
Machuca Espinoza, José Oscar
Madrid Gálvez, Rafael Antonio

Maghadon Valenzuela, Argelino C.
Magni Camino, Cecilia
Maigret Becerra, Mauricio A.
Maldonado Alvear, Javier Luis
Maldonado Bao, Miguel Enrique
Maldonado Díaz, Juan José
Maldonado Fuentes, José
Maldonado Gallardo, Luis E.
Maldonado Gatica, Víctor Joaquín
Maldonado Miranda, Manuel S
Maldonado Núñez, Víctor F.
Maldonado Sepúlveda, Jorge E.
Maldonado Ulloa, Héctor Hugo
Maldonado Urria, Raúl Fernando
Maldonado Velásquez, Jorge G.
Maldonado, Santiago
Malhue González, John Patricio
Malvino Campos, Héctor Juan
Mamani García, Juan Apolinario
Mamani López, Domingo
Mancill Hess, Edwin Ricardo
Mancilla Delgado, Juan
Mancilla Martínez, Ricardo D.
Manquian Calculef, Cardenio R.
Manrique Norambuena, Patricio
Manríquez Arroyo, Inés
Manríquez Díaz, Miguel H.
Manríquez Wilden, Luis Aníbal
Mansilla Coñuecar, Carlos H.
Mansilla Ruiz, Gladys
Manso Brizuela, Víctor Manuel
Manso de la Guardia, Manuel
Manso, Efraín
Manteira Marcelino, Miguel
Mantenegro Godoy, Sergio E.
Manuel Rivera, Juan
Manzano Cortés, Eduardo
Manzano Cortez, Osvaldo M.
Manzano González, Patricio E.
Manzo Santibáñez, Gastón R.
Mañao Ampuro, José Hernán
Marales Santos, José Eduardo
Marambio Silva, Joaquín Del C.

Marcarían Jamett, Manuel J.
Marcial Alarcón, Orlando
Marco, Felipe
Marchandon Valenzuela, Marcelino
Marchant Céspedes, Oscar E.
Marchant Ortiz, Isau Audilio
Marchante Hernández, Ismael
Marchat Sandoval, José Eduardo
Marchat Vivar, Marcela A.
Mardones Garcés, Frank
Mardones Jofre, Pedro
Mardones Román, Ernesto D.
Mardones Soto, Ernesto A.
Marengue Gaspar, Valencia
Marfull González, Gabriel A.
Margarían Jamett, Manuel
María Hernández, Rafael
María Izquierdo, José
Marilao Pichun, Moisés
Marín Álvarez, Héctor Gustavo
Marín Cortés, Guillermo Enrique
Marín Marion, Blas
Marín Martínez, Margarita Elena
Marín Martínez, María Paz
Marín Mejías, Pedro Vicente
Marín Novo, Esteban
Marín Novoa, Pedro Manuel
Mariqueo Martínez, Pedro A.
Marques Noble, Esteban
Márquez Agusto, Nelson José
Márquez Castro, Oscar
Márquez Martínez, Eugenio
Márquez Novo, Esteban
Márquez, Amado
Márquez, Roberto
Marrero Pardo, Salomón
Marrero Pulido, Francisco
Marrero, Reynaldo
Martell Guerra, Antonio
Martín Céspedes, Alberto
Martín Espinosa, Ramón
Martín Lara, Orlando
Martín Lizama, Jorge San
Martín Montero, Armando

Martín Pérez, Pedro E.
Martínez Aldana, José V.
Martínez Aliste, René Máximo
Martínez Andrade, Juan A.
Martínez Araya, Guillermo
Martínez Celis, Tomás R.
Martínez Concepción, Jorge
Martínez Enríquez, Helen
Martínez Fernández, Pedro
Martínez Ferro, Aurelio
Martínez Fraga, René
Martínez García, Ángel Donato
Martínez González, Ramón H.
Martínez Guerra, Fernando
Martínez Guillen, Huho
Martínez Gutiérrez, Vicente
Martínez Hernández, Diosdado
Martínez Herrera, Genaro F.
Martínez Hormazábal, Luis A.
Martínez Jaime, Max
Martínez Jiménez, Leonardo
Martínez Lara, Julio Antonio
Martínez Leyton, Gabriel R.
Martínez Limonta, Orelvis
Martínez Linares, Pablo
Martínez López, Rafael
Martínez Morera, Adalberto
Martínez Noches, Francisco H.
Martínez Norma, Felipe
Martínez Pérez, Juan De Dios
Martínez Robert, Antonio
Martínez Rodríguez, Mario Daniel
Martínez Rodríguez, Ricardo
Martínez Soto, Carlos Enrique
Martínez Soto, Carlos Enrique
Martínez Traslaviña, Marco A.
Martínez Valdés, Joael
Martínez Valenzuela, Domingo E.
Martínez Vera, Gustavo Hernán
Martínez Verdecía, Santiago
Martínez Zúñiga, Francisco
Martínez, Adiel Monsalve
Martínez, Caridad
Martínez, Leonel

Martínez, Roberto
Mascareña Díaz, Carlos
Masó, Braulio Contreras
Mata Costacairo, Evelio
Matamala Venegas, Luis Gilberto
Matas Rodríguez, Evelio
Matas Torres, Eugenio
Mateluna Gómez, Daniel de los A.
Mateluna Gutiérrez, Luis E.
Matías Castra, Israel
Matías Castro, Pablo
Matteau Aceituno, Humberto J.
Matulic Infante, Juan E.
Matus Hermosilla, Victoriano
Maureira Miranda, Edmundo
Mayorga Millán, Juan F.
Maza Carvajal, Enrique Antonio
Medel Rivas, Daniel José
Medina Cedeño, Luis
Medina Díaz, Eugenio
Medina Díaz, Julio
Medina Godoy, Sergio Nicolás
Medina Letelier, Nelson Joaquín
Medina Montes de Oca, José
Medina Riquelme, Domingo M.
Medina, Eduardo
Mejías Piedra, Tomás
Mejías, Roberto
Meléndez Ramírez, José Luis
Melgarejo Rojas, Santos David
Melin Pehuen, Manuel Segundo
Melipillan Aros, Jorge
Melo Farías, Joel Bernardo
Mellas Veliz, Juan Fernando
Mena Sánchez, Marcos David
Mena Sepúlveda, Pedro Armando
Menanteau Aceituno, Humberto J.
Méndez Broche, Izora
Méndez Esquijarros, Adaberto
Méndez Méndez, Daniel
Méndez Ortega, Luis Sergio
Méndez Pérez, Luis Olirio
Méndez Pérez, Luis Orlirio
Méndez Ramos, René Abelardo

Méndez Tacoronte, Mayulis
Méndez Valenzuela, José
Méndez Vásquez, Laura Rosa
Méndez Venegas, José Egidio
Mendoza Santibáñez, Justo J.
Mendoza Toro, Félix Alberto
Mendoza Villagrán, Renato M.
Mendoza Villavicencio, Jenaro R.
Mendoza, José F.
Mendoza, Pedro
Menéndez González, Juan
Menéndez, Edelmiro
Meneses Brito, Pedro Juan
Meneses Cisterna, Jaime Iván
Mesa Carbonell, José
Mesa Hernández, Antonio
Meza Arriagada, Víctor
Mezquita Ramírez, Manuel N.
Milián Gardía, Sabino R.
Milián Jerge, Alberto
Millahuinca Araya, Francisco S.
Miño Garrido, Hugo
Miño Garrido, Hugo Zacarías
Miño Logan, David Marcos A,
Miño Logan, Marcelo Esteban
Miño Salinas, Luis
Mirabal Sánchez, Francisco
Miranda Aguilar, Martín Gustavo
Miranda Clavijo, Lenin Cesar
Miranda Díaz, María Elena
Miranda Gálvez, Luis Alberto
Miranda Hernández, Joaquín F
Miranda Lizama, Manuel S.
Miranda Luna, David Ernesto
Miranda Martínez, Clodomiro
Miranda Martínez, Roberto
Miranda Segovia, Oscar Hermán
Miranda Vivar, Héctor Osvaldo
Miró Téllez, Teodoro
Misa López, Adalberto
Moffit, Ronnie Karpen
Mojica Barros, Mario Ernesto
Mola Hormazábal, Oscar Roque
Molina Candia, Enrique Segundo

Molina Dueñas, Eugenio
Molina González, Floripa D.
Molina Guerrero, José Gabriel
Molina Letelier, Oscar Enrique
Molina Rodríguez, Freddy F.
Molina Ruiz, Florentino Alberto
Molina Zambrano, Anastasio
Molina, Eduardo Pacheco
Molina, Hernán Sergio
Mollinedo Placencia, Jesús
Mondaca Vega, Ernesto R.
Mondaca Vega, Juan Francisco
Mondaca Zelada, Jaime Irinéo
Monroy Seguel, Leomeres
Monsalve Martínez, Odiel
Monsalve Sandoval, José E.
Monsalve, Bienvenido Molina
Monsalves Toledo, Waldemar S.
Montalvo, Roberto
Montecinos Díaz, Damasco Ulises
Montecinos Rojas, Joaquín S.
Montecinos San Martín, Marcos H.
Montecinos San, Martín Marcos
Montecinos Slavghter, Ricardo C.
Montecinos Verdejo, Fernando
Montelier Rodríguez, Lorenza
Montenegro Banítez, Camilo
Montenegro Davelido, Carlos
Montenegro, Sixto R.
Montero Mosquera, Armando F.
Montero Salazar, Edmundo E.
Montes de Oca, Eleodoro
Montes de Oca, Juan
Montesino Ramírez, Alberto
Montoya Torres, Mario Hugo B.
Mora González, José Tomás
Mora Gutiérrez, Fernando A.
Mora Orellana, Gilberto Antonio
Mora Osses, Sebastián
Mora San Juan, Luis del C.
Mora Serey, José Segundo
Mora, Juan Francisco
Moraga Muñoz, Enrique
Morales Álvarez, Carlos S.

Morales Álvarez, José Lenin
Morales Álvarez, José Leningrado
Morales Batista, Ismael
Morales Billagra, Enrique del C.
Morales Bustos, Luis Miguel
Morales Chávez, Enrique S.
Morales Díaz, Domingo de la C.
Morales Donoso, Luis
Morales Herrera, Juan J. M.
Morales Jaime, Andrés
Morales Jiménez, Emelio
Morales Lobos, Emilio
Morales Manhueza, Manuel A.
Morales Melzer, Enrique E.
Morales Menéndez, Francisco
Morales Muñoz, Henry Aníbal
Morales Muñoz, Luis Eduardo
Morales Pascual, Oscar
Morales Prida, Floreal
Morales Retamal, Pedro Abraham
Morales Sahueza, Prebisterio
Morales Salinas, Luis Fernando
Morales Vellenueva, Archibaldo
Moran Araya, Iván Florencio
Moreira Bustos, Segundo Osvaldo
Morejón Gil, Rogelio
Morejón Montero, Pedro
Morejón Valdés, Pedro
Morejón, José
Moreno Acevedo, Danilo Alberto
Moreno Bacallao, Eloy
Moreno Campusano, Héctor L.
Moreno Caviedes, Miguel Hernán
Moreno Díaz, Manuel Ernesto
Moreno Góngora, Melbar Acricio
Moreno Mena, Alfredo Andrés
Moreno Quezada, Manuel Jesús
Moreno Villarroer, Hernán E.
Moreno Villarroer, Luis Alberto
Moreno Villarroer, Luis Alfonso
Moreno, Garramasino
Morgan Rudeth, William A.
Morris Barrios, Mario
Morris Barrios, Mario Eduardo

Moscoso Moena, Fernando H.
Moscoso Quiroz, Raúl Eliseo
Moya León, Jesús
Moya Rojas, Ángel Gabriel
Moya Rojas, Miguel Ángel
Moya Zurita, Iván Nelson
Moya, Lumi Videla
Moyano Santander, Miguel A.
Mujica González, Gabriel
Mulet Marrero, Orlando
Mundaca Contreras, Eduardo O.
Munita Castillo, Patricio
Muñíz González, José Antonio
Muñíz González, Lázaro
Muñoz Aguyo, Luis Humberto
Muñoz Alarcón, Juan René
Muñoz Álvarez, Víctor Eduardo
Muñoz Aravena, Gonzalo R.
Muñoz Arévalo, Enzo
Muñoz Bravo, Luis Alberto
Muñoz Castillo, Rosario Aguid
Muñoz Contés, José Rafael
Muñoz Donoso, Washington R.
Muñoz Escobar, José Sergio
Muñoz Flores, Germán Eduardo
Muñoz Flores, Miguel Enrique
Muñoz García, Odalys
Muñoz González, José Luis
Muñoz Guajardo, Bernardo E.
Muñoz Hernández, Miguel A.
Muñoz Huechumir, Guillermo I.
Muñoz Lazo, Luis Miguel
Muñoz Maturana, Sergio Hugo
Muñoz Mesías, Carlos Abel
Muñoz Miranda, Ramos A.
Muñoz Muñoz, Heraldo Del C.
Muñoz Muñoz, Milton Alfredo
Muñoz Navarro, Irwin Eduardo
Muñoz Navarro, Jorge Eduardo
Muñoz Rivero, Alexis Eduardo
Muñoz Rodríguez, Dagoberto
Muñoz Rodríguez, Wuilzon G.
Muñoz Rojas, Hernán Antonio
Muñoz Rojas, Segundo H. A.

Muñoz Serpa, Julio Alberto
Muñoz Torres, Julio Alberto Luis
Muñoz Torres, Nelson Omar
Muñoz Ulloa, Mauricio A.
Muñoz, Pedro G.
Murga Medina, Eduardo Exequiel
Muría, Emiliano
Muriño, José Antonio
Muskatblit Eidelstein, Abraham
Nacimiento, Manuel de Jesús
Nahuel Huaiquimil, Juan Segundo
Nahuelcoi Chihuaicura, Bernardo
Nain, Heriberto Collio
Napoleón, Cesario
Naranjo Calderón, Rafael
Naranjo, Carlos José
Naranjo, Cristino
Naranjo, Wilson
Narváez, Jeannette Ingrid
Nash Sáez, Michel Selim
Nattino Allende, Santiago E.
Navarrete Clavijo, Marcos A.
Navarrete Solar, Juan G.
Navarro Andrés, Nicanor
Navarro Cáceres, Juan F.
Navarro Mellado, Sergio
Navarro Subiabre, Nibaldo
Navarro, Delia
Navarro, Guillermo
Navia Martínez, Ramón D.
Naya, Leoncio
Nazario, Luis Aurelio
Nechme Cornejo, Jecar Antonio
Negrete Castillo, Sergio Osman
Negrete Hernández, Manuel E.
Nehgme Cristi, Jecar Antonio
Neira Salas, Máximo Segundo
Nerváez Salamanca, Jorge P.
Nicol Anaya, José C.
Nicolls Rivera, Carlos E. Mario
Nieves Cruz, Luis
Nieves, Carlos
Nilo Arévalo, Juan Antonio
Noa Sanabria, Armando

Noel Vara, Amaury
Norambuena Canales, José del T.
Norambuena Cruz, Sonia Isaura
Nordenflycht Farías, Roberto S.
Noriega Duarte, Jorge Ramón
Nostare, Gerardo
Núñez Armas, Oscar
Núñez Bargas, Juan Bautista
Núñez Canelo, Jorge H.
Núñez Cantillano, Francisco R.
Núñez González, Eloy Emilio
Núñez González, Samuel Alfredo
Núñez Muñoz, Arturo Ricardo
Núñez Oryarzún, Manuel Genaro
Núñez Otaño, Luis
Núñez Valenzuela, Miguel A.
Núñez Vergara, Eduardo del C.
Núñez, Erasmo
Núñez, Manuel Lara
Ñanco, José Matías
Ñancuman Maldonado, José A.
Obando Coñue, Susana Estrella
Obregón Torres, Raúl Rodrigo
Ocampo Aldeacoa, Mario
Ocana Arrastre, Miguel A.
Ocaña Collazo, Rafael
Ocaña, Andrés
Ocara, Manuel
Oces, Fabio
Ochoa Mateo, Luis
Ochoa, Luis
Odualdo, Fermín
Oduardo, Eradio
Ojala Prieto, Rigoberto
Ojala, Ovedo
Ojeda Aguayo, Juan Ángel
Ojeda Disselkoen, Eduardo M.
Ojeda Grandon, Albasonia
Ojeda Prieto, Emilio
Ojeda Zulueta, Francisco Rafal
Ojeda, Emilio
Ojeda, Rigoberto
Olate Arigada, Marcos Antonio
Olea, Domingo

Oleart Rosales, Juana
Oliu Cordero, Federico
Oliva Espinoza, Abraham
Oliva Ramos, Santiago
Oliva Ramos, Santiago
Oliva Troncoso, Víctor Eduardo
Oliva Villalobos, Julio César
Oliva, Osvaldo
Oliva, Osvaldo
Olivares Becerras, Augusto
Olivares Blanco, Celso
Olivares Coronel, Iván Nelson
Olivares Estevens, Vicente
Olivares Jiménez, Dante V.
Olivares Jorquera, Raúl Jaime
Olivares Pérez, Bruno
Olivares Pérez, Juan Ramón
Olivares, Armando Cruz
Olivera Azaín, Pedro
Olmedo Moreno, Ricardo
Ona, José L.
Onelio Rodríguez, Olegario
Opaso Aravena, Cesar D.
Opaso Lara, Luis Humberto
Opaso Larrain, Francisco Luis
Oquendo, Raúl
Orama Orama, Andrés
Orayon, Felipe
Ordenes Simón, Juan Miguel
Ordenes Simón, Paulino Ernesto
Orellana Alarcón, Juan H.
Orellana Apablaza, David
Orellana Barrera, Miguel S.
Orellana Barrios, Luis Eugenio
Orellana Cuevas, Jaime Orobarel
Orellana Jara, Luis Alfonso
Orellana Pérez, Luis Emilio
Orellana Pino, Silvia del C.
Orellana Pinochet, Héctor
Orellana Rojas, Héctor Avelino
Orellana Villa, Pedro Juan
Oreola Acosta, José
Oreola Acosta, José Jr
Oriol Acosta, José

Orlando Álvarez, Luis
Orlando Valdés, Pastor
Ormeño Gajardo, Basco A.
Orrego Donoso, José Miguel
Orrego González, Jorge O.
Orrego Moscoso, Jorge Hernán
Orso Badilla, Carlos P. Dall
Orta Jopia, Rubén Eduardo
Orta, Belén
Orta, Ignacio
Ortega Alegría, Gilberto Antonio
Ortega Alvarado, Ricardo H.
Ortega Cuevas, Víctor A.
Ortega Donoso, Juan Luis
Ortega Fernández, Luis A.
Ortega, Domingo
Ortega, Efraín
Ortega, Hidelio
Ortega, José Miguel
Ortega, Laser
Ortega, Pedro Enrique
Ortega, Ramón
Ortigosa Ansoleaga, José María
Ortiz Acevedo, Juan Manuel
Ortiz Acevedo, Luis Celerino
Ortiz Barrera, Luis Armando
Ortiz Cid, Giovanna de las M.
Ortiz Miranda, Juan de Dios
Ortiz Orellana, Ramón Remigio
Ortiz Ortiz, Carlos Manuel
Ortiz Quiero, Juan Elías
Ortiz Valenzuela, Raúl M.
Ortiz, Octavio
Ortiz, Ramón
Osorio Ortiz, Luis Osvaldo
Osorio Pérez, Germán Aníbal
Osorio Rodríguez, María
Osorio Vera, José Sergio
Osorio Zamora, Jorge Ovidio
Ossa Galdames, Jaime Ignacio
Osses Malgarejos, Juan Agustín
Otero, Ibraín
Otis Fuller, Roberto
Otorola Sepúlveda, Pedro D.

Otts Flores, Luis Enrique
Oulloa Olivera, Claudio
Óvalos Castañeda, María del R.
Ovalla, Manuel
Oyarce Guarda, Martin A
Oyarce Oyarce, Juan
Oyarce Torres, Bautista S.
Oyarce, Carlos Patricio
Oyarce, Juan
Oyarzun Escobar, Jorge E.
Oyarzun Zamorano, Pedro E.
Oyarzun, Oscar Orlando
Pacheco Duran, Jorge Pedro
Pacheco Molina, Alfredo S.
Pacheco Monsalve, Javier A.
Pacheco Saavedra, Juan D.
Pacheco Sánchez, Mónica del C.
Pacheco Sepúlveda, Manuel R.
Pacheco, Jesús
Pacheco, Sócrates Ponce
Pachini González, Rosetta Gianna
Padrón Cárdenas, Antonio B.
Padrón Díaz, Ron
Padrón Trujillo, Amado
Páez, Cesar
Paillaqueo Catalán, Teobaldo José
Paineman Puel, Luz Marina
Painiqueo Tropa, Roberto
Palacio González, Alberto E.
Palacio Guarda, Iván Gustavo
Palacio Rojas, Gregorio Alberto
Palacio Toro, Esteban Alejandro
Palacio, Juan
Palacios García, Carlos
Palma Arévalo, Juan
Palma Coronado, Edinson Freddy
Palma Cortés, Ramón Antonio
Palma Moya, Pacifico Segundo
Palma Navarrete, Orlando G.
Palma Rodríguez, Juan Patricio
Palma, Jorge
Palomino Colón, José A.
Palomino Lamas, Germán Eladio
Palu, Félix

Pallera Norabuena, Adolfo Mario
Pan, Carlos John
Paneque, Jesús
Panes Muñoz, Gabriel Gonzalo
Parada Maluenda, José Manuel
Parapar, José
Pardo Aburto, Jorge Enrique
Pardo González, Sacaría Enrique
Pardo Tobar, Ricardo Guillermo
Paredes Cortinez, René
Paredes Lazcano, Cesar Gualdo
Paredes Trujillo, José Manuel
Parra Alarcón, Jorge Manuel
Parra Benítez, Marcelo R.
Parra Guzmán, Mario
Parra Quintanilla, Patricio H.
Parra Roldan, Fernando Iván
Parra Sandoval, Juan Francisco
Parra Sangueza, Juan Esteban
Pastene Ceballos, José Bautista
Patiño, Humberto Ricardo
Patten Tabares, William
Pavez Díaz, Sergio Osvaldo
Pavez Henríquez, Jorge Manuel
Pavez Pino, René Enrique
Paz, Saúl
Pedraza, Rafael
Pedrero Ferreira, Pedro Segundo
Peillaqueo Morales, Juana Maria
Pellegrin Friedmann, Raúl A.
Pena Verdecía, Miguel
Peña Brunes, Daniel Enrique
Peña Castro, Onofre
Peña Díaz, Sergio
Peña Escobar, Ricardo Osvaldo
Peña Hen, Jorge Washington
Peña Leiva, Edilberto
Peña, Elio
Peñaillio Vega, Luis Héctor
Peñalver Raguna, Ambrosio
Peñalver, Félix
Peralta Cardozo, Juan
Peralta Gajardo, Sergio Orlando
Peralta Vidal, Raúl Ricardo

Peralta, Alberto
Perdomo, Ángel
Perdomo, Eridio
Perdomo, Silvia
Pereda Calero, Reinaldo
Pereda Reyes, José
Peredo Daniel, Enrique
Pereira Cansino, Orlando Enrique
Pereira Luna, Sergio Omar
Pérez Balbontin, Luis
Pérez Cárdenas, Ricardo Abrahán
Pérez Clausel, Francisco
Pérez Espinoza, Víctor Omar
Pérez Flores, Pedro
Pérez Flores, Pedro Emilio
Pérez Gallardo, Norberto
Pérez Godoy, Pedro Hugo
Pérez Gómez, Julio
Pérez Jorquera, Raúl Humberto
Pérez López, Bebe
Pérez Loredo, Bartolo
Pérez Marambio, Ricardo
Pérez Mejía, Rolando
Pérez Menéndez, José Evelio
Pérez Morales, Ernesto
Pérez Navarrete, Ernesto Alfonso
Pérez Pérez, Lydia
Pérez Ríos, Carlos Luis
Pérez Santana, Hermán
Pérez Segundo, Enrique
Pérez Tacoronte, Yousel
Pérez Uveda, Jorge Segundo
Pérez Valdevenito, Roberto Andrés
Pérez Vargas, Dagoberto
Pérez Vargas, Iván Renato
Pérez Vargas, Mireya de Lourdes
Pérez, Alfonso
Pérez, Alfredo
Pérez, Avelino
Pérez, Gregorio
Pérez, Ramón
Pérez, Regino Germán
Pérez, Roberto
Periche, Roberto

Pero Panizza, Bruno Del
Perodin Almanza, Yaser
Pico, Francisco
Piedra, Benito
Pimentel, Gustavo
Pinales González, Rubén
Pincheira Díaz, Luis Landi
Pincheira Llanos, Luis P.
Pineda Ibacaches, Rafael Enrique
Pino Cortés, Claudio Patricio
Pino, Rafael Del
Pinto Coraca, Héctor Santiago
Pinto Coraca, Pedro Herman
Pinto Esquivel, Jorge Vernardino
Pinto Godoy, Juan Manuel
Pinto Menéndez, Juan Manuel
Pinto Rodríguez, Luis Armando
Pinto Viel, Guillermo
Piña Arratea, Cecilia Adelaida
Piñero Lucero, Carlos Alfonso
Pirgrim Roa, Mario
Pizarro Aranda, Artemio
Pizarro Nova, Carmen Ximena
Pizarro Rojas, Eliseo Enrique
Pizarro Vicencio, Oscar Ernesto
Pizarro, Héctor Manuel
Plaza Arellano, Manuel Benito
Plaza Díaz, Sara Beatriz
Plaza Narváez, Miguel Segundo
Poblete Hormasábal, Carlos Abel
Poblete Tropa, Juan Mauricio
Pobrete Carrasco, Rafael Edgardo
Pobrete Fernández, Gerardo F.
Poklepovic Braun, Pedro Raúl
Polanco Valenzuela, Oscar F.
Polo Aguiler, Mariano
Ponce Arias, Eligen
Ponce Contreras, Miguel Ángel
Ponce Quezada, Orlando Miguel
Ponce Silva, Samuel Antonio
Pontonholla, Avelino
Porma Cheuquecoy, Francisco P.
Porras, Daniel
Portal, Fidel Suero

Portales Socorro, Tito
Portuguez Maulen, Luis Antonio
Posada, Ángel
Pozo Jara, Luis Hermán
Prado, Aldo
Prats González, Carlos
Prieto Brito, Carlos
Prieto Suárez, Jesús
Prieto, Plinio
Puel Luz, Marina
Puel Villanueva, Segundo R.
Puentes Orea, Manuel Alfredo
Pugas Rojas, Ana María Irena
Pupo, Carlos Andrade
Queglas Maturana, Héctor A.
Quesada Oviedo, Víctor Manuel
Quevedo Álvarez, Raúl
Quezada Capetillo, Danilo W.
Quezada Núñez, José Díaz
Quezada Oquinton, Víctor H.
Quezada Yáñez, Marcos
Quian, Jorge
Quidel Reimay, Francisco
Quilan Cabezas, Jaime Antonio
Quintana Michelson, Sergio A.
Quintana, Raúl
Quintanilla Escobar, Jaime
Quintanilla Labra, Jorge B.
Quintanilla Palomino, Guido F.
Quintero Miranda, Eduardo Santos
Quinteros Martínez, Iván Alfredo
Quintul Muñoz, José Raúl
Quiroa Agusto, Francisco
Quiroga Rojas, Carlos Disiderio
Quiroz Nilo, Patricia
Quiroz Opazo, José Domingo
Quispe Choque, Donato
Rabelo, Pablo
Radamés, Juan
Ramel, Fidelio
Ramírez Amestica, Rogelio G.
Ramírez Artiles, Pedro
Ramírez Burgos, José Hernando
Ramírez Caballero, Antonio

Ramírez Diéguez, Juan
Ramírez Espinoza, Sergio M.
Ramírez García, Cosma
Ramírez García, Cosme
Ramírez González, Oscar Julio
Ramírez Iturriaga, Jorge A.
Ramírez Ortiz, Víctor Fernando
Ramírez Peña, Juan Guillermo
Ramírez Peña, Sergio Hernán
Ramírez Peregrín, Rosendo
Ramírez Pino, Héctor Leonardo
Ramírez Rubio, Robinzon
Ramírez Sánchez, Fernando R.
Ramírez Sepúlveda, Mario A.
Ramírez Torres, Pedro Luis
Ramírez Zurita, Manuel M.
Ramírez, Franklin Ramírez
Ramírez, Indalecio
Ramírez, Julio Cesar
Ramírez, Osvaldo
Ramírez, Porfirio
Ramón Castañeda, José
Ramón Ramírez, Juan Ramón
Ramón Rivera, José
Ramón Rivero, Juan
Ramón Rodríguez, José
Ramón, Ángel Vergara
Ramos Cáceres, Jorge Juan José
Ramos Kessel, Esteban
Ramos Tardío, Héctor
Ramos Verdecía, Rafael
Ramos Vergara, Ángel Clodomiro
Ramos Vidal, Guillermo
Ramos, Eduardo
Ramos, Raúl
Randolph Segovia, José R.
Rangel, Arturo José
Rangel, José
Rasales Sosa, Rafael
Ratier Noguera, Hugo Roberto
Raveli, Salustiano
Ravelo, Rolando
Rebolleo Méndez, Rosendo
Rebolleo Parra, Ricardo S.

Recaro Aguiar, Eneido
Regalón Acuña, Francisco
Regil Díaz, Evelio
Regino Crespo, Daniel
Reimundo Gil, Alfredo
Remberto Ramírez, Porfirio
René Pérez, Laureano
Reposo, José
Retamal Parra, Luis A.
Retamal Severino, Ramón E.
Retamal Soto, José Rolando
Retamal Velásquez, José G.
Retamal, Rosalindo del C.
Rey Alberola, Rubén
Rey Torres, Adolfo
Rey, Virgilio
Reyes Arzola, Marcos Aurelio
Reyes Averola, Rubén
Reyes Castillo, Javier Esteban
Reyes Castro, Miguel
Reyes Espinoza, Julio Enrique
Reyes Gajaldo, Rafael Agustín
Reyes Garrido, Manuel Lautaro
Reyes González, Ricardo E.
Reyes Lara, Juan Manuel
Reyes Manrique, Enrique H.
Reyes Martínez, Octavio
Reyes Ocaña, Valentín
Reyes Odín, Oscar
Reyes Rebolledo, Saturnino C.
Reyes Viada, Guillermo
Reyes, Antonio
Reyes, Clodomiro
Reynaldo Guinares, Martín
Riffo Figueroa, Julio Cesar
Riffo Pastenes, Orlando
Riffo Troncoso, Enriqueta C.
Rijas Fernández, Cornelio
Rin Martínez, Calde A
Ríos Bustos, Marcos Orlando
Ríos Castillo, Pedro
Ríos Céspedes, Ernesto Igor
Ríos Dalez, Jorge
Ríos Oliver, Ricardo

Ríos Portugués, Patricio E.
Ríos Pradena, Amado D.
Ríos Reyes, Eliecer
Ríos Traslaviña, Miguel Ángel
Ríos, Alicia Viviana
Rioseco, Ricardo G.
Ripoll Codoceo, Oscar Walter P.
Riqué Ruiz, Pedro
Riquelme Avilés, Roberto Adán
Riquelme Avilés, Waldo A.
Riquelme Briones, Erika del C.
Riquelme Briones, Juan A.
Riquelme Castillo, Luis F.
Riquelme Concha, Federico
Riquelme Garate, Ignacio H.
Riquelme Lemus, Marcelo A.
Riquelme Pacheco, Adán A.
Riquelme Pacheco, Francisco J.
Riquelme Pacheco, Jaime B.
Riquelme Ramos, Norberto M.
Riquelme, Julio Jaddad
Riquelme, Mariano A.
Riquelme, Misael Riquelme
Risquelme, Mario
Rivas Ovalle, Sebastián Rodrigo
Rivas, Felipe Pedro
Rivas, Quinteros
Rivera Aguilar, Jaime A.
Rivera Becerra, Pedro B.
Rivera Bello, Elías
Rivera Blanco, Jacinto
Rivera Carreño, Luis Francisco
Rivera Catricheo, Luis A.
Rivera Concha, Waldo Enrique
Rivera Cubillos, Germán R.
Rivera Duque, Manuel A.
Rivera Fierro, Rosa
Rivera Gajardo, Felipe S.
Rivera Linares, Fernando
Rivera Milián, Benancio
Rivera Milián, Estanislao
Rivera Nordet, Juan
Rivera Pérez, Emilio
Rivera Ramírez, José A.

Rivera Rodríguez, Nelson
Rivera Silva, Ricardo H.
Rivera, Alejandro Flores
Rivera, José Ramón
Rivero Gómez, Hugo E.
Rivero León, Rafael
Rivero Pérez, Luis Felipe
Rivero Pérez, Pablo
Rivero Ravelo, Gabriel O.
Rivero, Martín
Riviera Milián, Leocardio
Robaina, Lázaro
Robau, Mario
Robelo Jr, Pablo
Robelo Sr, Pablo
Robinson Figueras, Pedro
Robles Ortega, Pablo Marcelo
Robles Pantoja, Roberto Atzel
Roca Pérez, Máximo Antonio
Rocha Martínez, Rolando
Rocha Rocha, Domingo A.
Roche Valle, Santiago
Rodolfo Fuenzalida, Fernando J
Rodríguez Acevedo, Osmendo
Rodríguez Álvarez, Orlando
Rodríguez Anderson, Mario
Rodríguez Aqueveque, Florentino
Rodríguez Aqueveque, Juan E.
Rodríguez Arencibia, Luis Miguel
Rodríguez Báez, Juventino
Rodríguez Beruvides, Servando
Rodríguez Borges, José Ramón
Rodríguez Borges, José Ramos
Rodríguez Celis, Víctor René
Rodríguez Cifuentes, José
Rodríguez Cordero, Rolando Juan
Rodríguez Dalmau, Juan José
Rodríguez del Sol, Ángel B.
Rodríguez Díaz, Ernesto
Rodríguez Estrada, Belkis
Rodríguez Estrada, Bellido
Rodríguez García, Emeterio
Rodríguez González, Rigoberto
Rodríguez Hernández, José E.
Rodríguez Herrera, Nibaldo M.
Rodríguez Honojosa, Eric Enrique
Rodríguez Lazo, Daniel Eliseo
Rodríguez León, Arsides
Rodríguez Lima, Israel
Rodríguez Linares, José
Rodríguez López, Armando
Rodríguez López, Juan
Rodríguez Lugones, Benito
Rodríguez Martínez, Francisco
Rodríguez Martínez, Manuel
Rodríguez Mavan, Cecilio
Rodríguez Mayan, Cecilio
Rodríguez Mela, Aldo
Rodríguez Montelier, Lorenzo
Rodríguez Mosquera, José
Rodríguez Mzsel, Raúl
Rodríguez Naviera, Francisco
Rodríguez Novo, Esteban
Rodríguez Olave, Alfonso V.
Rodríguez Ordoñes, Juan
Rodríguez Pacheco, Hugo A.
Rodríguez Parajón, Fulgencio
Rodríguez Pedraja, Benito
Rodríguez Pinela, Manuel
Rodríguez Plaza, Lázaro
Rodríguez Puentes, Francisco
Rodríguez Rivero, Yolindys
Rodríguez Rodas, Pastor
Rodríguez Rodríguez, María E.
Rodríguez Sameillan, Armando
Rodríguez Santana, Carlos
Rodríguez Santos, Eduardo
Rodríguez Socorro, Rafael
Rodríguez Solís, Guillermo E.
Rodríguez Someillan, Amado
Rodríguez Someillan, Armando
Rodríguez Sosa, Domingo
Rodríguez Suárez, Omar
Rodríguez Tarafa, José
Rodríguez Torres, José S.
Rodríguez Vergareche, José R.
Rodríguez, Alejandro Rodríguez
Rodríguez, Claudio

Rodríguez, Elio
Rodríguez, Ernesto
Rodríguez, Genobebo
Rodríguez, José
Rodríguez, José Oscar
Rodríguez, Osvaldo
Rodríguez, Reinaldo
Rojas Acevedo, Juan Eliseo
Rojas Alcayaga, Roberto S.
Rojas Alfaro, Héctor
Rojas Álvarez, Roberto Walterio
Rojas Arce, Jean Eduardo
Rojas Arencibia, Rubén
Rojas Arencibia, Santiago R.
Rojas Ayala, Arturo
Rojas Castellanos, Jorge
Rojas Cortés, Hugo Manuel
Rojas Cortés, José Exequiel
Rojas Eirea, Anastasio
Rojas Fuentes, Manuel Tomás
Rojas Geraldo, Luis Eduardo
Rojas González, Carlos Héctor
Rojas González, Luis Alfredo
Rojas González, Patricio del C.
Rojas González, Rodolfo Ismael
Rojas González, Sergio W.
Rojas Marambio, Andrés
Rojas Miranda, Benito
Rojas Negri, Rodrigo A.
Rojas Orellana, Raúl Orlando
Rojas Osega, Juan Orlando
Rojas Pearce, Rodrigo Hugo
Rojas Riquelme, Juan de Dios
Rojas Rojas, Luis Antonio
Rojas Valenzuela, Luis F.
Rojas, Inocencio
Rojas, Ramón Luis
Rojas, Roberto de Jesús
Román Bustamante, Guillermo A.
Romero Corrales, Víctor E.
Romero Mena, José Luciano
Romero Reyes, Roberto R.
Romero Véliz, Juan Gualberto
Romero, Inocente

Romero, Narciso
Romeu González, Santos V. M.
Romo Escobar, Manuel Luis
Ronaldo Bonet, Félix
Ropert Contreras, Enrique
Roque del Toro, Benigno
Roque Martínez, Pedro
Roque, Braulio
Rosa Alegre, Francisco
Rosa Asenjo, Reinaldo Patricio
Rosa Fernández, Francisco L.
Rosales Gallardo, René del C.
Rosales Guerra, Isidro
Rosales Justiz, Roberto
Rosales, Eugenio
Rosas Águila, Teovaldo
Rosell, Francisco
Rubí Parra, Julio
Rubilar Gutiérrez, José Liborio
Rubilar Gutiérrez, José Lorenzo
Rubilar Gutiérrez, Manuel F.
Rubilar Salazar, Santiago
Rubio Cedeño, Heriberto
Rubio Faundez, Sergio Mario
Rubio Figueras, Ángel
Rubio Garrido, Luis Armando
Rubio Sánchez, Heriberto
Rudolf Reyes, Víctor Eugenio
Rueda Muñoz, Blas Enrique
Rueda, Blas Enrique
Ruiz Acosta, Antonio
Ruiz Beltrán, Antonio
Ruiz Blanco, Julio
Ruiz del Cristo, Manuel
Ruiz Mancilla, Juan Carlos
Ruiz Ramos, Moisés
Ruiz Rodríguez, Ricardo S.
Ruiz Roque, Pedro
Ruiz, Eugenio
Ruiz, Rodolfo
Ruiz, Serafín
Runca Runca, José Avelino
Ruz Díaz, Juan Antonio
Ruz Zañartu, Ricardo Delfín

Saavedra Bahamondes, Rudemir
Saavedra Chamorro, Francisco A.
Saavedra Gil, Armando
Saavedra González, José Gregorio
Saavedra González, Luis Eduardo
Saavedra Muñoz, Víctor Segundo
Saavedra Pérez, Teresita
Sabatier Rodríguez, Reynaldo
Sabino Artilles, Gustavo
Sáez Espinoza, Luis Onofre
Sáez Pérez, Orlando José
Sáez Sáez, Luis Antonio
Sáez San Martín, Joselín del T.
Sáez Valenzuela, Francisco
Safate Safate, Carlos Julio
Sainz Campos, José Antonio
Sainz, Adriano
Salas Cañizares, Juan
Salas Ovalle, Rosamel del Carmen
Salas Paradisi, Jorge Miguel
Salas Parra, Oscar
Salas Rojas, Jorge A. Marcelo
Salas Sotomayor, Mario Gabriel
Salazar Briceño, Alberto E.
Salazar Contreras, Carlos Helen
Salazar Jahnsen, Oscar
Salazar Leal, Teobaldo René
Salazar Quezada, María Noelia
Salazar Riquelme, Cesar E.
Salazar Veliz, Bartolomé A.
Salce Ascorra, Álvaro Agustín
Salcedo Muñiz, Ángel
Saldana Cruz, José
Saldías Cid, Diego Celso
Saldivia Saldivia, José Sofanor
Saldivia Villalobos, Teobaldo
Salgado Guzmán, Héctor
Salgado Morales, Miguel Segundo
Salgado Troquian, Alejandro
Salinas Flores, Carlos Vicente
Salinas García, Oscar Renato
Salinas Martin, Isidro Hernán
salinas Martínez, Gabriel
Salinas Muñoz, Wagner Eric

Salinas Toro, Sergio Eugenio
Salinas Velásquez, Javier A.
Salinas, Carlos Antonio
Sampson Ocaranza, José D.
San Gil Díaz, Tomás Devid
San Martín Inostroza, Exequiel O.
San Martín Poblete, Carlos E.
San Martín Sutherland, Arturo R.
San Martín, Pedro
San Román Rodríguez, Gilberto
Sanabria, Sergio
Sánchez Aldunate, Luis Agustín
Sánchez Allende, Martín
Sánchez Campertier, Carlos
Sánchez Carpente, Luis Carlos
Sánchez Carrera, Manuel A.
Sánchez Cayol, Samuel
Sánchez Espinoza, Susana del P.
Sánchez Guerra, Elizabeth
Sánchez Gutiérrez, Marcelino
Sánchez Hernández, Hiram
Sánchez Jiménez, Vicente
Sánchez Mejías, Luis Alberto
Sánchez Rojo, Nelson M.
Sánchez Suárez, Ismael
Sánchez Suluetas, Candido
Sánchez Vázquez, Rogelio
Sánchez Zamora, Pedro
Sánchez, Emiliano
Sánchez, Xistos
Sandoval Astorga, Jorge Luis
Sandoval Cares, Antonio O.
Sandoval Caro, Erika del C.
Sandoval Gómez, Segundo A.
Sandoval Ibáñez, Hugo F.
Sandoval Medina, Jerónimo H.
Sandoval Muñoz, José Orlando
Sandoval Puga, Segundo G.
Sandoval Sandoval, Mario E.
Sandoval Toro, Gabriel del C.
Sandoval Torres, Lisandro S.
Sandoval, Palermo
Sanguinetti Fuenzalida, Luis E.
Sanhueza Contreras, Oscar Omar

Sanhueza Ortiz, María Isabel
Sanhueza Salinas, Susana E.
Santamaría Cuyer, Victoriano
Santamaría Delgado, Rafael
Santana Alarcón, Raúl
Santana Bonilla, Elizardo
Santana Gómez, Héctor Arturo
Santana Molina, Mariano
Santander Alfaro, Patricio
Santander Valdés, Manuel S.
Santander Zúñiga, Omar Hernán
Santi Bañez, Eduardo Sporma
Santiago Bolaños, René
Santiago Castro, Marco Antonio
Santiago Hernández, Joaquín
Santibáñez Duran, Miguel Ángel
Santibáñez Roberto, Hernán
Santis Urriola, Raúl Fernando
Santos Abreu, Lázaro
Santos Muñoz, Domingo Elías
Santos, Arturo Deila
Santos, Dematto
Santos, Felipe
Santos, Francisco Deila
Santos, José
Santoya Lago, Ramón
Sanz Rumbaut, Melquíades
Sar Álvarez, Andrés
Sarabia Fritz, Arsenio Del C.
Sarabia González, Martín S.
Sarao Díaz, Juan Ignacio
Sardío, José Santiago
Sarmiento Cantillana, Leoncio
Schmidt Godoy, Guillermo E.
Schnever Xubero, Walter Carlos
Schouwen Vasey, Bautista V.
Sea Pizarro, Julio Andrés
Sedeño Montedia, Francisco
Segovia Gil, Leonardo Albino
Seguel Reyes, Norberto
Seguel Vidal, Demetrio De la C.
Seguería Cárdenas, Hildo
Segundo, José M.
Sepúlveda Beaza, José Esteban

Sepúlveda Bravo, Hernán Rafael
Sepúlveda Bravo, Juan Manuel
Sepúlveda Castillo, Domingo A.
Sepúlveda Catrileo, Raúl A.
Sepúlveda Farías, Adrian del C.
Sepúlveda Ferreira, Guido Héctor
Sepúlveda Malbran, Alejandro R.
Sepúlveda Mancilla, Nardo del C.
Sepúlveda Palavecino, Carlos A.
Sepúlveda Palma, Luis Enrique
Sepúlveda Rebolledo, Manuel J.
Sepúlveda Valenzuela, Bella Aurora
Sepúlveda, Justo Pastor
Sierra Castillo, Jaime Iván
Sigler Suárez, Armando
Silva Abarca, José Rosario
Silva Aguirre, Julio Eduardo
Silva Díaz, Carlos Jesús
Silva Díaz, Luciano del C.
Silva Fuentes, Sergio
Silva Iriarte, Héctor Mario
Silva Jara, Luis Alberto
Silva Jara, Luis Humberto
Silva López, Luis Alfonso
Silva López, Rolando de la C.
Silva López, Víctor Galvarino
Silva Oliva, Joel Guillermo
Silva Pacheco, Segundo Patricio
Silva Pozo, Emilio Segundo
Silva Soto, Ricardo Cristian
Silva Tejeiro, José
Silva, Andrés Silva
Silva, Luis Osvaldo
Silva, Sánchez
Sivera, Reimundo Emeterio
Sobarzo Luque, Pedro S.
Sobarzo Núñez, Héctor Patricio
Socarrás, Domingo
Socarrás, Ramiro Almeida
Soladan, José Alfonso
Soladana, José Alfonso
Solano García, Salvador
Solar Miranda, Jorge Ricardo
Solar Welchs, Luis Pedro

Solari Longo, Ricardo Aldo
Soler Puig, Rafael
Solís Núñez, Bernardo Isaac
Solís, Juan Luis
Solorza González, Bernardo E.
Solórzano, Walfrido
Sopena Inojosa, Sabino
Sopo Barreto, Rogelio
Soria Espinoza, Carmelo Luis
Sosa Delgado, Renato
Sosa Hernández, Sergio
Sosa Rodríguez, Carlos
Soto Cárdenas, Hernán
Soto Cárdenas, Víctor M. Rolando
Soto Cerda, Juan Ramón
Soto Herrera, José Antonio
Soto Marín, Adolfo
Soto Martínez, Marino
Soto Medina, Luis Alberto
Soto Muñoz, José
Soto Plutin, Manuel
Soto Quintana, Pedro Antonio
Soto Sepeda, Vicente Ramos
Soto Silva, Luis Horacio
Soto Valdés, Alberto Toribio
Soto Vega, Juan Carlos
Soto, José Miguel
Soto, Luis Alberto
Stappung López, Mario Emiliano
Stay Stay, Gilberto Del Carmen
Stokle Poblete, Gloria Ana
Suárez Amoró, Anselmo
Suárez Esquivel, Eduardo
Suárez Esquivel, Estrella
Suárez García, Eliecer
Suárez Luque, Armando
Suárez Mata, Manuel
Suárez Pérez, René
Suárez Rizo, José
Suárez Suquet, Armando
Suárez Suquet, Manuel
Suárez, Felipe de la Caridad
Suárez, Sixto
Suazo Sandoval, Julio Celestino

Suazo Suazo, Luis Segundo
Superby Jeldres, Mario Edmundo
Tabaquero, Eulogio
Tabares Alfonso, Roberto
Tabera Prades, Pedro
Taberna Gallegos, Freddy M.
Tamargo Gutiérrez, Rolando
Tamario, José
Tamayo Jiménez, Rolando
Tamayo Lezcano, Luis Enrique
Tamayo Reyes, Antonio A.
Tamayo Reyes, Antonio Artemio
Tamayo Salgado, Eduardo
Tamayo, Ángel
Tan Tixdale, Julio
Tang Taxier, Julio
Tapia Aguilera, René Hernán
Tapia de la Puente, Rogelio H.
Tapia Delgado, Juan de Dios
Tapia Guzmán, Marco Javier
Tapia Leyton, Oscar Eugenio
Tapia Muñoz, José Alejandro
Tapia Tapia, Benito de los Santos
Tapia, Rubén
Tapias Muñoz, José Alejandro
Tapias Rojas, Miguel Ángel
Taquias Vergara, Manuel S.
Tarafa Machado, José
Tardío Hernández, Benjamín
Tardío Hernández, Blas
Tardío Hernández, Camilo
Tarton Molina, Julio
Taulet, Mario
Téllez Cisneros, Ramón
Téllez, Francisco
Teodorovic Certic, Nenatd
Teodorovic Sertic, Nenad
Thomes Palavecinos, Segundo E.
Thorn Valenzuela, Gustavo P.
Tiburcio, Filomeno
Tierno Regueiro, Alfredo
Tobar Coron, Rosa Blanca
Toha González, José
Toledo Betancourt, Carlos

Toledo Betancourt, Carlos Jr
Toledo Carbajal, Ángel Domingo
Toledo Cortez, Eduardo
Toledo González, Luis Segundo
Toledo, Jorge
Toledon, José Alfonso
Torecella Rivero, Luis
Toro Castillo, Luis Alberto
Toro La Barca, Mario Antonio
Toro Ortiz, Martín Eugenio
Toro Toro, Jorge Manuel
Torres Aguayo, Paola Andrade
Torres Aguayo, Paola Andrea
Torres Aguayo, Soledad Ester
Torres Ahumada, Víctor Roberto
Torres Antinao, Luis Omar
Torres Arenas, José Fernando
Torres Gaete, Oscar Segundo
Torres González, Celso
Torres González, Nelson Mario
Torres López, Filiberto
Torres Martínez, Ibraín
Torres Muñoz, Manuel Urbano
Torres Pérez, Enrique
Torres Quintana, Joaquín
Torres Rivera, Luis Carlos
Torres Tello, Macarena Denisse
Torres Torres, Benito Heriberto
Torres Treto, Armando
Torres Velázquez, Mario Cesar
Torres Villalba, Freddy Jimmy
Torres, Rafael
Toy Vergara, Jorge Arturo
Traical Huenchuman, Juan S.
Tramolao Pastene, Ramón
Tran Huynh, Que Phuong
Tranamil, Luis Curivil
Transito Villagra, Emperatriz del
Travesa Aguiar, Enrique
Travieso Duro, Antonio
Travieso, Julián
Triana Guillen, Luis
Triana Salazar, Luis
Triana Salazar, Placido

Triana, Pablo
Tribons Batute, Emilio
Trimillo, Eliberto
Trimiño Guerra, Lorenzo
Troncoso Pérez, Guido Raúl
Troncoso Saavedra, Pedro E.
Trujillo Amador, Gerardo
Trujillo Correda, Nelson
Trujillo García, Lorenzo
Trujillo Lucero, Juan Antonio
Tudela Cortez, Armando Camilo
Turruggi Bombatch, Frank K.
Ugalde Jiménez, Pedro
Ugalde Pérez, Amado
Ugarte Gutiérrez, Atilio Ernesto
Ugarte Román, Marta Lidia
Ulacia Montiel, Ruperto
Ulacia, Roberto
Ulacia, Ruperto
Ulloa Carrillo, Juan Carlos
Ulloa Olivera, Claudio
Ulloa Sáez, José Iván
Ulloa San Martín, Emilia M.
Ulloa San Martín, Emilio
Ung Roque, Enrique
Ur Hechevarría, Humberto
Urbina Bravo, Rolando Hugo
Urbina Díaz, Domingo Antonio
Urbina Díaz, Luis
Urbina Díaz, Luis Alberto
Ureta, Evelio
Urra Casas, Ana María
Urra Lagos, Mercenorio
Urra Parada, Raúl
Urrieta Castillo, Leonardo Baltazar
Urrieta Díaz, Carlos Albertos
Utrera Cortez, Álvaro Rodrigo
Valdebenito Carlos, Rosendo S.
Valdebenito Espinoza, Carlos R.
Valdebenito Juica, Wilson F.
Valdebenito Medina, Francisco A.
Valdebenito Vira, Roberto E.
Valdenegro Arencibia, Juan M.
Valdenegro Carrasco, Lila L.

Valderas Angulo, Arturo J.
Valderas Mancilla, Flavio H.
Valdés Galaz, Manuel N.
Valdés Sepúlveda, Edelmiro A.
Valdez Chávez, Mario A.
Valdez Moreno, Lino Fidel
Valdez Pozo, Jova del T.
Valdivia Araya, Javier Edgardo
Valdivia Contreras, Luis Alberto
Valdivia González, Oscar D.
Valdivia Valdivia, Aliro del C.
Valdivia Valenzuela, José E.
Valdivia Vásquez, Miguel Ángel
Valdivia Vásquez, Segundo F.
Valdivia Vázquez, Víctor E.
Valdovino Pérez, Sergio H.
Valencia Cáceres, Manuel J.
Valencia Calderón, Manuel E.
Valencia Castillo, Julio S.
Valencia Hinojosa, Juan
Valencia López, Juan Fidel
Valencia Norambuena, Manuel A.
Valencia, Luis Armando
Valenzuela Álvarez, Basilio A.
Valenzuela Bastias, Julio G.
Valenzuela Ferrada, Luis M.
Valenzuela Figueroa, Luis A.
Valenzuela Flores, Alex A.
Valenzuela Levi, José J.
Valenzuela Leyva, Luis O.
Valenzuela Mella, Oscar S.
Valenzuela Olea, Humberto A.
Valenzuela Pondrecky, Recadeo
Valenzuela Rivera, Fernando A.
Valenzuela Salazar, Héctor D.
Valenzuela Scheumann, Ricardo L.
Valenzuela Valenzuela, Julio
Valenzuela Varriento, Jorge P.
Valenzuela Velásquez, Claudia A.
Valenzuela Velásquez, Víctor H.
Valenzuela, Alcibíades
Valenzuela, Jorge O. V.
Valverde Briones, Carlos A.
Valladares Caroca, Oscar E.

Valladares, Julio del T.
Valle Pérez, José M.
Vallejos Aguilera, Nilson H.
Vallejos Buschman, Marta A.
Vallejos Ferdinad, Guillermo O.
Vallejos Ferdinad, Osvaldo
Vallejos González, Luis A.
Vallejos Ramos, Jorge
Vallejos Ramos, René D.
Vallejos Villagrán, Álvaro M.
Valles Cortez, Juan Carlos
Van Yurick, Edwin F.
Vanini, Jane
Vara Aleuy, Rubén
Vargas Arencibia, Carlos A.
Vargas Barrientos, Pedro L.
Vargas Contreras, Juan A.
Vargas Díaz, Florencio A.
Vargas Fernández, Félix M.
Vargas Gallardo, Guillermo C.
Vargas Lizama, Pedro Jaime
Vargas Miranda, Luis O.
Vargas Quesada, Rubén
Vargas Salazar, Ángel Patricio
Vargas Sepúlveda, Bernardo A.
Vargas Silva, Juan Manuel
Vargas Valenzuela, José M.
Vargas, Manuel de la Cruz
Varó, Abel Eugenio
Vásquez Carlos, Germán
Vásquez Castañeda, Enrique Z.
Vásquez Castañeda, Vicente A.
Vásquez Escobar, Jorge E.
Vásquez Godoy, Ernesto
Vásquez Guajardo, Romelio A.
Vásquez Martínez, Hugo Rivol
Vásquez Matamala, Jorge
Vásquez Matamala, Jorge M.
Vásquez Ortiz, Juan R. A.
Vásquez Peña, Hugo H.
Vásquez Rivero, Juan F.
Vásquez Romos, Emilio G.
Vásquez San Martín, Erasmo J.
Vásquez San, Martín E. Juvenal

Vásquez Silva, Juan Bautista
Vázquez Fredes, María E.
Vázquez Muños, Luis J.
Vázquez Saenz, Jaime E
Vázquez Sepúlveda, Héctor M.
Vázquez Silva, Juan B.
Veas Salinas, Jaime A.
Veas Valdivia, Luis E.
Vega Bizama, Iris Yolanda
Vega González, Arturo
Vega González, Arturo
Vega Ramírez, Luis E.
Vega Rivera, Víctor Hugo
Vega, Oscar
Vegas Barrios, Jaime N.
Vegas González, Oscar
Vegas Pemjean, Marcos A.
Vegas Riquelme, Víctor H.
Vegas Salazar, Sergio O.
Vegas Sisterna, Alonso del T.
Vegas Tapia, Jaime Alberto
Vegas Vásquez, Florentino S.
Vegas, Julio Roberto
Velásquez Aguilar, Jorge A.
Velásquez Calderón, Hilda I.
Velásquez Molina, Héctor F.
Velásquez Velásquez, José E.
Velásquez, Esal Velásquez
Velásquez, Gregorio Velásquez
Velázquez Vargas, Rubén A.
Velázquez, José R.
Velez Aguilera, Luis Alberto
Veliz Ramírez, Héctor
Veloso Araya, José Segundo
Veloso Meriño, Lidia Ester
Veloso, Gilberto Victoriano
Venegas Gautier, Héctor A.
Venegas Islas, Grober H.
Venegas Labra, Jorge Patricio
Venegas Muñoz, Elizabeth del C.
Venegas Silva, Luis Alfonso
Venegas, Claudio S.
Venegas, Rachel E.
Venturelli, Oscar R.

Vera Almarza, Ida A.
Vera Contardo, Bernardo R.
Vera Linares, Marisol de las M.
Vera Muñoz, Enrique Eduardo
Vera ortega, Fernando Isidro
Vera Soto, Juan Segundo
Vera Tapia, Boris Aroldo
Vera Torres, Pablo Renán
Vera Vergara, Héctor Fernando
Veras Figueroa, Sergio E.
Veras Oyazun, Juan
Verdajo Contreras, Luis Albaerto
Verdejo Santibáñez, Emilio G.
Verdejo, Exequiel del C.
Verdugo Herrera, Sergio O.
Verdugos Bustos, Oscar René
Vergara Corso, Luis E.
Vergara Doxrud, Héctor P.
Vergara González, Luis A.
Vergara Inostroza, Pedro J.
Vergara Muñoz, Gabriel G.
Vergara Ortega, Leonardo Patricio
Vergara Sepúlveda, Julio
Vergara Toledo, Eduardo A.
Vergara Toledo, Pablo Orlando
Vergara Toledo, Rafael Mauricio
Vergara Umaña, Jorge Alberto
Vergara Valenzuela, Lucia Orfilia
Vergara Vargas, Fernando G.
Vergara, José Adan
Vernal Honores, Jorge Lenin
Vicencio Arriagada, Blas Javier
Vicencio, Héctor O.
Vicenti Cartagena, Néstor L.
Vidal Aedo, Jesé Edmundo
Vidal Arenas, Hugo A.
Vidal Hinojosa, Florindo Alex
Vidal Ibáñez, José A.
Vidal Molina, Abel A.
Vidal Ovalle, Jaime B.
Vidal Panguilef, José Maceo S.
Vidal Paredes, Vicente del C.
Vidal Pereira, Rudy Freddy
Vidal Tejeda, Víctor Iván

Vidal, Edmundo J.
Vidaurrazaga Manríquez, Gastón
Videla Álvarez, Juan Félix
Vielma Luengo, Edurado G.
Viera Ovalle, Francisco E.
Vila Leal, Víctor Hugo
Vilches Urrea, Aída Rosa
Vilches Yáñez, Juan S.
Vilches Yañez, Juan Santiago
Vilugron Reyes, Jorge Orlando
Villablanca Villanueva, Ramón A.
Villafranca Vera, Jaime Edison
Villagas Sepúlveda, Rudecindo O.
Villagra Astuillo, José C.
Villagra Cruz, Humberto Javier
Villagra Garrido, Víctor Segundo
Villagra Rojas, Juan Pedro
Villagran Villagran, José Luis Tito
Villagran, José Villagran
Villalobos Díaz, Alejandro Delfín
Villalobos Díaz, Manuel J
Villalobos López, Humberto
Villalobos Moraga, Waldo R.
Villalobos Perinetti, Sonia del R.
Villalón, Juan Calderón
Villanueva Ramírez, Sigifredo
Villar Moraga, Elías R.
Villarroel Díaz, Máximo Reimundo
Villarroel Espinoza, J. de D. Espinoza
Villarroel Latin, Ofelia Rebeca
Villarroel Mella, Isaías Alejandro
Villarroel Nazara, Pedro Segundo
Villarroel Rivera, Luis Antonio
Villarroel, Víctor M.
Villaseca Díaz, Jorge Bernardo
Villaseñor Jara, Juan Antonio
Villavella Araujo, Arturo Jorge
Villevicencio Medel, Osvaldo E.
Vivancco Herrera, Nicolás H.
Vivanco Carrasco, Celsio Nicasio
Vivanco Díaz, Ramos Luis
Vivanco Vázquez, Víctor J.
Vivanco Vega, Hugo E.
Vivar Mella, José Amador
Viveros Flores, Gabriel José
Vizcarra, Carlos M.
Walker Arangua, Joaquin
Walsh Río, Sinesio
Wall Cortés, Luis Guillermo
Was, Bartolo
Wegner Millar, Absalon del C.
Weibel Navarrete, José Arturo
Weibel Navarrete, Ricardo Manuel
Weitzel Pérez, Patricio Lautaro
Wenten Valenzuela, Manuel
Windo Barrios, Víctor Hugo
Wood Gwiazdon, Ronald Williams
Woodward Iribarri, Michael Roy
Yanques de la Cerda, Luis Arturo
Yáñez Ayala, Evaristo S.
Yáñez Calfupan, Sofía Eleonor
Yáñez Carvajal, Alberto Amador
Yáñez Duran, José Florencio
Yáñez Figueroa, Patricio A.
Yáñez Hernández, Domingo S.
Yáñez Martínez, Juan Carlos
Yáñez Orellana, Juan Benigno
Yáñez Palacios, Pedro Juan
Yáñez, Dagoberto Yáñez
Yavenes Apablaza, Ernesto A.
Yavenes Yavenes, Simón Eduardo
Yueng Rojas, Jorge Rubén
Zabala Barra, Rubén Federico
Zacarías Díaz, Alberto
Zalazar Arrue, Juan Carlos
Zalazar Hlaczik, Claudia Victoria
Zamora Meléndez, Juan Cristian
Zamora Portilla, Pedro Germán
Zamora, Alberto
Zamorano Aranguiz, Robinson
Zamorano Cortés, Mario F.
Zamorano Donoso, Mario Jaime
Zamorano González, Víctor M.
Zamorano Valle, Miguel Ángel
Zani Espinosa, Luis Armando
Zapata Águila, Carlos

Zapata Andrade, José F.
Zapata Banda, Luis Orlando
Zapata Carrasco, José Ananías
Zapata Rivas, Raúl Iván
Zarate Alarcón, Pedro Antonio
Zavala Gallegos, Miguel Ángel
Zavala López, Héctor Gregorio
Zayas, Dámaso
Zelaya Suarzo, Carlos Hugo
Zenón Viera, Diego
Zenteno Araneda, Arioste Emilio
Zerega Ponce, Víctor Osvaldo
Zerguera Canosa, Aquilino
Zerguera, Aquilino
Ziede Gómez, Eduardo Humberto
Zorrilla Rubio, Jorge Lautaro
Zuleta Francisco, Rafael
Zuley, Eligio

Zulueta Sánchez, Cándido
Zunaeta Dattoli, José Rienzi
Zúñiga Aceldine, José Rafael
Zúñiga Aceldine, José Segundo
Zúñiga Adasme, Luis Hipólito
Zúñiga Aguilera, Francisco A.
Zúñiga Arellano, Víctor Miguel
Zúñiga Llanquilef, Ariel Eduardo
Zúñiga Sánchez, Ramón Víctor
Zúñiga Urzua, Gabriel Ángel
Zúñiga Vergara, Ernesto Enrique
Zúñiga Zúñiga, Eduardo Fernando
Zúñiga, Chicho
Zúñiga, Ignacio
Zúñiga, Luis Isaías
Zúñiga, Martín
Zúñiga, Víctor Hugo
Zurita, Iván